To Eddie, with Best l
from the

No Hero, Just a Survivor

A personal story with
Beaufighters and Mosquitos of
47 Squadron RAF
over the Mediterranean and Burma
1943 - 1945

G R T (Bob) Willis MBE DFC

For Joan, Catherine, Ian, Andrew and Howard

First Published in Great Britain in 1999
by Robert Willis Associates Limited
19 Rectory Lane, Emley, Huddersfield

First reprint August 2000

Reprographics by
Aniseedball, Huddersfield.
Printed and Bound in Great Britain by
Enterprise Print, Long Lane, Honley, Huddersfield.

ISBN 0 9537178 0 1

47 Squadron RAF was fully engaged as an active service Squadron from June 1940 to August 1945 firstly in East Africa, followed by North Africa, India and Burma. It is very moving to read of the committment, heroism and courage displayed by all ranks in the Squadron during these years. Serving on the Squadron for over three and a half years, I welcome this opportunity to pay tribute to my old comrades and to remember with gratitude all those Squadron members who gave so much, often their lives, to achieve the ultimate victory.

Group Captain H Fishwick RAF (Retired) MBE MID
(ex RAF Apprentice)

Henry V prior to Agincourt:

> 'Gloucester, 'tis true that we are in great danger
> The greater therefore should our courage be.'

Henry V Act IV Scene I - Wm Shakespeare

CONTENTS

List of Illustrations

FOREWORD

If one mentions the role of the Royal Air Force, and other Allied air forces, during the Second World War, the popular perception is about the heroic Few who fought and won the Battle of Britain, and the thousands of airmen who were involved in the long and weary bombing campaigns over Occupied Europe. But there were other campaigns, that in their own way, contributed to the defeat of the Germans, the Italians and the Japanese.

This narrative is about one RAF pilot, who never experienced hostile action over North West Europe, but completed many operations in the battles for the islands in the Aegean Sea, and later in the campaign that drove the Japanese from Burma before their surrender. I was a member of No 47 Squadron, Royal Air Force, which was formed in March 1916 and, with only a short interval, continues in service today. It is perhaps appropriate that the squadron was formed in Yorkshire, for this pilot and my navigator were also very proud of their Yorkshire heritage.

47 Squadron was formed on 1 March 1916 at Beverley in the East Riding of Yorkshire and is still, in the new millennium, an active Royal Air Force Squadron on Hercules C-130 Transport aircraft based at Lyneham in Wiltshire. This is a very proud squadron with a most distinguished history illustrated by its motto 'Nili Nomen Roboris Omen', which may be translated as 'Our strength is as the strength of the Nile'; reminding one of the squadron's early history when it served with distinction in both Russia and the Sudan. Based at Khartoum from 31 October 1927 the squadron adopted as its badge the demoiselle crane, a native of southern Russia, set against a background of blue and white stripes depicting the convergence of the Blue and White Nile at

Khartoum. The squadron has never failed to live up to its motto, of which more later. From 1939 to 1945 this squadron played a continuous and very active role, firstly against the Italians in Abyssinia and Eritrea, then against the Germans in the Mediterranean and finally, with great fortitude, against the Japanese in Burma.

There were many dangers and hazards in air operations in all theatres of war, but this story vividly illustrates the added difficulties of operations out of remote airfields in mountainous country, with nothing that even resembled home comforts at the end of a long day or night's work.

The end of the war in Europe was of little consequence to those who were still fighting - at the extreme range of the aircraft's endurance, and, sadly suffering very high losses of gallant airmen. In compiling this narrative I was proud to have been a member of 47 Squadron that fought in those remote and sometimes forgotten campaigns.

Thus on 20 November 1943 I joined a 'mobile' squadron in the Western Desert which had already covered many thousands of miles from Khartoum in the Sudan to Eritrea, north to Egypt, westward across North Africa to Tunisia and then back to Libya.

Periods of intense activity, punctuated by weeks of frustration and boredom, was to be a common experience during my squadron service. I believe a little less of the obsession with secrecy would have helped to explain some of the factors behind the many changes in policy we were to experience. Waiting around and re-training for new roles requires some explanation if boredom and frustration are to be contained. In the overall plan most individual's contribution in achieving operational objectives was comparatively small, but the personal risks were often considerable.

Joining a squadron on active service was the ambition of every trained pilot, and indeed of all aircrew, once all the training hurdles had been jumped. The training, spread over months and years, had been long, the skills required were often amended or modified, and there was always the anxiety that perhaps one did not have the aptitude or ability to pass the numerous tests and assessments in the air and on the ground. Most, if not all, of my colleagues gave little attention to the thought that an accident of posting to a particular operational squadron could ensure that, despite all their personal skill, survival was at best only 50%.

I was exceptionally fortunate in teaming up, as a 'twin engine' operational pilot, with a most competent navigator/wireless operator, 'Tommy' Thompson, a fellow Yorkshireman from Dewsbury, trained in Canada, who joined me at Crosby on Eden, now Carlisle Airport, on 11 July 1943. We were to fly together on operations and later at Middleton St George No.13 Operational Training Unit until I left the Royal Air Force on 30 May 1946, a time span of nearly three years. The comradeship and dependence upon each other forged a very special relationship which we always treasured, until Tommy died suddenly of a heart attack on 9 April 1988.

In six years of operational flying against the Italians and Germans in North Africa and the Japanese in Burma, broken only by training, stand by, on rest, or moving bases, 47 Squadron was home to many courageous airmen who did not return. In the unique experience of serving on the squadron from November 1943 to July 1946 the emotional impact in losing colleagues with whom I was closely associated was, over time, quite considerable. I was to feel a deep sense of sadness and horror in seeing so many inspiring friends and colleagues destroyed by the fortunes of war. This book is particularly dedicated to the memory of Flying Officer Arthur Unwin, temporary Commanding Officer of 'A' Flight for a few days in November 1943, lost with his navigator, Sergeant Ken Farmer, on 13 February 1944; Squadron Leader L H Skinner, Officer Commanding 'A' Flight and his navigator, Warrant Officer H F Laing, killed on 2 February 1945; Warrant Officer Ken Thomas, a close friend, and his navigator, Warrant Officer Tommy Bashford, killed on 8 February 1945; Flight Lieutenant Al Scott, Officer Commanding 'A' Flight, killed on 14 April 1945; Wing Commander Filson-Young DFC, Officer Commanding 47 Squadron from November 1943 to May

1945, and his navigator, Flight Lieutenant R C U Waters, killed on 15 May 1945. Circumstances surrounding many other aircrew losses and achievements during my time on the squadron and in training to become an operational pilot are in the ensuing narrative. Perhaps, as survivors, many of us were sustained and supported by our Christian beliefs in the struggle to rid the world of evil oppressors.

ACKNOWLEDGEMENTS

It would have been impossible to write this book without the benefit of many personal records, including all my letters to Joan who served as a nurse in Edinburgh Royal Infirmary during my time on 47 Squadron, and who was to become my wife. Of equal importance has been the ready help and consent of past 47 Squadron members of the 1943/45 period who have given very freely of their notes, photographs and reminiscences, which are much appreciated.It has also been most pleasing to receive continuous encouragement and help from those past and present members of 47 Squadron who I have been privileged to meet either at the squadron's base in Lyneham, or on their home ground in the UK, Ireland, Canada and Australia.

My special thanks for all this help goes to all my old squadron colleagues, G/Capt Harold Fishwick RAF (Rtd) MBE MID, the late Tony Norris, Bill Powell, Maurice Jones, Bob Milne, Jimmy Gibson, Reg Davis, Bill Hughes, Mike Mackay, the late Doc Bamford, Nick Colley, Doug Terry, Bob Barrett, Grant Flook, Dick Taylor and all my many friends in 47 Squadron Association. Much help was also given by Stan Perrett and Charlie Tomalin with whom I shared many training experiences. I am indebted to Jimmy Gibson and Gordon Thewlis for several photographs of the Burma campaign.

Many books have been written on the experiences of aircrew in those momentous years of the early forties. I have learnt a lot about the wider picture surrounding my own activities as I have studied these publications over the years. I shall always be grateful to these authors and whose books are listed in the bibliography at the end. Thanks are also extended to Owen Clark for his most valuable research into the squadron operational losses from June 1943 to March 1944.

Nothing could have been achieved without the help and courtesy of the Public Record Office in Kew, which I gratefully acknowledge. To my immediate helpers, Paulette Huntington, who prepared all the maps and photographs, typed and corrected the script, to Jimmy Gibson and Des Curtis who read the narrative and gave much useful advice, and to my wife Joan, who tolerated all the time spent on the project, I extend most grateful thanks.

Bob Willis,
September 1999

CHAPTER 1
BACKGROUND AND EARLY YEARS

My father was a veteran of the First World War serving in the Kings Own Yorkshire Light Infantry from 1916-1919, was wounded and met my mother, a Ward Sister in Sheffield Royal Hospital, where he was recuperating in 1919. They were married at St. Emmanuel Church, Sheffield in 1920 by my grandfather, the incumbent vicar.

Father and mother settled in Barnsley, South Yorkshire, where I was born on 20 June 1921, followed over the next eight years by two sisters and two brothers. Father purchased on an instalment basis from his own father a small wholesale food business in the town. Father's mother died at her family home in County Leitrim, Ireland, when father was but two years old. His father remarried which ultimately led to my father severing all communication with his own father until shortly before the outbreak of World War ll.

After the General Strike of 1926 to the early 1930s father found business very hard going. He was still paying his own father, through solicitors, for the business acquired in 1922. There was a lot of unemployment in Barnsley. I remember well the dole queues at the Labour Exchange as I walked into town from the Grammar School, usually to play chess at the YMCA or to browse in the Public Library. In the later 1930s business improved, father paid off his debt to his father and also managed to buy out one or two small competitors. We moved from our small terraced house to a newly built four bedroom detached house, on the outskirts of Barnsley, for which father paid £500. Winning a scholarship in 1932 gave me a place at Barnsley Grammar School leaving, with reasonable School Certificate results, at the age of sixteen to join father in his business. It was taken for granted that I, as the eldest son, would go into the family business, then trading as R T Willis and Son. Father, pre-occupied with surviving the 1930s, and mother, having her hands full with a fairly large family establishment to maintain, had little time available to encourage my academic endeavours. Pocket money of twopence per week depended upon attendance every Saturday morning at father's Barnsley Warehouse to deliver on foot small parcels of sundry groceries to local corner shops in the terraces and courtyards of central Barnsley. At least I became well acquainted with the cohesion and self support prevalent in these working class communities, who largely depended on the coal and glass industries. This experience, which I never regretted, was to stand me in good stead as a future employer amongst the down to earth, honest and straight talking communities of South Yorkshire. Father's business in 1937 had grown to comprise three small food warehouses, one in Barnsley with two others to the north and south of Sheffield, employing in all around thirty people, mostly women. My personal ambition and expectations in those days were very modest, confined to activities with the Boy Scouts, the local church, football and cricket, walking in thc country and reading books of travel, exploration and history. The culture and confining lifestyle of the time centred very much on the need to have a job. Without a job there was only the dole; with a job went just one week's holiday in August known as 'Barnsley Feast' week. Those who could afford to stay in a modest boarding house departed for the most part to Blackpool or the east coast.

After a brief holiday with my sister Maisie in the Lake District I joined the family business in the autumn of 1937. To succeed in the future and to win the respect of father I would have to prove that I could eventually be a good salesman and turn my hand to any task. Starting on the bottom rung, I was soon to learn that even sweeping up had an element of skill attached. All energies were devoted to proving that one day I would respond effectively to real responsibility. There was no time for girl friends.

After two years as a warehouse assistant in Barnsley I was promoted to assistant manager at father's warehouse in Eckington, a mining village six miles south of Sheffield. This was a welcome escape from father's eagle eye, able to work and live away from home. The business at Eckington was a very modest affair with a staff of six supplying local family owned corner shops on a wholesale basis. Most supplies to the warehouse came in by rail still using some horse drawn drays besides motor transport to complete the final stage. The average wage of our male employees was £3 to £3/10/- per week. At the age of eighteen I was paid the quite handsome wage of £3 per week of which 30/- (£1.50) was paid to my landlady for full board and lodging. 50/- (£2.50) would buy a suit. Many were the families who managed on even less. Having no dependants I even opened a bank deposit account. Arriving at Eckington in July 1939 I took up lodgings with a miner and his wife, Cyril and Ethel Garratt, in their two up, two down terrace house at 41 Station Road. They were to prove to be real friends then and post war. Change was in the air as Poland came under pressure from Germany to hand over the Baltic port of Danzig. I read the daily newspapers with interest and some anxiety.

On 1 September 1939 the Germans invaded Poland. On the following Sunday, 3 September 1939, I was at home in Barnsley listening to the radio and the declaration of war that day in defence of Poland. That evening, returning to Eckington through Sheffield by bus, householders were already digging air raid shelters in gardens and allotments in anticipation of the expected air raids. Until the day in August 1941 when I finally donned the uniform of an airman in the Royal Air Force, my responsibilities in the Eckington warehouse continued. Very soon we had to come to grips with shortages, with food rationing introduced on 8 January 1940. To follow was an ever changing pattern of rationing and registration for available supplies. Part of the warehouse was requisitioned by the Ministry of Food to store emergency supplies of margarine. Our part in the war effort was the receiving, dispatch and recording of large quantities of 'Stork' and 'Echo' margarine as it was fed into the food chain under the rationing regulations. The autumn and winter of 1939/40 appeared a little unreal, referred to in the newspapers as the 'phoney war'. On 9 April 1940 Germany invaded Norway. The war was back in the forefront of our minds. On 10 May Germany invaded Holland and Belgium and Churchill became Prime Minister.

We listened daily to the radio during the battle for France, always encouraged by Churchill's radio broadcasts. Immediately after Dunkirk several soldiers came to the village for a brief rest, finding accommodation in the streets and houses around my lodgings. They were given a warm welcome by my landlady and her husband who with their friends and relations provided hospitality and rest from the stresses the soldiers had endured. Despite Dunkirk, and the anxiety that a German invasion could take place at any time, there always appeared to be a quiet confidence that in the end we would win through.

Rumour and speculation were rife. In the village there was a strong belief that we had spread oil on the sea and set the English Channel on fire to prevent a German invasion. Against this background what contribution could I make in the overall struggle against Germany? Choice was available before conscription decided my future role. The inspiration in wishing to join the Royal Air Force arose from the victory in the Battle of Britain. Every evening, during the months of August and September, as we listened to the radio, we noted with great relief and satisfaction the tally of enemy aircraft destroyed. The opportunity was soon to come as advertisements appeared in the newspapers urging young men, of proven fitness and with a reasonable educational background, to volunteer for training as aircrew in an expanding Royal Air Force. At the age of nineteen the thought of volunteering to train as a pilot in the Royal Air Force appeared a little unreal - but what an opportunity! With the fall of France, and then Dunkirk, followed by the fight back in the Battle of Britain, I was certainly enthusiastic to have a go. At least, I would be able to break away from the narrow confines of the family business.

CHAPTER 2
JOINING THE 'HOPEFULS'

Usually I travelled home for weekends in Barnsley by bus through the centre of Sheffield. The decision to volunteer was made on Saturday afternoon 19 October 1940. I climbed two flights of stairs and walked into the Royal Air Force recruiting office on the second floor of the Cutlers Hall, Church Street, Sheffield. 'I would like to volunteer to be a pilot in the RAF', was my greeting to the RAF Sergeant sitting behind the desk. Brief particulars were taken; date of birth, residence, occupation, education. 'Yes, you could be suitable material, you will be contacted for interview and to undergo a medical examination. Continue in your work, we will call you'. Back home that evening mother was concerned, her brother had been killed on the Somme only 24 years before. Father had little to say, as with diminishing supplies for his warehouses, and more severe rationing being implemented, I would be off his hands. To me it was opening up a new world where I would be free of the constraints and expectations of parents who had never paid much attention to my ambitions. I was the eldest son, I should know my place, I was expected to join the family business. Both parents were products of their time. We were locked into a typical middle class hierarchy. Continuing to work in the Eckington warehouse, I had a much longer wait than expected. It would be just over three years, on 26 November 1943, before I flew my first operational flight in a Beaufighter over the Mediterranean with 47 Squadron.

Life had to go on. I joined the local fire watching service, being issued with a tin hat and a whistle. During the winter of 1940/41 the blitz was at its height. Coventry was devastated on the night of 14 November; Sheffield was severely bombed on the nights of the 12 and 15 December.

When the air raid sirens sounded, our refuge in Station Road was the steps down to the coal cellar, only used if there appeared to be a lot of activity overhead. Little emotion was shown by our neighbours as we watched the red skies from the fires of the Sheffield blitz. There was just a whispered hope that friends and relatives in the city were alright. On the night of 12 December the nearest bomb to fall in our vicinity fell harmlessly in a field a quarter of a mile away. After the Sheffield blitz relief convoys of emergency food supplies came in by lorry, parking in Prince of Wales Road, a main artery running from the blitzed area to the south of the city. I drove into the city in our small van the morning after the first major blitz to see what a volunteer could do, but with the emergency services at full stretch and coping very well, there was no immediate need for unskilled volunteers. War had come to Sheffield, with burnt out buildings and rubble blocking the roads in the Don Valley at the east end of the city. Walsh's, Sheffield's largest department store, from which I had purchased a Christmas present only a week before, was a burnt out shell. It transpired that the two raids on the city had rendered 16,000 people homeless and killed nearly 200. Later in the same month Liverpool and Manchester were to suffer similar assaults.

On 21 April 1941 the eagerly awaited travel warrant arrived with instructions to report to RAF Cardington, an Aircrew Receiving Centre, near Bedford, for a medical examination and, if successful, attestation into the Royal Air Force Volunteer Reserve as a prospective pilot. After two days in Cardington, which had been the home of the ill fated R100 and R101 airships, I was pronounced fit for aircrew, along with several other men of similar age, given an Airman's service/pay book and assigned my service number, 1430437. Back home to wait, yet again, for a posting. At Cardington we were told there would be a fairly long delay, even though training programmes for aircrew were being expanded as fast as possible. The wait was longer than expected but, to demonstrate commitment, all prospective aircrew awaiting call up were issued with a small RAF lapel badge. Records in the Public Record Office indicate that by the spring of 1941 there were ten thousand potential pilots awaiting initial ground training. To reduce this waiting time, which, if known, could cause bad publicity in the press, a new Aircrew Receiving Centre was opened in June 1941 at Regents Park in London which could handle some five thousand recruits. On 11 August 1941 the call came to report to the Lords Cricket Ground, part of the Regents Park Aircrew Receiving Centre.

We were billeted in newly completed but empty luxury flats in St. Johns Wood with meals in Regents Park Zoo. They may have been luxury flats but our accommodation was basic; three biscuits (small mattresses) on the floor, two sheets, two blankets - and as many prospective aircrew in one room as could find space on the floor for a rudimentary bed. Little did we know at the time that ground staff recruits slept between blankets only, no sheets. We underwent a series of interviews, including one in front of a selection board of four senior officers to assess aircrew suitability. Why do you want to be a pilot? What activities have you been involved in since leaving school? A scouting background scored quite well. I was passed on to the next stage. Seven days in St. Johns Wood quickly passed, with extensive medical checks, written aptitude and numeracy tests together with the issue of a uniform, gas mask and supporting kit, including standard issue boots. Despite regulations, whenever I had the opportunity boots were discarded for shoes It transpires that the brief given by the Air Ministry to the Regents Park Aircrew Receiving Centre was to sift and select. Special teaching was given to any recruit who fell below the accepted standard in mathematics until he was good enough to go forward. Failure to reach the required aircrew standard could be for a variety of reasons such as educational attainment, being colour blind or having other physical problems. Despite undergoing rudimentary aptitude and numeracy tests pilot selection in 1941 appeared to be rather haphazard with most emphasis placed upon physical fitness. It was not until mid 1942 that more comprehensive grading and evaluation systems were introduced, designed to reduce the high wastage rate when as many as 25% of potential pilots at Elementary Flying Training School failed to make their first solo flight. With the object of reducing this high wastage aircrew cadets were, from 1942, allotted to specialist categories of pilot, navigator or bomb aimer after attending a grading school where flying ability was assessed.

For the time being the London blitz was over. The Germans were fully stretched in the east after invading Russia on 22 June. The nightly exodus to the shelter of the London Underground network still took place. Friends were quickly made and amusing incidents laughed at, such as the experience of our first medical held in the Long Room at Lords, with photographs of all our boyhood heroes on the walls. Our St. Johns Wood group lined up for a preliminary medical inspection, known as an FFI (Free From Infection). The Medical Officer walked down the line with a Corporal in tow - the command was, 'Drop your pants - lift up your testicles and cough', as the Medical Officer stopped in front of each man. The recruit next to me did not understand the word 'testicle' and hesitated - substitution by the common usage 'balls', brought quick understanding - so much for potential aircrew. The week was quickly over with most of our group of about thirty men given a train pass to Scarborough and told to report to the Crown Hotel to commence ground training at No.10 Initial Training Wing (ITW). The headquarters of this establishment, with Wing Commander A H H Gilligan AFC as Officer Commanding, was the Grand Hotel dominating the cliff overlooking the South Bay. We enjoyed the basic rank of AC2 (Aircraftsman 2nd Class). Rather proudly and to identify us as aircrew cadets we sported a white flash in our forage caps. More friends were made as we shared rooms in the Crown. One very close friend in particular has remained to this day - Stan Perrett who, after qualifying as a Wellington pilot, lost a leg in a Wellington crash on take-off, on Malta in October 1943.

ITW was an introduction to Royal Air Force discipline through the Daily Routine Orders - reveille at 06.30, breakfast 07.30. First parade in front of the 'Crown' at 08.30. Dinner was at 12.30, a second parade at 13.50 with tea at 16.30 and lights out at 22.15. Food was modest, to say the least, with most of our off duty time looking for fish and chips or black market bacon and eggs. Six of us occupied a front room on the first floor of the Crown Hotel, one of Scarborough's best hotels situated on the South Bay looking out to sea, with a wide esplanade in front. In all, two hundred aspiring pilots, plus the permanent staff, occupied the hotel which normally catered for a maximum of about sixty guests. Scarborough had been selected along with other seaside resorts, such as Torquay, as suitable venues to enhance the fitness of potential aircrew. We turned out on parade twice a day for the next two weeks, with boots and buttons polished, onto the esplanade in front of the hotel. Drill was conducted by a Corporal who soon let us know that he was a professional footballer from Millwall Football Club. He enjoyed the exercise far more than we did, instructing us how to salute, form up in threes, present arms, march and carry out basic drill sequences. At the daily inspection we were quite certain that his main pre-occupation was to get our hair cut even shorter. Many years later Jimmy Gibson, who served on 47 Squadron, told me he had to have his hair cut four times in three weeks as a recruit in 1942 at No.1 Aircrew Receiving Centre.

Other basic training followed, including Morse code, aircraft recognition, the principles of flight, meteorology and the RAF code of discipline and procedure. Morse code practice, using an Aldis lamp, was conducted between an upper floor of the Grand Hotel and the beach below. Most of the beach was covered with anti-invasion barbed wire. A small patch about one hundred yards long had been left in the South Bay which we occupied for this signalling practice. After nearly two weeks in Scarborough we received news that our course was to be terminated early. A group of about sixty men from the Crown was to embark by sea for Southern Rhodesia. Once there we would complete our ITW course and then proceed to Elementary Flying Training School. Other trainees at the Crown Hotel, on completion of ITW training, were scheduled to go to the USA for training under the 'Arnold Scheme'. As potential aircrew we were made up to Leading Aircraftsman and issued with two kit bags, which gave me room to pack a few luxuries, such as books, expecting to be away from the UK for an indefinite length of time. Only seven days leave was granted even though I could be away for the duration of the war whether I qualified as a pilot or not. I guessed that a posting to the Middle East from Rhodesia was my most likely ultimate fate. Although the future was certainly a little uncertain neither I nor my colleagues worried very much. In August 1941 with the weather warm and sunny Scarborough had proved to be a pleasant posting. Beer was still plentiful, for us the war seemed far away. We now had a new ally as Russia fought desperately to stem the German invasion. At least, we could see that the Russian front had relieved the pressure on the UK.

After seven days at home, I reported to the Royal Air Force Personnel Dispatch Centre, West Kirkby, Liverpool, for kitting out with tropical kit, including topees (which were seldom worn), plus the usual injections, including smallpox vaccination, anti-tetanus and anti-typhoid. On 30 August 1941 a hundred and ten U/T (under training) pilots entrained from Liverpool to Gourock. Our ship for the voyage to Durban, South Africa, was the 'Empress of Russia', a coal fired, vintage passenger liner now moored at Gourock at the mouth of the Clyde. Late afternoon, with our kit piled on the quayside, volunteers were called for to load the pile of kitbags onto the ship - I did my share hoping that I would eventually see one of my kitbags as it went into the hold; the other was for use on the voyage. On board were about five thousand military personnel, reinforcements to our commands in the Middle East, India and points further east. The RAF U/T pilots were allocated part of a mess deck with long tables and hammocks slung over; one hammock space per man. Only our small RAF contingent would disembark at Durban. Two days after boarding we were on our way amidst a convoy of about forty assorted cargo and passenger ships, protected by a variety of naval vessels. Our lead ship was the 'Dominion Monarch', a well known modern cargo liner, a little larger than the 'Empress of Russia'. Our first port of call was to be Freetown, the capital of Sierra Leone, then a British colony off the west coast of Africa, where the ship was due to replenish its stock of coal. During the first few days of the voyage there was a lot of dashing about by our naval escort, with some depth charge explosions on the outer perimeter of the convoy. Muster stations were organised for emergencies, if torpedoed, and life rafts identified, but many of us were too sea-sick to worry overmuch.

As far as we could tell, there were no serious incidents on the voyage south, with our naval escort reducing as we approached Freetown, a hot and humid port where we were obliged to stay on board as the re-coaling went on. There was coal dust everywhere. Waiting and watching the coaling, we amused ourselves tossing pennies into the sea to see them retrieved by native boys diving from assorted canoes. After two days in port the convoy reassembled and headed south for Durban. We crossed the equator with the usual fun and games organised by Army personnel, including a visit from Father Neptune and his attendants. During the voyage we were left largely to our own devices, apart from a series of lectures by one of the doctors on board over the precautions necessary in the South African climate to keep a clean bill of health. A great deal of emphasis was given in these lectures, not only to us but also to other personnel on board, on the dire consequences of sex with native women. As our average age was only 20, in the culture of the 1930s, one could only say that our experience and knowledge of those matters were very limited. As we sailed south the sea was calm, the sun shone, the war and the rough North Atlantic seemed far away. My pocket chess was a great boon. It was a very pleasant voyage, no chores, apart from queuing three times a day for the usual basic diet in which corned beef hash with potatoes and prunes with custard played a major role. The convoy rounded the Cape of Good Hope and, six weeks after leaving Gourock, the 'Empress of Russia' tied up at the quayside in Durban.

So we parted from our Army friends who went on to Suez or across to Bombay, and perhaps to Malaya and Singapore. It was early October 1941. On 7 December the Japanese bombed Pearl Harbour. Moored alongside the jetty in Durban harbour as we arrived was 'HMS Repulse', a formidable looking battle cruiser in sombre grey paint, soon to be sunk by the Japanese Air Force along with 'HMS Prince of Wales' on 10 December 1941. Later, as we heard of the Japanese successes in Malaya and Burma, we speculated

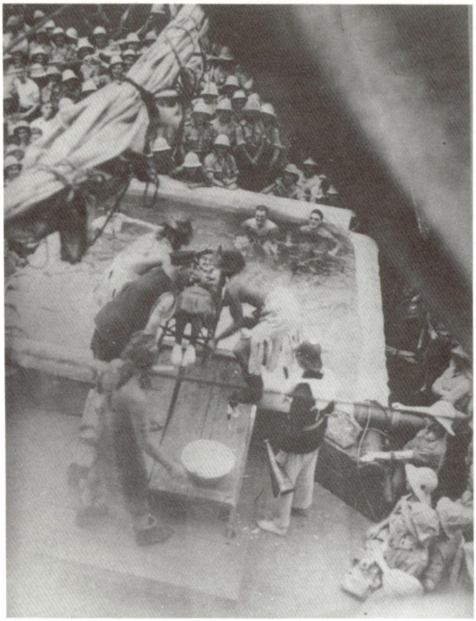

GRT Willis Archives

September 1941
'Crossing the line'.
S.S. Empress of Russia.

GRT Willis Archives

GRT Willis Archives

Hut 25, Hillside Camp, Bulawayo. Back, l to r, Ian Thompson, Pearce, Reeve, Thompson, McMillan, MacLachlen, Willis, Ovenstone, Turner. Front, l to r, Rae, Rowe, Murray, Perrett, Tyler, Vean.

Left: Bulawayo, September 1941, l to r: Bob Willis, Harry King, Stevenson (Aussie), Bert Vice, Stan Perrett.

GRT Willis Archives

and wondered at the fate which possibly befell our fellow passengers on the 'Empress of Russia', the 'Dominion Monarch' and other troopships in the convoy. No doubt many went on to reinforce the troops in India, Malaya and Singapore. After several weeks in cramped and crowded troopships, they would have had little time to acclimatise to the humid and enervating conditions of the Far East before they were fighting for their lives against the invading Japanese forces. We did not know at the time of the trauma and suffering which would befall the POWs held by the Japanese, who could be deemed to be lucky if they even managed to survive. Singapore surrendered on 15 January 1942 nine weeks after our arrival at Hillside Camp, Bulawayo, Southern Rhodesia (Zimbabwe).

Approaching from the sea on a brilliant sunlit day, Durban was a very attractive sight with its tall white waterfront buildings glistening in the sun. It really did look like a New World, far removed from the grey and grimy cities of northern England from where many of us had come. As the troopships sailed into the harbour past the whaling station to discharge a few passengers and replenish stores, 'The Lady in White', a soprano, sang her welcome to South Africa. This welcoming performance was carried out for each troopship for most of the war. We disembarked with relief, collected our kitbags, and piled into lorries to be billeted in the rather uncomfortable concrete buildings of the Durban Clairwood Racecourse. From these very drab surroundings we were rescued by the white inhabitants of Durban who soon made themselves known. I was looked after, fed right royally and shown the city by a Mr and Mrs Mate of 27 Rorvik Avenue, Durban. Mr Mate was a supervisor on the South African Railways. I was made very welcome in their house, so much so that correspondence with them continued for some years after the war. Stan Perrett and I teamed up together. We enjoyed seeing the shops, being pulled in rickshaws by the muscular Zulus and, apart from the high humidity, found the city a very welcome change from the austerity and blackout at home and on the ship coming out.

After a couple of weeks in Durban our contingent, along with other prospective aircrew who had arrived in Durban before us, were put on a sleeper train bound for Bulawayo, in Matabeleland, the western part of Southern Rhodesia. The overnight journey across Natal, around Johannesburg, through the Transvaal, west to Mafeking (Mafikeng), north through Bechuanaland (Botswana) to the border with Southern Rhodesia and then into Bulawayo, took two days. Memories are of a flat, very dry landscape, on the horizon gleaming white spoil heaps from the gold mines on the Rand, with native boys scrabbling on the track looking for pennies thrown to them when we stopped to take in water for the two giant locomotives pulling the train at a steady thirty miles an hour or so.

This was a journey of a little over one thousand miles. West of Johannesburg the train stopped for a couple of hours at Mafeking (Mafikeng). Accepting an offer of a sightseeing tour by car from one of the welcoming party at the station, we were shown the only two important buildings in town, namely the jail and the local hotel. After seeing the jail we were soon in the hotel being plied with South African 'Lion' lager by our host. As a keen Scout, Mafeking was interesting to see as the town tenaciously defended, under Baden Powell, during the Boer War only forty two years before our visit. It was still a relatively small outpost of modest bungalows with the usual corrugated tin roofs, clustered together in a flat and dusty landscape; but it was an important communication centre on the north west border of the then Union of South Africa. The defence of this uninspiring township must have been a miracle of improvisation.

Over the border, and through the Bechuanaland Protectorate (Botswana), the train clattered steadily across a flat and arid plain along the edge of the Kalahari Desert. It was late in the day as we arrived at Plumtree, just over the Southern Rhodesia (Zimbabwe) border, and into Bulawayo a little over two hours later. It had been a comfortable and interesting journey from Durban made more so by the local white inhabitants who turned out at all the stations en route to wish us well and cheer us on our way with free drinks and eats. Nearly three weeks had elapsed since our arrival in Durban. I am sure we wondered just a little as to what lay ahead.

CHAPTER 3
THE RHODESIAN AND SOUTH AFRICAN EXPERIENCE

It was early November 1941 as we drew into Bulawayo Central Station. Bulawayo was once the kraal of Lobengula, the king of the Matabele people, who came from Zululand under Mzilikazi in 1837. Bulawayo as a name simply means 'killed', stemming from the original name of 'Gubuluwayo' given by Lobengula when he built his first kraal of that name at the foot of the Matopos Hills, some sixteen miles south of the present town. Subsequently Lobengula moved his kraal to the present area of Bulawayo where the water facilities were better able to cope with his large entourage. The name Bulawayo commemorated Lobengula's victory over some of his people who had refused to accept him as king after his father's death.

Bulawayo, as we arrived in late 1941, was a splendid looking town founded in 1893 with a population of thirty thousand of whom some twelve thousand were Europeans. The town was rightly referred to as 'the Gateway to the 'Rhodesias' with its airport, railway and road system leading north to Salisbury (Harare) and beyond. Here was a prosperous town, the centre of a farming and extensive cattle ranching district, supported by a modern manufacturing infrastructure including food production, brewing, printing and steel production together with all the supporting industries and services. Arriving with the jacaranda in full bloom bordering the wide and straight town centre streets gave us an instant uplift. It was a marked contrast to the blacked out towns and cities we had left behind. The colonial style houses with their verandas, the colonnaded shops, and the elegant municipal buildings, including the City Hall and Clock Tower facing onto the wide Eighth Avenue, made a great impression. High on a plinth in Eighth Avenue stood a statue of Cecil Rhodes, who was largely responsible for encouraging the drive north from South Africa of white settlers and miners looking for gold and land to farm in the 1890s. Just off Eighth Avenue was Central Park with its manicured lawns, flower beds and access to the swimming baths in Same Parrenyatwa Street, destined to be a favourite rendezvous after lectures. We were at the end of a long journey of over eight thousand miles, and the future looked very promising as we entered this new country. We were not to be disappointed.

Our train party of over one hundred trainees, still with two kitbags each, was driven to our new home, Hillside Camp, to be our base for the next four months as we awaited posting to an Elementary Flying Training School. Here, enduring the spartan comfort of ITW (Initial Training Wing) we continued with the training programme cut short over two months ago at Scarborough. Hillside Camp, formerly Bulawayo's agricultural showground situated at the edge of town, had its own security problem. More than one accommodation hut had been burnt down before our arrival through the activities of some dissident settlers, members of the Osawabrandvaag, who disapproved of the entry of South Africa and Rhodesia into the war. Along with the Askari guards, rotas were established amongst the trainees to patrol the perimeter and hopefully to intercept any intruders. With little training, we lay in the bush on the outskirts of the camp during the night hours, sporting a .303 rifle with a clip of bullets. The turn of our contingent came around about once a month. Thankfully, there were no incidents to report.

We were quartered in long huts constructed from wattle covered with white painted hessian and with concrete floors and thatched roofs. Our arrival had swollen the number of trainees so much that our living quarters were just being completed as we arrived. Hut 25 was to be home for sixteen aspiring trainee pilots, each with a small locker, plus beds comprising timber platforms, with a straw mattress, sheets and blankets. The best place for our uniforms proved to be the rafters overhead. At the entrance to each hut was a large metal container to be used before retiring for the night if relief was required from the South African 'Lion' lager consumed in town. The container was duly emptied by native workers early the next morning. Meals were taken in a large thatched dining hall furnished with benches and long tables. The food was excellent as we were introduced for the first time to delicacies such as sweet corn, sweet potatoes and paw paw.

As at Scarborough, early morning parade started the day, held in the parade ring formerly used for show animals. The tradition had to be maintained that drill instils discipline and a culture of obedience; you could well believe that if it moves salute it, otherwise paint it white! Later experience of operational flying proved to many of us that a policy of blind obedience doesn't always extract the best performance. Discipline is no substitute for good leadership. As we moved in to Hillside, a large party of Australian trainees moved on to Elementary Flying Training. They certainly demonstrated an independence of spirit the night before leaving by substituting the Commanding Officer's pennant, flying from its flagstaff in front of the Headquarters building, with a pair of lady's knickers. The pennant was posted back the next day. I don't suppose the CO was amused. Being Australians, they demonstrated a scepticism for authority which we from the UK could not match.

The influx of trainees from the UK had imposed substantial pressures on the flying training facilities at both the Elementary and Advanced Flying Training Schools. Consequently we stayed four months at Hillside before flying training could commence. This period of waiting was taken up with lectures held at Kumalo No.21 Advanced Flying Training School outside Bulawayo. Lectures covered navigation theory, aircraft instruments, armaments, meteorology, engine theory, aircraft recognition, and the theory of flight. Lectures were over by midday and with weekends free we were able, through the very generous hospitality offered by local residents, to develop many friendships and see a great deal of the country. Southern Rhodesia, only settled by white farmers and traders a mere fifty years before, freely gave substantial and early support to the Empire Air Training Scheme. In early 1942 trainees came from the United Kingdom, Australia, South Africa, Greece and Rhodesia destined for eight newly established Air Stations. This training programme, with financial and material contributions from the UK and the USA was backed up by a white population in Rhodesia of only forty five thousand, supported in a wide range of services by the native population as well. In all, seven thousand six hundred pilots qualified in Rhodesia between 1940 and 1945. The Rhodesian experience encouraged many of these trainees to become permanent citizens after the war, with the white population increasing to around three hundred and fifty thousand, falling to about two hundred and fifty thousand in the years after independence.

We had arrived during the summer season with its warm sunny days, the occasional shower and some cumulus clouds after midday. The overall climate was quite tolerable giving ideal flying conditions in a country about five thousand feet above sea level. Further to the west was the Kalahari desert, an area to be avoided during flying training. This was, for the white population, still a frontier country with many of them first generation settlers.

Shortly after our arrival Stan Perrett and I were invited to the home of a Mr and Mrs R W J Ballantine who lived at 101 Grey Street, the road which led from Hillside to the town. Later they were to move to 30 Cawston Street. Their small bungalow, with the usual corrugated tin roof and veranda, had been their home since they emigrated from Scotland. Mr Ballantine had built the first flour mill in Bulawayo and was now enjoying retirement. Several picnics were organised by our hosts using their car, an American Buick, to visit places of interest in the adjoining Matopos Hills with their caves and rock paintings. On other days the Ballantines drove us through the flat and dry savannah (or in RAF slang the 'Bundu'), which abounded with wildlife, including elephant and buffalo. One notable journey Stan Perrett and I made, again with our hosts, was to the Khami ruins, thirteen miles to the north west of Bulawayo, where an ancient Shona stronghold had been

GRT Willis Archives

Left: December 1941, Bulawayo, Southern Rhodesia. Mr and Mrs Balantyne and 'Peter'.

Below: Shagani Memorial, Worlds View. Alf Sheldrake and Bob Willis.

GRT Willis Archives

Above: May 1942, Gatoona Airfield near Salisbury (Harare), Southern Rhodesia, Tiger Moths from 25 EFTS.

GRT Willis Archives

Below: Belvedere, Southern Rhodesia, 25 EFTS. Trainee Pilots, l to r: Bob Willis, Bert Vice, Stan Perrett, Jack Bonner at Gatoona Airfield.

GRT Willis Archives

overwhelmed by the Rozai of the Changemire dynasty from the Zambezi around 1680AD. We explored and photographed the terraced ruins of brick dwellings and forts overlooking the gorge through which the Khami River runs. The stone buildings of this advanced Shona civilisation was largely destroyed by these new invaders from the Zambezi. There had been a human presence on this site, now largely deserted, for the past one hundred thousand years. Quite close by we picnicked on the rocks overlooking the Khami Dam.

Equally generous hospitality was extended to Stan and me from Alf and Freda Sheldrake at their home on 36 Clark Road. Alf ran an electrical supply business which supplied and fitted generators to the farms on the veldt. He did all manner of electrical contracting and supply, having come out from Newark in Nottinghamshire to escape the depression of the 1930s. In 1956 Alf and Freda visited us in England with their two little girls, Rose and Heather, when on a visit to Alf's relatives in Newark. Using the Sheldrake's large General Motors car, favourite activities were fishing and swimming in the Matopos Dam, or picnics out in the veldt. Alf took us by car to see 'World's View', situated on the bare granite rock of the Matopos Hills, 50km south of Bulawayo, where Cecil Rhodes and Dr. Jameson are buried in simple graves hewn out of the rock. 'World's View' also contains the Shagani memorial to Major Wilson and his party of soldiers and settlers who were all killed in the Matabele rising of 1893. The Matopos Hills with their outcrops and granite boulders interspersed with green valleys of long grass and bush were very popular for picnics. By the 1940s all signs of conflict with the native population had been swept away. Two major towns with all modern amenities had been built, Bulawayo and Salisbury (Harare).

From late 1939 the British Government was keen to support and encourage the Rhodesian Air Training Group, eight thousand miles from the UK. The preferred location of the Air Ministry for aircrew training was Canada, but due to delays in negotiating the terms of the Canadian Air Training Scheme, the Rhodesian model was initiated in partnership with the colonial government of Rhodesia who were very eager, without any quibble, to play a full part in the war effort. The enthusiasm for the Rhodesian project was so great that as early as May 1940 the first training station was opened at No.25 EFTS, Belvedere, near Salisbury, to be followed shortly after by No.26 EFTS at Guinea Fowl near Gwelo, a small town on the road and rail link between Bulawayo and Salisbury. On Sunday 7 December 1941 the Japanese attacked the United States Pacific Fleet at Pearl Harbour, sinking or seriously damaging five battleships, fourteen smaller ships and two hundred aircraft. Whilst waiting for our flying training to start, the news that Japan was now ranged against us was a surprise. However, with the United States now fully committed to our cause, I am sure we were quite convinced that it would only be a matter of time before Germany, Italy and Japan were defeated.

In the meantime, Stan and I were determined to see with our friends, as much as possible of the surrounding country. Victoria Falls was a priority destination, visited on one weekend in January 1942 when a party of six of us from Hillside including Stan and I booked into the Victoria Falls Hotel. Just fifteen years after the Union Flag was hoisted in Salisbury in 1890 the building of this hotel was started. Outside the main towns we were obliged to take precautions against malaria, with mosquito nets mandatory overnight in the Victoria Falls Hotel. With fly screens on the windows and doors, plus large electric fans on the ceilings of the public rooms, everything possible was done to make the hot and humid climate tolerable. Air conditioning was a luxury yet to come. The journey, first class by train, was very comfortable, and, for us out from the UK, the height of luxury with the native 'boys' attending to our every need. The distance to Victoria Falls by rail from Bulawayo is about two hundred and eighty miles. Approaching the Falls, the train passed through dense bamboo forest with the climate becoming much warmer and humid as we dropped down from the five thousand foot plateau to the Zambezi River valley. The Falls were quite spectacular, with the Zambezi River plunging more than three hundred feet down a sheer chasm. Up river from the Falls the Zambezi is over a mile wide, containing many palm dotted islands. We took many photographs, declining to ride on the trolley car from the hotel to the view points overlooking the Falls and the Zambezi. The trolleys were originally provided for Edwardian ladies who were pushed along the rails by trolley boys. The track was pulled up a few years after our visit. At the hotel a local resident offered to take us by car over the Zambezi bridge to Livingstone, a town on the other side of the Falls in Northern Rhodesia, now Zambia. Livingstone in 1942 was a one street town of colonial buildings plus one hotel with six or seven cars around. In recent times, around Livingstone and the Falls area, many Stone Age tools have been discovered with clear signs that humans lived and settled around the Falls two million years ago. Many of the Stone Age tools discovered are now housed in a museum in Livingstone, today an important tourist centre. In 1942 the only local attraction, apart from the Falls, was the Livingstone game reserve through which our host drove us to see the zebra, giraffe, wildebeest and innumerable monkeys.

At last on 26 March 1942 I was posted with Stan to No.25 Elementary Flying Training School at Belvedere, ten miles or so to the west of Salisbury(Harare). This airfield, referred to as a grass strip, was in a large field fenced off and carved out of the flat savannah on the outskirts of Salisbury. The station was set out in the traditional Royal Air Force style complete with flagpole, in front of the station HQ, flying the Royal Air Force ensign and the Station Commander's pennant. As we arrived, passing the guardroom and sentry at the gate and seeing the neatly parked yellow painted Tiger Moths drawn up at the edge of the field, we knew that serious business was about to begin. We had excellent quarters with real beds - no longer hard wooden pallets on the floor. Unlike Hillside, we could no longer walk into town, but had to rely on station transport, which was somewhat limited.

A day in Salisbury, attractive as the city was, did not lend itself to any spending spree. With less than £1 a week to spend, the main attraction was always going to be a restaurant meal, a glass of Lion lager or just a walk in Salisbury Park. Excessive high spirits, together with too much Lion lager one Saturday evening, found the writer bundled into a taxi back to camp out of harm's way. This was an occasion not to be repeated! The town centre, with its American cars, was where the predominantly white population enjoyed the luxuries offered by the department stores and shops in Monica Road and First Street. The white stone buildings, arcaded shopping streets and segregated population were the product of a colonial regime which, after much bitter strife, would ultimately surrender to majority rule.

We were Course No.27, quite a mixed bunch with 33 from the UK, 4 from Rhodesia and 18 from Australia, under the Chief Flying Instructor, Squadron Leader E Fulford. My first flight, in a dual control Tiger Moth on 31 March 1942, was a familiarisation exercise of twenty five minutes with Flying Officer Chilvers as instructor. The De Havilland Tiger Moth, powered by a Gypsy Major 130hp engine, giving a maximum speed of a little over 100mph in level flight was a widely used basic trainer. This small two seater dual control biplane taught us all the basic skills required for safe flying. It was an aircraft which generally allowed the pupil to correct mistakes. Subsequent service aircraft were not nearly so tolerant.

I was then assigned as a pupil to Flight Lieutenant Loat, who I soon discovered was a very impatient individual. His command of the English language down the speaking tube between instructor and pupil, embracing all the unprintable Anglo-Saxon words, was an experience not to be forgotten. Normally ten to twelve hours tuition was needed to go solo. Some exceptional pupils went solo after eight hours instruction; anything under ten hours was considered quite good. Flight Lieutenant Loat was determined to have me solo before the ten hour deadline, so after nine hours and forty five minutes in the air I was dispatched on my first solo. All went well until the landing, when I misjudged the height and hit the ground with a severe bump, breaking the undercarriage. It was a very humbling experience standing beside the broken aircraft waiting to be picked up by the 'crash' wagon. More unprintable words from Flight Lieutenant Loat, followed on the next day with another twenty minutes with him in the air and then off again on my own - this time completed successfully. My instructor, to give him credit, must have had some confidence in my abilities. Despite the strong language, I was certainly thankful to be given a second chance. Over the next four years of continuous flying this was the only aircraft I ever damaged through misjudgement or, what was euphemistically called, 'pilot error'.

The course at No.25 EFTS was for twelve weeks until 21 June 1942. Thankfully, after going solo, I acquired a new instructor, Pilot Officer Chaldecott who was much more 'pupil friendly'. Perhaps my first instructor was frustrated, as some instructors apparently were, at being thousands of miles away from 'active service'. During my brief experience of his teaching he was the only pilot who ever made me air-sick. The innumerable spins and low flying 'buzzing' of his girlfriend's bungalow, out in the country, are still vivid memories. Much of the subsequent flying programme was conducted from a satellite airfield at Gatooma, about an hour's journey from Belvedere, which we reached bumping along rough roads in the back of a three ton truck. We left Belvedere at around 6am to take advantage of the cooler part of the day. Gatooma was out in the bush ('bundu') surrounded by a featureless landscape with few landmarks, which made it imperative to keep a sharp eye on the compass. It was inadvisable to get lost or run out of fuel and then have to make a forced landing in the bush. It was far from certain that you would be found quickly. Flying training covered a whole range of exercises including instrument flying, aerobatics, formation flying, forced landings, steep turns and cross country. Towards the end of the course I was introduced to night flying, comprising one hour and twenty minutes of continuous take-off and landings by the light of 'goose-neck' paraffin flares and a 'chance' floodlight at the start of the take-off and landing area. Instrument flying in the Tiger Moth was supplemented by exercises in a 'Link Trainer', a simulator in which the pilot was completely enclosed in a blacked out cockpit where all that could be seen was the illuminated instrument panel. Following instructions into the head set, I practised in these simulated conditions the art of instrument flying in nil visibility. Link Trainer practice, essential to maintain blind flying skills, was to continue throughout my flying career. Lectures on navigation, engine theory, meteorology and aircraft recognition continued as at ITW. Having completed nearly forty eight hours solo day and night by the end of the course I was assessed as an 'average' pupil. The stage was now set for more advanced training. Along with most of our course Stan also passed out successfully, although around twelve or so of our original colleagues had dropped out for various reasons. Pupils who were 'washed out' as pilots always found the disappointment difficult to cope with, having come eight thousand miles to achieve a personal ambition. They were re-mustered mostly as observers or air gunners under training.

Stan and I had missed our Rhodesian friends in Bulawayo very much. We kept in touch by mail, but as Salisbury was about two hundred and forty miles from Bulawayo, personal contact was impossible. The war news at this time was rather depressing as we read in the Rhodesian press of the capture of Mandalay on 2 May and the surrender of Tobruk on 21 June, followed by the advance of Rommel's Afrika Corps to the Egyptian border. Thirty three thousand troops surrendered at Tobruk to German forces of perhaps half that number, much to Churchill's dismay. Other setbacks, such as the critical loss of shipping in the Atlantic during 1942, we did not know about at the time.

From Belvedere Stanley and I were posted to No.20 Service Flying Training School at Cranborne, again quite close to Salisbury. We were now made up to the exalted rank of Acting Sergeants, but with no extra pay, possibly to lessen the blow if we failed on the next leg. Before posting to Cranborne decisions had to be made as to who would be trained as single engine pilots (fighter pilots) or twin engine pilots (bombers, etc.). The decision in both Stan's and my own case was for single engine training, an experience which was to stand me in good stead some eighteen months later. No.20 Service Flying Training School was a well equipped station with modern workshops and a concrete runway. It was the home to North American Harvards, a modern advanced trainer supplied under lend-lease from the States. For most aspiring pilots the Harvard was a big leap forward. Climbing into the front cockpit of this aircraft, with its array of instruments, control column, toe brakes and 550hp Pratt and Whitney Wasp engine up in front to give a maximum speed of 205mph, was a far cry from the basic Tiger Moth. The Harvard was a two seater, all metal, single engine monoplane with retractable undercarriage, constant speed airscrew and an enclosed cockpit. The pilot under training, converting from the Tiger Moth, sat in front of the instructor, the aeroplane being equipped with dual control. We learnt to treat the Harvard with respect, not difficult to fly but it was not easy to fly well.

Enjoying a week's leave, between Belvedere and Cranborne, Stanley and I celebrated our twenty first birthdays in Umtali (now Mutare). Umtali, a small mining township close to the Mozambique border, was located at the foot of Christmas Pass, on the main road and railway from Salisbury to Beira on the Indian Ocean. In the 1940s Beira was a popular holiday venue for the white Rhodesians, being their nearest point to the sea. The distance from Umtali to Beira was about two hundred and fifty miles, and from Salisbury to Beira about five hundred miles. We travelled first class by train, booked in to a small but comfortable hotel, and then contacted the local gold mine manager, Mr Tyler, who had offered to show us around the 'Iona' mine when we arranged the holiday. The search for gold was the compelling reason that brought the white settlers into Rhodesia in the first place; but gold in the quantity that existed at the Rand in South Africa has never been found. We were picked up by car and taken to the mine. The mine, according to our host, was only profitable because of cheap native labour. A continuous flow of rock, mostly hacked out by pick and shovel, came to the surface in large iron buckets to be machine crushed and then poured into tanks for treatment under the cyanide process. A day's mining might extract enough gold the size of a tennis ball. The gold was kept in the office safe prior to shipment to South Africa for further refining. After visiting the mine workings we had the dubious pleasure of handling a ball of gold, when Mr Tyler opened the safe for our benefit. Donning overalls, down the mine we went in a large open bucket. It was similar to a small but deep open cast coal site with tunnels cut into the hillside. All the miners, many stripped to the waist, were recruited from the neighbouring native villages. With no credit to ourselves we took little interest in the miners. This country, at the time, was part of the British Colonial culture and we were part of that inheritance

Returning to our hotel for two 21st birthday dinners, one on the 18th June for Stan and one on the 20th for mine, we drank to our health and absent friends, speculating as to what the folks back home were doing. Mail came by sea and took up to eight weeks to reach us. For a few days we enjoyed a mixture of horse riding and walking as we absorbed the atmosphere of open space, with a backdrop of mountains in neighbouring Mozambique and the spectacular waterfalls on the Odzi River. Houses, scattered in the valleys and occupied by European farmers or ranchers, were generally roofed in corrugated iron with the mandatory veranda. Roads connecting towns consisted of two parallel concrete strips designed to carry one car or truck in either direction. Driving on strip roads across the veldt was guaranteed to be a bumpy experience as avoiding action had to be taken from vehicles hurtling towards one's own. The question always was; who gave way first?

Returning from Umtali to Cranborne, there followed five months continuous training. After five hours and twenty minutes of dual instruction I completed my first solo in a Harvard. Training at Cranborne was divided into two parts, initial and advanced. The first nine weeks of initial training with instructor Flying Officer Andrews were devoted to acquiring the basic flying skills. Andrews, a man of few words, not given to offering much praise and encouragement, demonstrated and instructed take-off and landing, stalling, spinning, aerobatics, steep turns, low flying and instrument flying. These were all basic skills to be acquired before any advanced training could begin. As at Belvedere, we were under the clear impression that some of the instructors, especially if they were married, were unhappy at being sent out to Rhodesia instead of a posting to a front line squadron nearer home. Some above average pupils, on gaining their 'wings', were kept in Rhodesia for training as instructors to allow some repatriation to take place.

After successfully completing a flying test by the Chief Flying Instructor, Squadron Leader Hamilton, I passed on to the advanced stage on 17 August with one hundred and sixty hours flying in my log book. On 7 September 1942, in RAF parlance, the 'Flying Badge' was awarded. However, the wings presentation was deferred until the completion of the advanced section of the Harvard course. What happened if one failed the advanced section was never explained. I was rather pleased to learn that out of forty six pupils I was third from the top in the wings exam. This exam covered Navigation, Armaments, Meteorology and Signals. Navigation and Signals were practical as well as theoretical. Total marks were 82.1%. However, my performance in general flying was only rated, at 69%, as average.

Occasionally in the Sergeants Mess we would speculate on how far Japan would advance, having pushed the British ground forces out of Burma. There were even rumours that if the situation worsened, with a Japanese invasion of India or Ceylon, we would be dispatched with our Harvard trainers, suitably armed with a single .303 machine gun in the starboard wing plus bomb racks, to render support to the defenders. Fortunately we gave little attention to these rumours and concentrated on earning our coveted 'wings'.

Before commencing advanced training Stanley and I, given another two weeks leave, accepted an invitation to stay at Tobaus Farm at Arcturus, about forty miles from Salisbury. We journeyed there by post lorry, a large canvas covered truck which carried passengers, freight and post to outlying farms. The journey took most of the day. Unfortunately, for much of the time we were on the farm I was in bed with 'flu. This was the only time I was ill, apart from 'gippy' tummy, in the service. Our hosts, Mr and Mrs Stobart, were very understanding and took my indisposition in their stride. Their bungalow was brick built with the usual tin roof. The veranda was covered in fine mesh with screens on all windows and doors to keep out flies and mosquitoes. These precautions were essential if one was to enjoy a 'sundowner' on the veranda at the end of the day. I did manage to see and photograph the farm with its cattle being dipped and the oxen in harness doing the heavy work in preparing the land for the tobacco crop. We watched the natives dig irrigation ditches and visited their kraal on the farm about a mile from the Stobart's bungalow. It was a new experience for us to watch the native women grind maize by hand and carry water from the well in pots on their heads. What the men earned paid for maize, vegetables, beer and the right to have a hut on the farm. The Stobarts were first generation settlers bringing the bush into cultivation through growing tobacco.

Back from leave, the training for the next ten weeks was a serious business indeed. We started with a pep talk from Squadron Leader Stratton, the OC of the Advanced Training Squadron. Thankfully, I had left behind the dour Flying Officer Andrews. Guided by various instructors, who turned out to be a friendly lot, we practised formation tactics, low flying, bombing, cross country navigation, instrument flying and night flying. Fighter tactics, and interception tactics, also played their part. The course proved to be stimulating and quite demanding with my last flight on 27 November 1942. Three days later Stanley and I were presented with our 'wings' by the Chief Ground Instructor, Squadron Leader Cousins at an informal and hurried parade in his office. We were on an immediate posting to No.21 Service Flying Training School at Kumalo, outside Bulawayo, for conversion to twin engine aircraft prior to attending a General Reconnaissance Course at George in Cape Province, South Africa.

On our advanced flying course at Cranborne there had been three fatal casualties out of fifty trainee pilots. Accidents arose for a variety of reasons, such as collisions whilst practising formation flying, stalling on the landing approach or misjudgments when low flying, all usually from lack of experience. All the aspiring pilots on my course attended the three military funerals. It was a sobering experience to hear the 'Last Post' sounded by a single bugler followed by a volley from the RAF escort over the open grave. These sad events enhanced the resolve to avoid a similar fate. The parents of trainees killed would never know the full circumstances of their deaths out in Rhodesia, apart from the fact that it was a flying accident on a training course. Another very sad experience occurred later when, driving down a strip road near Bulawayo with one of the instructors, I was taken out to a crashed Oxford which for some reason had fallen out of the sky. Skin tissue from the two occupants was still to be found adhering to the wrecked airframe. Again eight thousand miles from home one wondered about the families of those involved in this tragic accident. A telegram, followed by a brief letter of condolence from their Commanding Officer, saying that "following a flying accident we regret"...........would be the sad ending. At least Stanley and I had survived so far.

We had started at Cranborne as a course of fifty pupil pilots. By the time we qualified and earned our 'wings', our numbers were down to forty six. The urge to qualify was fostered by a strong competitive spirit. Every aspiring pilot that had got so far lived with the fear of being 'scrubbed'. For me it was difficult to contemplate the personal disappointment and blow to my self esteem if I failed to make the grade. This fear was a great motivator. Looking back, if we could survive the stresses of flying training we should be able to cope with the hazards of operational flying which lay ahead. Four or five of our course identified as star pupils were commissioned as Acting Pilot Officers. The rest of us were now fully paid Sergeant Pilots! Those commissioned went onto further training in Rhodesia to qualify as instructors. During our stay in Cape Province, we were saddened to hear that Ian Thompson of our course, subsequently commissioned, had been killed in a flying accident in a Harvard. In due course and as far as practicable, the whole Southern Rhodesia air training scheme had to be self sufficient. With a shortage of operational training units in the Middle East the maximum use of Southern Rhodesian facilities was desirable. Quite sensibly a large proportion of pilots trained in Rhodesia were posted to the Middle East. The length of time spent at Service Flying Training Schools in Rhodesia depended to some degree on the demand for pilots both in the UK and the Middle East. We were yet to see the large scale expansion of Bomber Command from 1943 to 1945 but already demand for fighter pilots, as opposed to bomber or multi engine aircraft pilots, was being modified.

My sudden and unexpected posting for twin engine training demonstrated the increasing demand for pilots of multi engined aircraft. I had spent the previous five months being trained as an embryo single engine fighter pilot. The theory and practice was to acquire sufficient skill to be capable of destroying enemy aircraft in the air and to act in a ground attack role. Particularly important was the ability to shoot straight. Much time had been spent on target practice against a drogue towed behind another aircraft. However for me the Royal Air Force had other ideas. Both Stan and I were to be switched to twin engine aircraft with a possible future role in the Mediterranean or back in the UK on Coastal Command.

Our training in Belvedere and Cranborne allowed us much less free time in Salisbury than we had enjoyed at ITW in Bulawayo. A visit to the cinema in Salisbury where, much to our surprise, the ladies and gentlemen wore evening dress, or an evening in a restaurant or bar to enjoy a meal, plus Lion lager, was usually the most off station relaxation we could manage. The cinema and restaurants were patronised exclusively by the white population. The native population was totally segregated as far as social activities and living areas were concerned. We were in Mashonaland where most of the native male population worked on the farms or in the towns in all manner of semi skilled occupations, under a paternalistic colonial government. Salisbury, now Harare, was and still is the capital of the country. Here, hospitality from the white population was again very generous but, due to training pressures and distance from town, difficult to take up. Apart from the brief excursions to town, Stan and I only managed to accept a few off duty invitations to dinner, followed by an evening playing bridge, with a retired widow and her daughter who lived in a large brick bungalow on the outskirts of Salisbury.

On 1 December 1942 we left Salisbury for Bulawayo, travelling by train and truck to Kumalo for immediate conversion to twin engine flying in Oxford aircraft. The Airspeed Oxford was a twin engined monoplane and valued training aircraft, powered by two Armstrong Siddeley Cheetah engines of 370hp each, to give a maximum speed of around 180mph in level flight. Fitted with dual control, this aircraft had the same advanced features we had mastered on the Harvard which made conversion from one to the other comparatively easy. Six days after my last flight in a Harvard, I was taking lessons at Kumalo on the Oxford. From 21 April 1941, when I first reported to Cardington Aircrew Selection Centre, to 27 November 1942 it had taken nineteen months to get so far, with two hundred and forty seven hours flying logged.

The crash conversion course to Oxfords lasted exactly two weeks after which I was deemed to be reasonably proficient on the type, flying solo after three and a half hours dual instruction. Most of the available time was taken up in take-off and landing exercises, namely ‘circuits and bumps’. There was a small amount of single engine flying and instrument flying to complete the course. We contacted our old friends the Ballantines and Sheldrakes, but with the course so short all we managed was a couple of weekends with these old friends. Back in the mess, the notice board confirmed our posting to South Africa.

CHAPTER 4
SOUTH AFRICA AND BACK TO THE UK

On 19 December 1942 we were on the train to No.61 General Reconnaissance School at George, Cape Province, arriving just before Christmas. The journey across Africa was done in style with first class accommodation provided. We stopped at Mafeking again, it was raining, there was no welcoming party, we stayed on the train. For most of two days the train steamed across open veldt, through Kimberly arriving at George, two hundred and fifty miles east of Cape Town, early on 22 December 1942. South African Army transport conveyed us from the station to the airfield described as No.61 Air School. Miraculously Stan and I were still together although our group of aspiring GR pilots from Rhodesia was now a mere handful, six of us in all, from our original 'Wings' course of forty six. The accommodation in wooden barrack huts proved to be excellent. With a large quota of Cape 'coloured' personnel on the station, all our wants were more than adequately catered for. There was to be no flying or lectures for us until after Christmas as many of the South African Air Force instructors were away on a few days leave. In the meantime transport was laid on each day to the beach at Mussel Bay, a few miles away. In the six days over Christmas much of the time was spent swimming and surfing or walking on the white sands of the bay. Christmas dinner was a splendid feast in the Sergeant's Mess with roast turkey and Christmas pudding. It was midsummer, very warm and sunny. Not knowing or really caring what lay ahead, we made the most of these very pleasant surroundings. On future weekends Knysna and the 'Wilderness', a prime holiday spot not many miles away, became the favoured destination. Knysna with its lagoons, warm climate and pleasant beaches was an idyllic retreat, with some very fine swimming. The local residents, many of whom were retired, were very friendly taking us into their homes and to church on Sunday. Again there was total segregation with the original native population living well away from the beaches and lagoons of Knysna, unless they were live-in house servants.

The GR course was intellectually demanding embracing dead reckoning navigation over the sea, the ability to use a sextant, and astro-navigation. Examinations had to be passed in DR Navigation, Compass, Meteorology, Reconnaissance, Coding, Ship Recognition, Photography and Astro-Navigation. For the first time since leaving the Grammar School I had to swot hard to be sure of passing. All our group worked hard. There was a rumour that failing resulted in an undesirable flying job.

The school was administered by the South African Air Force who provided most of the instructors. For much of the training I assumed the role of navigator, tracking over the Indian Ocean in an Avro Anson in flights of up to four hours. On my first flight on New Years Day 1943, I was assigned the 'highly prestigious' role of third navigator. As the course progressed I was 'promoted' to first navigator. To add a little spice to these flights passing shipping was identified and a watch kept for any possible U Boats venturing into the area. Following ground training, all training in the air was in the RAF's original coastal reconnaissance aircraft, the trusty Anson, a twin engined monoplane powered by two 350hp Cheetah engines and able to carry three pupils on these exercises. Experience gained included some night flying, embracing search and find techniques and astro observations, together with some daytime low flying over the sea to familiarise us with that environment. Despite passing all the theoretical exams with above average marks of 87%, I was thankful when the flying exercises were over. Stretched out full length in the nose of an Anson, low flying over the sea, estimating wind speed and direction or squinting through a bomb sight was, for me, tedious and uncomfortable, not helped when I managed to rip my right knee on the undercarriage crank handle. A three inch scar still bears witness. The Anson undercarriage had to be manually retracted hence the crank handle. Thankfully it was never suggested that I should be a navigator; coping with a bubble sextant in a pitching aircraft and trying to keep the star, previously identified, in the centre of the bubble, was not my ambition. As for our leisure activities, the time at George passed too quickly.

On 26 February 1943 as the course ended, posted up in the Mess were our future destinations. Of the six Sergeant Pilots from our course in Rhodesia all except myself were to entrain for Durban and then by ship to the Middle East, including Stan my closest friend since our days in Scarborough eighteen months ago. For some obscure or statistical reason I was destined for the UK. Ahead lay the challenging task of completing operational training on a front line aircraft, prior to joining a squadron. Stan's experience was not unique. After operational training on Wellington bombers at Shallufa Operational Training Unit on the Suez Canal, he was posted to join 221 Coastal Command Squadron on Malta. On 23 October 1943, on only his second operational flight his aircraft, a Wellington bomber with a crew of six, crashed at the end of the runway on take-off and caught fire. Stanley was pulled clear of the aircraft severely injured. After a long period in hospital in Malta he was invalided home.

Years later I was to hear from him the full story of his last flight. The aircraft, destined for an anti-submarine patrol, was carrying a full complement of depth charges. The crash followed an aborted take-off by the pilot due to air speed indicator failure. As the Wellington was taking off Stan, as second pilot and as part of the cockpit drill, called out the indicated airspeed to the pilot who would then know when sufficient speed had been achieved to pull the 'stick' back with his heavy load and become airborne. Stanley called down the intercom 'no airspeed indicator'. The pilot had to make a quick decision, to take-off by 'feel' and jettison the depth charges before attempting a landing without an air speed indicator, or to abort the take-off immediately. In the event, the pilot decided to abort the take-off halfway down the runway. The aircraft overshot the runway with the brakes hard on. With the airfield buildings looming ahead the pilot swung the aircraft round as it crashed into an aircraft hangar. A concrete block fell onto the cockpit, trapping Stanley by the legs. The aircraft broke into two halves on impact and caught fire. Stanley was only able to extricate himself because the floor below his seat caught fire and collapsed. He rolled onto the ground and was pulled clear by the fire tender crew. The depth charges were thrown clear as the aircraft broke into two halves on impact and fortunately failed to explode. Of the other members of the crew, the rear gunner was killed but the remaining four members, including the pilot, escaped without serious injury. Fortunately, and largely due to the courage of the fire tender crew, all the aircrew were pulled clear before over a thousand gallons of fuel went up in a great ball of flame. Stan's injuries were severe burns and the ultimate loss of a leg. After two years in training, and just two flights on operations, Stanley's future was a long stay in hospital, discharge from the RAF and a disability pension. Stanley, much to his credit, ultimately rejoined his old firm of insurance brokers, and pursued a very successful career until retirement. Shortly after Stan's discharge from hospital in England, my parents offered him the opportunity of a holiday at the family bungalow in the country near Barnsley. My sister Maisie took him in hand, which helped him to feel welcome and gave him the opportunity to meet my family. I was quite unaware of this hospitality at the time, being myself in the Middle East, having completed operational training in the UK after returning from South Africa.

With the GR course successfully completed, no time was wasted before entraining to Cape Town to wait for a suitable ship bound for the UK. On the train, as it travelled over the open veldt, my attention was drawn to a huge bonfire surrounded by at least twenty to thirty cars. It was early evening just after sunset on a fine but dark night. A companion in the coach, in answer to my enquiry, said it would be a gathering of the brotherhood - the Osawabrandvaag - who were opposed to South

Africa's entry into the war. Whilst at George we were alerted to the danger of hit and run cars when walking back to camp from the town of George during the hours of darkness. Stanley and I, walking back from George one evening, only escaped this fate by dodging behind a tree at the side of the road as a large saloon car with headlights full on swerved towards us. We heard of other servicemen who had narrow escapes in similar circumstances. It was a stark reminder that South Africa had only joined the Allies by passing the necessary resolution in the Parliament at Cape Town by a very slim majority.

Joining several other aircrew in Capetown waiting for a berth I was to learn that an old colleague at Cranborne, Sergeant Walshaw, a fellow Yorkshireman from Doncaster, who had sailed for the UK a few weeks before, had been torpedoed and lost at sea. I just hoped we had a fast ship. Walking down Adderley Street, with its shops and double decker buses, we could have been in London on a warm summer's day. Another day was given over to a ride in the cable car to the top of Table Mountain. It was a clear day with fine views of the city and harbour. Still waiting, much of the next two weeks was spent fifteen miles south of Cape Town on the beach at Muizenberg reserved for 'whites' only!

On 13 March 1943 I sailed from Capetown on the American liner 'Mariposa', along with another newly qualified Sergeant Pilot, Charlie Tomalin. We became lifelong friends; Charlie, also from Kumalo and No.61 Air School, George, subsequently joined 248 Squadron on Beaufighters and Mosquitos, engaged in anti-shipping strikes in French and Norwegian waters. The 'Mariposa', before Pearl Harbour, was a cruise ship of the Matson Line, when it was engaged in sailing between Los Angeles, San Francisco and the Hawaiian Islands. Arriving in Capetown, bound for the UK as an American troopship, Charlie and I, along with half a dozen RAF aircrew, were given berths aboard. The ship was crowded with a mixture of American and British servicemen being repatriated from the Middle East for various reasons. The ship had sailed from Suez via the Cape as the Germans were still able to attack convoys in the central Mediterranean area. Movement on the

'Mariposa' was restricted, with at least one deck given over to servicemen requiring hospitalisation, including cholera victims. The Americans, who comprised the majority on board, placed armed guards to keep unauthorised persons away from the hospital area. I shared a cabin with three other British NCOs; all Special Forces veterans from the Middle East who turned out to be interesting characters. One, who had performed as a stuntman before the war by diving into what he described as a 'damp sponge' in Blackpool Tower Circus, had a fund of gruesome stories to tell of Special Forces activity against the Germans on Crete. How to quietly dispose of German guards using a Commando knife and then place plastic explosives in aircraft parked on Heraklion airfield was described in horrific detail. This kind of wartime activity could only be carried out by a very special type of personality. I was not one of those. The ship sailed north through the Atlantic at top speed, without any naval escort, expecting to outpace any waiting U-boats. The voyage was uneventful, arriving at Gourock on the Clyde in just under three weeks. No sooner had we docked than Charlie and I, together with our kit, were bundled onto a train in the late afternoon, destination Harrogate, North Yorkshire. As usual, nobody told us what to expect. We were hungry, with no English money and back to the blackout Arriving in Harrogate on 2 April 1943 tired and bemused, sometime around midnight, we were driven to an hotel at Pannal Ash, just outside Harrogate. We had arrived at No.7 Personnel Reception Centre. After two days there, kitted out with a fresh uniform, a train pass and following a quick phone call home, I turned up on leave to a rather surprised family. I had been away for nineteen months; operational training was the next stage. There was quiet satisfaction at having got so far. Records at Kew(Public Records Office) now show that only 64% of those who started flying training in 1941/42 as pupil pilots succeeded in obtaining their 'wings'.

CHAPTER 5
A TEAM TRAINED FOR WAR

As I left England in August 1941, two months after Germany attacked the USSR, an Allied victory seemed to be far away. Back to England in April 1943, despite Japan's entry into the war, ultimate victory, followed by a better and more stable world, seemed certain. My family at home were coping very well and fortunately not worrying too much about me. I was to learn for the first time that mother had been seriously ill whilst I was in Rhodesia but was now fully recovered. After two weeks leave, mainly spent visiting friends and seeing staff who were still in father's business, I received a telegram sending me on my way to Little Rissington, No.6(P) Advanced Flying Unit. This station in picturesque countryside on the edge of the Cotswolds served, for many years after the war, as the Central Flying School. Here along with Charlie Tomalin I was to have a six weeks refresher course on Oxfords, including a week at Pershore in Worcestershire on Link Trainer exercises simulating Standard Beam Approach landings. Until arrival at Little Rissington all flying training to date had been conducted in ideal weather conditions. A refresher course was badly needed; I had not been at the controls of an Oxford for four months. It was essential to adapt quickly to the very different flying environment of the unpredictable British weather. The course was a crash refresher course, including one week devoted to night flying exercises. It was early summer 1943 and fortunately for me the weather was reasonable. The assessment at the end was 'average on Oxfords'. Whilst on this course higher authority had to decide what role I should fill as a pilot, considering my previous training and in the light of current RAF needs. Considerable interest was displayed in the mess as the posting lists were put up at the end of each course.

My posting was to Crosby on Eden, No.9(C) Operational Training Unit to fly Beaufighters. Unfortunately I was to part company with Charlie Tomalin who was posted to the OTU at East Fortune near North Berwick, also to fly Beaufighters, ultimately to join 248 Squadron on anti-shipping strikes. Thankfully Charlie survived, completing 47 sorties, ending the war as a Flight Lieutenant and a much loved friend to many on 248 Squadron. After completing the Operational Training Unit course I could expect a posting to a squadron. I enjoyed the flying both at Little Rissington and later at Crosby on Eden. Unlike later experience at Crosby, accidents on Oxfords at Little Rissington were few, although one aspiring pilot had his ambitions abruptly terminated when he managed to taxi an Oxford into a double decker bus transporting airmen around the airfield. Fortunately, there were no serious injuries but much amusement in the mess.

On 21 June 1943, after seven days leave having just managed to celebrate my 22nd birthday with a family party, I arrived at Crosby, near Carlisle, to train for operations flying the Beaufighter. The training started on a Beaufort, a twin engined aircraft all metal monoplane, still used by torpedo squadrons in attacks on enemy shipping. The Bristol Beaufort, until superseded by the Beaufighter, was the RAF's standard torpedo-bomber. The aircraft carrying a crew of four, was powered by two Bristol Taurus radial engines giving a top speed of around 250mph. This aircraft, fitted for training with dual control, had to be mastered before attempting to fly a Beaufighter. There was no dual control available on a Beaufighter but if one could handle a Beaufort, which had rather similar flying characteristics, one should be sufficiently competent to fly a Beaufighter.

The Beaufighter was designed and manufactured by the Bristol Aeroplane Company Limited at Filton outside Bristol. It was produced as a successor to the Beaufort, which had seen a great deal of service as a torpedo strike aircraft. The Beaufighter was a very robust all metal aeroplane weighing just under ten tons fully loaded and powered by two Bristol Hercules air-cooled, sleeve-valve engines, carrying a crew of two, the pilot and observer. It was to prove a very versatile aircraft, being used extensively as a night fighter and intruder aircraft besides being a torpedo bomber and rocket firing strike aircraft, serving in all theatres. Most of my time on Beaufighters was spent flying the Mark X powered by two 1735 horse power Hercules engines. Training flights were generally on the earlier Mark Vl powered by two 1670 hp Hercules engines, giving a maximum speed of around 300mph.

My first flight in a Beaufort at Crosby was on 23 June 1943, followed by solo on the type four days later. With four more days experience on the Beaufort the time came to switch to the Beaufighter. The Beaufighter was a very powerful aircraft in comparison to the Beaufort. We were warned that the power of the Hercules engine and the torque induced could cause the aeroplane to swing off the runway if not promptly corrected. We prospective pilots had to be satisfied with a demonstration flight. On 5 July, after one hour and fifty minutes in the air standing behind the pilot, Pilot Officer Henderson, as he demonstrated the basic characteristics of the aeroplane, I found myself in the aircraft all alone and taxiing out to the end of the runway for my first solo. We had been told to expect a sudden surge forward which would give us a sharp jolt in the back as we released the brakes and opened up the engines to full power. And so it was.

All went well on take-off and, after nearly one hour in the air familiarising myself with the controls and instruments, a successful landing took place, remembering to carry out all the in-flight sequences many months of training had instilled. Most pilots I was later to fly with had great confidence in the inherent strength of this aircraft, often put to the test in violent evasive action if attacked by single engine fighters such as the Me109. We were impressed with the heavy armament carried, particularly the four 20mm Hispano cannons, although they were prone to jamming. Supplementing the four cannons were six .303 Browning machine guns. This was standard armament which could be complemented or modified when armed with bombs, rockets or torpedoes. Each Hispano cannon carried a magazine of two hundred and fifty rounds plus one thousand rounds for each Browning machine gun, giving the pilot tremendous fire power for sustained attacks on ground targets. Before firing, the standard gun sight would be swung into place. The cannons were fired by pulling a trigger and the machine guns by pressing a button, both located on the control column. Some protection to the pilot was given by a bullet proof toughened glass windscreen and an armour plated partition behind the pilot's seat. The aircraft was equipped with the standard fighter aircraft bucket seat allowing the pilot to sit on his parachute to which was attached a canvas container holding a dinghy and CO2 bottle. After sitting on this pack for four or five hours the CO2 bottle, an essential item necessary to inflate the dinghy if parachuting into the sea, could begin to feel very uncomfortable. This was a small price to pay and re-assuring on flights over the sea. As possible future Coastal Command aircrew, we had to master all the skills necessary in flying at high or low level, in various formation formats and in all weathers, mainly over the sea. One feature of the Beaufighter which we were to appreciate, especially when operating in the Mediterranean, was the high speed of over two hundred and fifty knots, which could be extracted at low level if jumped by enemy fighters. We were soon to learn what a high level of concentration was required when flying at the very lowest level in formation with other aircraft.

It was now time to team up with an observer. Observers combined the duties of navigator and W/T (radio) operator. They were justly proud of their observer brevet - an 'O' on a single wing. Our pilots' course of ground instruction was now joined by an equal number of observers. After training together in class for two or three days the instructor suddenly asked us to team up into pairs, pilot and observer. The RAF system was to allow aircrew teams to come together through their own natural preferences. I looked around. Tommy Thompson was there, a Sergeant Observer and, most importantly, a fellow Yorkshireman. I said, "Are you OK?" He just said, "Fine" and that was it. We flew together, without a break, for the next three years.

The downside at Crosby was the loss of two good friends I had trained with in Rhodesia. One evening at the local pub Jack Beanland, a fellow

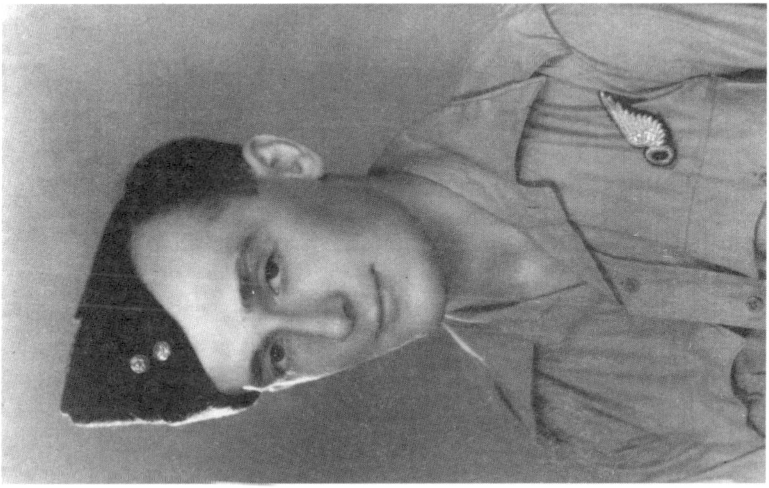

GRT Willis Archives

The team trained for war, far left, the author Bob Willis and left, Tommy Thompson.

Sergeant Pilot, drank too much despite beer being in short supply. The next morning, 16 July, after two days of poor visibility and low cloud, the weather cleared with a full flying programme ahead. Waiting our turn in the crew room Jack turned to me, 'I feel awful, I don't think I should fly.' He had a hangover. 'Why don't you report sick?'. 'I can't do that, I'll have to go.' Jack's observer, Sergeant Philcox, a young fresh faced bright eyed and most unassuming young man had no idea that his pilot was feeling unwell. They were dispatched on a local flying exercise. Twenty minutes later their Beaufighter 5335 was over the airfield on one engine, the port engine stopped with the propeller feathered. Jack had practised single engine landings on the Beaufort. Could he cope with the Beaufighter? There were two golden rules: maintain forward speed well above the speed at which the aircraft stalls and never turn into the dead engine. We rushed out of the crew room to watch this emergency landing. Fascinated we could see he was in serious trouble, flying over the centre of the airfield uncertain how to make an approach onto the runway. With the port engine feathered he was required to make a right hand circuit as opposed to the standard left hand (anti-clockwise) approach. His airspeed fell off, the aircraft appeared to hover and suddenly stalled at fifteen hundred feet, falling out of the sky. I covered my face with my hands, I could not bear to watch. A loud explosion, a fierce fire and that was the end of Jack Beanland and his young observer. We rushed across to the burnt out wreckage on the edge of the airfield, soon to walk away saddened and much chastened. Later that same day Tommy Thompson and I took off in Beaufighter 455 on our very first flight together on a formation exercise. I never enquired if he had any qualms. Wisely no time was allowed to dwell upon the tragedy that had overtaken two families.

Another friend, Jack Powell, a colleague from Rhodesia and South Africa, and one of our group at Victoria Falls in January 1942, was dispatched over the Atlantic on a long distance navigation exercise. Despite having a small reserve, accurate navigation was essential on this type of exercise to avoid the risk of running out of fuel. On this day, 22 July, Jack's petrol ran out as he was just two hundred feet up on his final approach onto the runway. Both engines cut out, the aircraft dropped out of the sky, on the edge of the airfield. Jack was killed, Sergeant Weatherman, his observer, was injured. Crosby had suffered its fourth fatal accident in just nineteen days, with the first on 4 July when Beaufighter L223 crashed ten miles south of the airfield. The pilot and observer Pilot Officer Carner and Pilot Officer Sedgeley were both killed. On 11 July Sergeant M M Vinton and his observer, Sergeant H J Shallow, lost their lives as they crashed close to the airfield when attempting a forced landing in Beaufighter X8036. Crosby opened our eyes to the hazards and risks of operational flying, although at this stage we were confident it wouldn't happen to us.

The intention was to train us in a variety of specialist activities applicable to coastal operations. A crew's ultimate destination could be to a squadron employing a variety of roles involving torpedoes, rockets, low level bombing, or day and night intruder operations. Crosby introduced us to rockets with our Flight Lieutenant instructor stating: 'You are not to take any notes, these are highly secret weapons, they are known as RPs - rocket propulsion weapons'. A Beaufighter could carry eight sixty pound high explosive rockets, four under each wing on individual racks. On 30 July 1943 Tommy and I, in Beaufighter 128, were over the range near Whitehaven on the Cumbrian coast, on our first practice rocket firing exercise. Beaufighters equipped with RP proved to be a most effective weapon against German coastal shipping towards the end of the war, as well as being extensively used in other theatres, such as the Far East.

Tommy and I were members of No.12 Course at Crosby from 23 June to 10 August 1943. Despite the sad loss of friends through accidents it was a happy posting. Carlisle was not far away. Notwithstanding all the shortages in the shops and with little beer in the pubs, the sheer challenge of flying a front line aircraft kept us keyed up and determined to succeed and acquire all the necessary skills. Tommy, with an F24 hand held camera, took some excellent aerial photographs of prominent landmarks off the West coast of Scotland. Lighthouses, such as

Corsewall north of Stranraer, were favourite rendezvous. It was a rocky and picturesque terrain we came to know well in all its changing moods and weather conditions. Low flying in formation down the Solway Firth, fighter evasion tactics and cine camera air to air exercises were exhilarating. This was training for action to come with no thought of any dangers ahead. Live for the day; it was far more important to know which local pub had beer, even if it meant going to the back door. As a counter to our carefree attitude, a lot of effort was quietly given to improving our chances of survival. 'Tee Emm', a popular training manual featuring Pilot Officer Prune, a cartoon character, was widely distributed. Pilot Officer Prune, a creation of cartoonist Bill Hooper, managed to survive disaster after disaster in a highly humorous way. Prune may survive and walk away - we may not. Crew room walls were liberally papered with Pilot Officer Prune posters driving home the message. Prune was reputed to say that "a good landing is one you can walk away from". We had to do better than that.

The station was very good at organising football matches, mess dances, social evenings and concerts by ENSA. The ladies in the NAAFI came in for some light hearted ribbing, which they took in good part, although it was rumoured that the 'tea and wad' they sold was not much better than prison food. The local ATC were often on the station, no doubt to raise the enthusiasm and qualifications of future recruits for life in the Royal Air Force.

Ground studies and link training continued in parallel to flying exercises. 'Escape' briefing was given on action to take if forced down over Europe. We were expected to attempt to make our way back to the UK if at all possible. One apparent safe haven was the 'red light' district of Paris, although getting there rather depended on having some civilian clothing. No mention was made of the Middle East or of India and Burma. Dinghy drill and swimming exercises in Carlisle swimming baths were part of 'escape' briefing, although these excursions usually turned out to be very hilarious affairs. More than one trainee ended up in the water fully clothed. We enjoyed a typical Cumbrian west coast summer, a few sunny days followed by weather systems driving in from the Atlantic bringing frequent rain and poor visibility. Despite the weather, every opportunity was taken to give us maximum flying experience. My end of course assessment was again 'Average' with seventy eight hours on Beauforts or Beaufighters.

During these seven weeks at Crosby Tommy and I became firm friends and a good operating team. Confidence in our individual abilities was to stand us in good stead when the inevitable emergencies arose. We were both from Yorkshire, he from Dewsbury, and with similar home backgrounds. It was Tommy who introduced me to Joan Nowell, then a clerk in the rates office at Dewsbury Town Hall, having joined the local authority after leaving the Wheelwright Grammar School in Dewsbury. Little did we know that he was to be our Best Man when Joan and I were married in November 1945. Tommy was going to introduce me to Joan on our next leave as he was concerned at my lack of a girlfriend. Tommy, who also worked at Dewsbury Town Hall before joining the RAF, always maintained that Joan considered him to be a little too pushing - so perhaps I would have better fortune!

With the end of the course came the news that we were to be trained as a torpedo strike crew. After training we could be posted either to join an anti-shipping strike squadron in the Mediterranean or to a squadron based at North Coates, near Grimsby which, at the time, was engaged in anti-shipping strikes off the coasts of Holland and Denmark. In the event, married men on the course had priority for a home posting.

Our posting on 16 August 1943 was direct from Crosby on Eden to Castle Kennedy, No.2 Torpedo Training Unit. The airfield was in a pleasant setting near the village of Castle Kennedy four miles east of Stranraer. It turned out to be a three week crash course, involving up to four sorties in one day. Theory training on torpedoes was by a lieutenant from the Navy. He had few teaching skills but a wry sense of humour. Opening the lecture with 'I'll tell you all about torpedoes' he then drew the outline of a torpedo on the blackboard, filling in the main control mechanisms. From then on every moving part was referred to as a 'gubbins'. This 'gubbins' goes into that 'gubbins' and so he went on. I do not think we were any the wiser at the end of the lectures, but we did find the teaching style entertaining. One message we did understand; 'don't lose a torpedo by dropping it badly' - the penalty could be a Court Martial. This was no joke. We had to take care as torpedoes were valuable costing £6,000 each or £400,000 at today's prices. At the same time our instructor informed us that a Beaufighter cost £25,000. If you wrote one off through carelessness, you were also in trouble as £25,000 then would price a Beaufighter at around £2 million each today. Torpedoes were lost if one was released with the aircraft in an unstable position, nose up too much or if the wings were not straight and level, or if the speed or height were not correct. Height from the sea was to be 150 feet, range 1,000 yards and speed 180 knots, using a calibrated bar on the windscreen to set the deflection according to the estimated speed of the target. We were expected to drop the torpedo correctly both in practice and when being shot at. There was a small tailplane attached to the torpedo designed to keep it stable as it flew through the air prior to entering the water. The tailplane broke off when the torpedo hit the water at an angle of 171/2°, all depending on a correct release by the pilot. The torpedo would be pre-set to run at a depth of about eight feet and armed to explode on impact or if set at magnetic to explode under the keel of the target ship. The rather difficult torpedo course at Castle Kennedy was taught by some very experienced instructors who had already dropped torpedoes from Beauforts or Beaufighters in action. We were fortunate in having Squadron Leader G D (Bill) Sise, a New Zealander, later Group Captain G D Sise, DSO and Bar, DFC and Bar, as one of our chief instructors. For operational leadership over the North Sea he had just received his first DSO. He proved to be an inspirational instructor, later commanding the Banff Mosquito Wing, being regarded as Coastal Command's leading 'ship buster'. By the end of the war he had completed one hundred and fifty sorties. His skill, amply demonstrated on our course, must have been a significant factor in his survival. Operational training took place flying Beaufighters at low level in a designated area of the Clyde estuary, releasing torpedoes at a target buoy. Cameras, aimed at the target and also focussed on the instrument panel, measured performance. The practice torpedoes, known as attack runner torpedoes (ART) were, of course, unarmed with buoyancy chambers in the nose which enabled them to be picked up by a naval launch and re-cycled. At the commencement of training, we used concrete torpedoes in dummy attacks as they were expendable! We left Castle Kennedy on 9 September having completed three weeks intensive training in the air and on the Link Trainer simulator. During the final few days there were demanding exercises in formations of nine or twelve aircraft against various naval vessels, such as HMS Cardiff and HMS Isle of Guernsey. All went well with another 'Average' proficiency in my Log Book. We were sorry to hear, shortly after leaving on 11 September, that a Beaufighter on a training torpedo exercise crashed into the sea off Turnberry, both pilot and navigator being killed. Fortunately on our course, although we had one or two accidents with aircraft swinging on take-off, there were no serious mishaps.

Just before departing for two to three weeks leave the posting notices went up. Tommy and I were destined for the Middle East to join a torpedo squadron based in the Mediterranean. We were to ferry a Beaufighter Mark X LZ331 to Cairo. We would be called, during our leave, to report to RAF Llandow just west of Cardiff to collect this aircraft, and fly to No.304 Ferry Training Unit at Port Ellen on Islay in the Hebrides. Here, facing the Atlantic north of the Mull of Kintyre, we were to participate in fuel consumption tests and navigational exercises.

Before flying to Islay, Tommy had been hoping to introduce me to Joan during our leave. Arrangements were in hand for us all to meet up in Dewsbury, which was Tommy's home town and where Joan lived at the time. Unfortunately, the expected leave was abruptly shortened by a telegram home, sending us both by train to Llandow and forcing the cancellation of our proposed Dewsbury meeting. Photographs were hastily exchanged by post. By good fortune, Tommy persuaded Joan to write to me at Islay, before he left Dewsbury. From the time of Joan's first letter to me on 9 October 1943 to July 1945 we corresponded weekly with eighty four of my letters and telegrams from overseas still surviving, thanks to Joan. At the time that we were departing for the Middle East Joan decided to make her own contribution to the war effort by enrolling as a student nurse at Edinburgh Royal Infirmary. My first letter to Joan, from Islay in reply to hers, dated 12 October 1943, heralded weekly correspondence we increasingly appreciated, until we were able to meet face to face in Edinburgh some twenty one months later. On 10 August 1945, less than four weeks after my return to the UK, we were engaged to be married.

It was a two hours and fifteen minute flight, with Beaufighter LZ331, from Llandow to the airfield facing the Atlantic at Port Ellen. Arriving on 2 October 1943 the summer was over, Islay appeared a bleak and desolate place. It felt and looked like winter, very wet and windy as we settled into a draughty Nissen hut with several other Beaufighter crews and no fuel available for the stove. The change of environment from Rhodesia and South Africa to Islay was something of a shock. In my first letter to Joan I bluntly said, 'No matter what you do, don't for the love of Mike, visit this part of Scotland. Imagine a Yorkshire moor in winter in the middle of the Atlantic and you have a fair description of Islay. I am rather keen on seeing as much of the world as I can, but I have not many ambitions as far as Scotland is concerned.' How wrong I was about Scotland, and the Hebrides in particular. As our family grew up in the years after the war all Scotland, especially the Inner and Outer Hebrides and Orkney, became and still are our favourite holiday locations. My war time impressions of Islay, coloured by service life on the island, were rather biased. Port Ellen was a small township clustered around the harbour, with two whisky distilleries which, unfortunately from some of the airmen's point of view, were securely locked up. One Saturday Tommy and I ventured to walk from the airfield to Port Ellen, a distance of four miles, which on our arrival appeared to be completely closed down for the weekend. There was not even any sign of life on the Air Sea Rescue Launch moored in the harbour nor at the Coastguard viewing platform above. The only person on this walk either to or from Port Ellen that we were able to speak to was the road sweeper, diligently attending his stretch of windswept road, quite oblivious to any war which was going on.

Over the next fourteen days we carried out navigation exercises and fuel consumption tests on our aircraft LZ331. Our longest flight was a navigation exercise over the Atlantic with one turning point at Rockall, a tiny rocky outcrop in mid-Atlantic, approximately 250 miles west of the Outer Hebrides. We were airborne for six hours and fifty minutes covering one thousand and thirty six nautical miles. Of Rockall we saw no sign, four hours of the flight were in cloud, certainly giving us the opportunity for concentrated instrument flying and accurate Dead Reckoning navigation. Ferry training was not without its hazards. Just before we arrived a Beaufighter and its crew were reported lost at sea on 2 October, with another one crash landing at Wigtown, a satellite airfield, on 17 October, the crew being killed. Perhaps it was as well that our stay on Islay was scheduled to be brief.

Our Nissen huts, built of corrugated iron sheets, were completely uninsulated. The ends were bricked in round the windows and door. They were dreadfully cold with just the one large coal/coke burning stove for heating, together with a rationed fuel supply. We understood that all wood within the vicinity had long ago been chopped up by enterprising airmen. Fuel had run out; in desperation, we even tried burning emergency flares. Being without fuel, a council of war was held. With cold winds and driving rain and all our fuel expended, we could only assume that the previous occupants must have been extravagant. A reconnaissance party was dispatched and soon reported no shortage of fuel behind the Officers Mess. Not to be denied, a raiding party of volunteers was organised who, under the cover of darkness, ensured that this fuel stock became somewhat depleted. At least we had greatcoats to supplement the blankets on the beds. The ablution blocks with their cold concrete walls, little hot water and no plugs in the wash basins, were not places to linger in. Perhaps the spartan conditions were viewed as being good training, prior to facing the harsh realities of overseas service.

On 22 October we left Port Ellen behind as we flew LZ331 to Portreath in Cornwall and then on to St. Mawgan just north east of Newquay. It was a very welcome change from the cold winds and inhospitable conditions of Islay to the warm breezes of Cornwall. Although it was late October 1943, the airmen on the airfield at St. Mawgan were quite relaxed, with some when off duty sunbathing or lying under the aircraft wings to shelter from the sun. That evening we walked on the beach at Newquay, a small portion of which had escaped barbed wire enclosure, to savour the last of the English climate for at least a couple of years. Three nights were spent in a Bed and Breakfast. Together with Tommy my navigator, (the term we always used from now on, instead of Observer), I reported to the airfield each day, for tropical kit and inoculations. I did not forget to send a postcard to Joan with our new address, HQ RAF Cairo.

Back to Portreath on 25 October, we were briefed to fly our Beaufighter the next day to Rabat in Morocco. To avoid the possibility of interception by enemy aircraft the first leg of our course was south west into the Atlantic before turning south east to Rabat. Instructions were that if we were slightly off course, short of fuel and close to the coast of Portugal, then head for Gibraltar. Gibraltar, with its short runway jutting out into the Mediterranean, left little room for error. The approach and circuit were tight to avoid any overflying of neutral territory.

Taking off on a warm sunny late autumn day, the flight to Rabat on 26 October 1943 was uneventful, taking six hours and thirty five minutes. We had covered one thousand one hundred and ten nautical miles, close to our maximum range. Rabat was an airfield with a runway of pierced steel planking laid in interlocking sections onto the levelled semi-desert floor. Woe betide any aircraft unfortunate enough to swing off this runway. At the very least the soft sand ripped off the undercarriage and tipped the aircraft onto its nose. As we came in to land seeing a crashed Beaufighter, which had recently suffered this fate, certainly concentrated the mind. Rabat brought us face to face with the Arab world. The first shock was the toilet, a hole in the floor with two foot plates. We had not been warned but they were certainly cleaner and more hygienic than what was to come.

Two days later, as we prepared to take-off for Castel Benito in Tunis, a British private soldier approached. 'Are you going to Cairo?' he asked. He was, so he said, from an Army Headquarters detachment in Cairo. 'Yes we are,' was the response. 'Well I've just been to England. I've had a lift to Rabat, will you take me on to Cairo?' We asked, 'What happened?' 'I had leave in Cairo so I decided to hitch hike to England to see my family. I'm now going back'. 'You can stand in the well at the back of the pilot,' which he did. Perhaps this was a foolish thing to do. If any mishap had befallen us there could have been serious consequences. The well contained the escape hatch through which escape by parachute was made in an emergency, but it was exceptionally difficult to get into from the pilot's seat. We flew our unofficial passenger, who had no parachute, all the way to Cairo West where he disappeared immediately after landing. The flight from Rabat to Cairo entailed two further refuelling and overnight stops, firstly at Castel Benito, seventeen miles south of Tripoli, (No.17 Staging Post) and the following day at El-Adem outside Tobruk in Libya, (No.12 Staging Post). Castel Benito, a large dusty airfield on a sloping site, was crammed with assorted aircraft of the RAF and USAAF. This was a major base supporting the 5th and 8th Armies as they pushed through southern Italy, against stiff opposition, on the road to Rome.

Landing at El Adem on the afternoon of 29 October 1943 coincided with an opportunity to hear Vyshinsky, the Russian Deputy Minister of Foreign Affairs, give an address to all the officers and airmen not on duty. During his speech, given in the airfield cinema, a surviving Italian hangar, Vyshinsky insisted that the Allies open a second front without delay. As he addressed his audience in Russian, translated by a Russian speaking RAF interpreter, it was interesting to see in the flesh the notorious special prosecutor of the many purge trials held in Moscow and featured in the newspapers during the Thirties. These big public treason trials were engineered by Stalin to execute many of Russia's leading politicians and generals who, he believed, posed a personal threat. As we listened we were not to know just how many politicians and serving military personnel were sent to their deaths by Vyshinsky on trumped up charges. We were to meet this Russian delegation again when they visited 47 Squadron a few weeks later at Gambut, a desert airfield thirty miles or so to the east of Tobruk.

On 30 October 1943, five days after leaving the UK, we landed at Cairo West (Heliopolis). In the distance were the Pyramids and the Sphinx. In no time we were on our way to RAF Eastern Mediterranean Headquarters in Cairo by three ton truck, or 'gharrie'. Without ceremony we scrambled into the back, together with our kit. We were soon to experience how little was the respect given to the local population by some members of the British Forces. Approaching the city from the airport our RAF driver decided that a taxi in front was taking up too much room on the road. He drove the truck close alongside the taxi at high speed, and then with a sharp twitch of the steering wheel gave the taxi a severe bump on the side, demonstrating in the driver's view Anglo-Saxon superiority. The damage to the lorry was minor compared to the taxi. The passengers in the taxi shook their fists and shouted as we sped away. We were not an army of occupation - or were we?

We reported to HQ Cairo as a replacement Beaufighter crew ready to join a torpedo squadron based on the North African Coast. To our surprise there did not appear to be any great rush to send us on. With six days in Cairo, shopping and warding off the shoe shine boys, time passed pleasurably enough. The accommodation in Sister Street, close to the 'red light' district was very comfortable. We kept well away from the temptations of this well known area, going to the open air cinema instead. Posting to HQ 201 (Naval Cooperation) Group at Alexandria was the next stage. Taking a train from Cairo to Alexandria was an experience in itself, with passengers clinging to the roof, doors and locomotive as we clattered through the Nile delta, past its

GRT Willis Archives

1943, Bob Willis (Above) and Tommy Thompson with Beaufighter LZ331 ferried from the UK to Cairo West.

GRT Willis Archives

GRT Willis Archives

GRT Willis Archives

Above: December 1943, Muhamed Ali Square, Alexandria.

Left: December 1943, Bob Willis and Tommy Thompson on leave in Alexandria.

innumerable villages, vast stretches of water and paddy fields. On arrival we were soon ensconced in a very pleasant RAF leave hostel with good beds and clean sheets. Despite the Beaufighter aircrew losses of which we were to learn about later, we surprisingly were granted more free time, using the extra days to explore this historic city. Here was an opportunity to see the Roman ruins of Alexandria. Tommy came along rather reluctantly, 'Oh God, are we on to this kind of thing again?' he would exclaim. He suffered for my curiosity as we explored the ancient Roman ruins of Alexandria, with my camera put to good use. We even sought out King Farouk's Palace with little to see because of its high surrounding walls. Witnessing rioting and street demonstrations both in Cairo and Alexandria, we were soon aware of a ground swell of discontent against the government and King Farouk in particular - a foretaste of things to come. How was the war progressing as we waited for our squadron posting? The Afrika Corps was out of Africa. Italy had surrendered on 3 September. The Russians had advanced to the River Dnieper. The Germans were putting up stiff resistance on the road to Rome and had taken over all the islands in the Aegean from the Italians.

Early on 20 November 1943, three weeks after arriving in Egypt, Tommy and I were collected, along with our kit, by the usual canvas covered three ton truck and driven to LG 91, a barren landing ground and transit camp at Amyria just west of Alexandria. Then, on the same day, we were flown by Wellington bomber to El Adem, just inland from the port of Tobruk. We were on our way to join a Torpedo Beaufighter squadron, No 47. Immediately on arrival at El Adem we had to scramble aboard a lorry as the squadron was on the move to a new base at Gambut, a large desert airfield on the edge of the escarpment about forty miles east of El Adem. Arriving late in the afternoon, the first task was to report to the Adjutant, Flight Lieutenant E W (Ted) Hunter, a pleasant individual, whose background was as a director and Company Secretary of a department store in Oxford. Ted Hunter having joined the squadron two months before, was to become quite a father figure to we aircrew with his unflappable air, much helped by his advanced years. We collected and erected the standard issue ridge tent designed to hold six airmen, or two aircrew, and settled in the sergeants' lines. Newcomers were given few luxuries but at least we had a tent for two on the desert floor. For most airmen on the squadron these tents, which you could barely stand up in, left little room for kit or personal luxuries. At least we had some space for our few personal belongings. Non-commissioned aircrew were supposed to have reasonable comfort, provided they found it for themselves. We soon learnt that the trick was to search through all the debris left by retreating or advancing armies and which littered the desert around us. I soon had enough scrap metal, wire and extra 'acquired' blankets to make a makeshift mattress which, raised off the floor on old ammunition boxes, served for four months as quite a comfortable bed. Commissioned ranks had the benefit of standard issue camp beds and canvas wash basins. No such luxury for non-commissioned aircrew, although we all faced the same hazards and needed to be able to sleep in some comfort to unwind after missions. We were soon to learn how much better American aircrew were accommodated when we came in contact with their squadron of Mitchell bombers (B25s) of 310 Bombardment Group, USAAF, who shared Gambut with us, together with the Beaufighters of 603 Squadron and the Marauders of 24 Squadron SAAF. We were now, along with the Mitchells, Marauders and Beaufighters of 603 Squadron, under the authority of the AOC Air Headquarters Eastern Mediterranean as operational squadrons of 201 (Naval Cooperation) Group, based at El Adem and Gambut, and forming 235 Wing.

We arrived at 47 Squadron as replacement aircrew, along with Sergeant Pilots Bill Powell, Sid Appleton and Ken Thomas together with their respective navigators. Bill Powell shared a tent next to ours with his navigator Maurice Jones. We made a very close 'foursome' which survived our whole time on the squadron. No time was lost as I was allotted to 'A' Flight under the temporary command of Flying Officer Arthur Unwin - all other senior officers of 'A' Flight having become recent casualties.

CHAPTER 6
A SQUADRON FOR ALL SEASONS

As time went on, we soon learnt what a distinguished history lay behind the name of 47 Squadron. From the day of its formation on 1 March 1916 at Beverley in the East Riding of Yorkshire to November 1943 when Tommy and I joined the Squadron at Gambut in the Libyan desert, 47 Squadron had always played an active role at the cutting edge of British Foreign Policy.

In the early part of 1916, equipped with various aircraft including the BE2, Vickers Bullet, Bristol Scout, DH2, Armstrong Whitworth FK3 and FK8, the operational task had been to protect East Yorkshire and Hull from German Zeppelin raids. In September 1916 the squadron moved out of Beverley to Salonika (now Thessaloniki) in north east Greece. Here the task was to support the Allied land forces engaged against the Bulgarian forces in Macedonia. Flying hundreds of sorties to the end of World War 1 many severe blows were inflicted upon the Bulgarian Army, particularly when they were retreating in the latter part of 1918.

In April 1919 the squadron was on the move again, this time to Southern Russia in support of General Denikin's White Russian forces against the Bolsheviks. Following political pressure at home, when questions were asked in the House of Commons expressing concern at the RAF's presence amidst a foreign country's civil war, 47 Squadron's continuing support of the White Russians necessitated the removal of RAF insignia from uniforms and aircraft to be replaced with a tri-coloured logo of blue, yellow and red as an identification badge. This design was also made up into the flag under which they were fighting. This logo, with blue in the centre flanked by red and yellow, remains the squadron's distinctive emblem to this day. The squadron at this time had about fifty aircraft in southern Russia comprising DH9s and Sopwith Camels, operating along a front which stretched for two thousand miles. With fluctuating fortunes and with the tacit support of the British government wide ranging operations took place in support of the White Russians. The squadron in southern Russia was commanded by Lieutenant-Colonel (Wing Commander) Raymond Collishaw, a much decorated Canadian pilot. (In 1940 Raymond Collishaw, as an Air Commodore, commanded 202 Group in the Western Desert.) Eventually after many vicissitudes, and with considerable difficulty, the squadron was evacuated from the Crimea at the end of 1919 moving in February 1920 to Helouan, thirty miles south of Cairo on the east bank of the River Nile. Helouan was destined to be home for the next seven years. During this period the squadron pioneered air routes between the major cities of the Middle East such as Cairo, Amman and Baghdad including the establishment of airfields, much needed during World War ll. On 31 October 1927 the squadron was on the move again, this time to Khartoum in the Sudan where it was to remain until 1940. Here at Khartoum a major role was to pioneer more air routes, this time both across Africa from east to west and down to the Cape through East Africa. All this experience must have been invaluable after June 1940 when accurate maps were required of the terrain and landing grounds for the planned destruction of the Italian forces in East Africa. By 1940 47 Squadron consisted of 'A', 'B' and 'C' Flights of Vickers Wellesleys and 'D' Flight of Vickers Vincents with one Supermarine Walrus. The Wellesley was a two seater single engine monoplane with two machine guns and a bomb carrying capacity of 2,000 pounds. The only hostile activity, prior to June 1940, was a certain amount of anti personnel bombing of rioting tribes in southern Sudan. In March 1940 'D' Flight left 47 Squadron to become 223 Squadron. The Wellesley was to remain with the squadron until replaced by the Bristol Beaufort in 1942.

Inside a Beaufighter cockpit.

GRT Willis Archives

November 1943, Gambut 'Ready to go'.

GRT Willis Archives

GRT Willis Archives

November 1943, Dispersal, Gambut, Libya.

GRT Willis Archives

Left: 4 December 1943, Beaufighter X LX898 'W'.

GRT Willis Archives

Right: January 1944, Gambut outside the parachute tent, l to r, Tommy Thompson, Ken Thomas and Bob Willis.

GRT Willis Archives

Left: 14 december 1943, Beaufighter JM410 'E' with the wing tip shot off by an Arado 196.

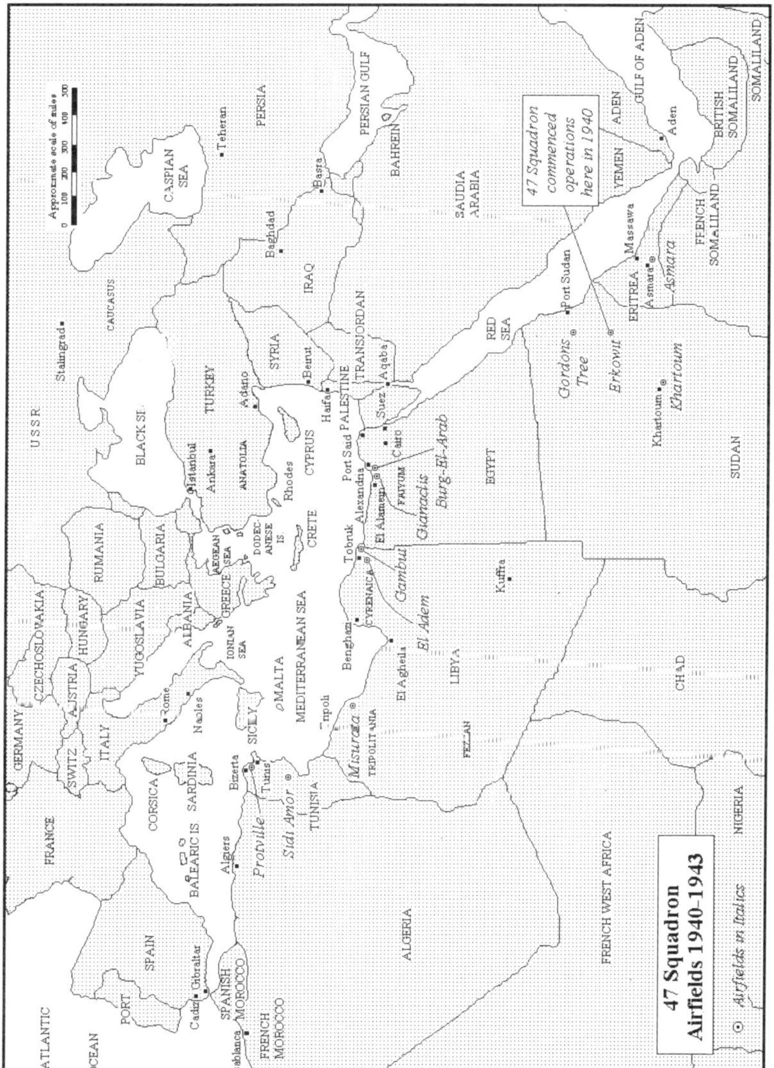
47 Squadron
Airfields 1940-1943
Airfields in Italics
47 Squadron commenced operations here in 1940
Approximate scale of miles
MEDITERRANEAN SEA
BLACK SEA
CASPIAN SEA
RED SEA
PERSIAN GULF
GULF OF ADEN
ATLANTIC OCEAN
Gordons Tree
Erkowit
Khartoum
Asmara
Burg-El-Arab
Gianaclis
Gambut
El Adem
Misurata
Sidi Amor
Protville

On 11 June 1940, following Hitler's successes in the Low Countries and France, Italy declared war against Britain. In May 1940 the squadron had moved to Erkowit, an airfield sixty miles south of Port Sudan and close to the Red Sea, being well placed to harass the Italians in Eritrea. From 11 June 1940, for the next eighteen months, the squadron played a major role in the defeat of the Italian forces in Eritrea, Abyssinia and Somalia. Using their Wellesley bombers the squadron flew continuous sorties against the major Italian airfield at Asmara, inflicting a great deal of damage to the facilities. Asmara surrendered on 1 April 1941. Along with other RAF squadrons, 47 also flew many other sorties against airfields and troop concentrations from their base at Erkowit and later from the captured airfield at Asmara. It is easy to forget that in 1940 there were several brigades of trained native troops in Italian occupied East Africa who Mussolini believed would occupy Egypt and British East Africa during 1941. He was to receive a rude awakening as British and South African troops, attacking on three fronts from the Sudan, Kenya and from Berbera, on the northern coast of Somalia, steadily defeated all the Italian forces and their native allies. These demoralised and defeated enemy forces in East Africa, who early on had lost control of the air, were to play no further part in the war after November 1941.

Joining the squadron at Gambut in 1943, we soon appreciated that the groundcrew cherished the distinguished history and spirit of the squadron just as much as the aircrew. Some groundcrew members, now servicing Beaufighters at Gambut, had performed the same duties on Wellesleys at Khartoum in March 1940, before Italy had even entered the war. A remarkable record was kept by some of these groundcrew which, thanks to Nick Colley, Bob Barrett, Dick Taylor and Grant Flook, all qualified tradesmen as LACs on the squadron, was written up in 1976. Quoting from these memoirs, they record the consistent bombing raids by the Wellesleys on Italian forces and the airfield at Asmara, with the loss of several Wellesleys and their crews between May 1940 and November 1941. Nick Colley recorded five aircrew killed on 13 and 16 July 1940 naming them as Wood, Baxter, Nelson, Styles and

Clark. They were not to be forgotten by those airmen who saw them fly out against the Italians.

On 2 November 1940 the squadron moved back to Khartoum from Erkowit and then in December 1940 to an air strip known as 'Gordons Tree'. The Commanding Officers in these early forays against the Italians were Wing Commander J G Elton DFC followed by Squadron Leader J E Pelley-Fry who was succeeded on 26 December 1940 by Squadron Leader G R Magill (later Air Vice-Marshal G R Magill CB CBE DFC and bar). As a New Zealand airman, he is remembered by the groundcrew as 'Digger Magill' and was much liked and respected, being in the habit, as Nick Colley was to recount many years later, of "chatting up the erks and keeping the finger out". Magill had many successful sorties from June 1940 to April 1941 earning his first DFC. On 16 October 1940 the squadron Wellesleys were caught by surprise on a forward strip at Gedaref from where they were scheduled to conduct night operations. At 0406 hours four CR32 bi-plane fighters supported by three CR42s and one CR79 strafed the parked Wellesleys. Eight Wellesleys and two Vincents were set on fire and completely destroyed. Fortunately ground casualties were only minor. These losses were soon replaced by Wellesleys from 14 Squadron, who along with Blenheims from 45 Squadron, had co-operated with 47 on many occasions.

Activity from December 1940 through to May 1941, with the squadron based at Gordon's Tree under Magill, was very intensive in support of the Allied Army as it pushed into Eritrea and Abyssinia. A detachment was based at Kassala on the Sudan/Eritrea border following its capture, with the whole squadron moving to Asmara in May 1941 as the Italian forces in Abyssinia surrendered. In April 1941 Squadron Leader M Cooke succeeded Squadron Leader Magill as Commanding Officer. Cooke's successor in November 1941, Squadron Leader D M Illsley, was killed shortly after arrival, crashing in the mountains. His grave is in Asmara cemetery.

The route from Addis Ababa to Asmara taking a direct flight path is close to many mountains of over thirteen thousand feet. Pilots were briefed to fly at specified heights to clear these mountains, particularly if the visibility was poor. At least one pilot decided there were more interesting ways to fly over these spectacular mountain ranges as narrated many years later by Dick Taylor, a Corporal Airframe Fitter, who joined 47 Squadron at Erkowit, and left four years later from Rangoon bound for the UK. He recalled guiding a Wellesley of the squadron as it taxied in at Asmara after a flight from Addis Ababa in September 1941. Out of the aircraft jumped the pilot, Flying Officer James and an Army captain with his kit, flown as a passenger from Addis Ababa. Of the navigator Sergeant Bonner there was no sign. James had called out on leaving the aircraft, "Sling my hat out Bonner". There was no response. James looked around, perhaps Bonner had rushed off to relieve himself; James looked into the aircraft, no sign of Bonner. "Where's the navigator?", James addressed the captain. "Oh he jumped out about three hundred miles back, I thought he was on a special mission!" About four days later Bonner turned up, having narrowly escaped a rather unpleasant end, at the hands of the native tribesmen. It was alleged that captured Italians in native hands were passed to the local women folk who made sure the prisoners would never be fathers again. Fortunately Bonner was able to identify himself by brandishing his identity, i.e. a document, invariably referred to as a 'Goolie chit', carried by all British serving personnel in the Abyssinian campaign, written in Sudanese, Eritrean, Abyssinian and Italian, embossed with the stamp of the Abyssinian Emperor, Haile Selassi. This document stated that the holder was to be taken safely to the nearest military establishment whereupon his helper would be rewarded. Bonner maintained that his pilot refused to fly at the regulation height over the mountains, preferring a route down the valleys. He warned the pilot over the intercom that he would get out if flying down the mountain valleys continued. No response from the pilot. Bonner pocketed his emergency rations and water bottle, opened up the rear canopy of the gunners position, clipped on his parachute and out he went. He was a married man and did not relish the thought of coming to a sticky end in a mountainous cul-de-sac. James, who broke the regulations, probably put the navigator's action down to excessive 'twitchiness'. This was one episode which did not reach the public records. It is interesting to note that until the end of the war in Burma, 47 Squadron aircrew always referred to their escape document, then written in Burmese, as a 'Goolie chit'.

الى كل عربى كريم

السلام عليكم ورحمة الله وبعد فحامل هذا الكتاب ضابط بالجيش البريطانى وهو
صديق وفى لكافة الشعوب العربية فنرجو ان تعاملوه بالعطف والاكرام وأن تحافظوا
على حياته من كل طارئ ونأمل عند الاضطرار أن تقدموا له ما يحتاج إليه من طعام
وشراب وأن ترشدوه إلى اقرب معسكر بريطانى أو أمريكى وستكافئكم ماليًا
بسخاء على ما تسدونه إليه من خدمات . والسلام عليكم ورحمة الله وبركاته .

القيادة البريطانية العامة فى الشرق

To all Arab Peoples - Greetings and Peace be upon you. The bearer of this letter is an Officer of the British Government and a friend of all Arabs. Treat him well, guard him from harm, give him food and drink, help him to return to the nearest British soldiers or American soldiers and you will be liberally rewarded. Peace and the mercy of God upon you.

The British High Command in the East

'A Goolie Chit'

Squadron Leader E B Grace now assumed command as the Squadron moved in December 1941 from Asmara to LG87 at Burg-el-Arab, a windy, dusty airfield twenty miles west of Alexandria on the escarpment overlooking the Mediterranean. The groundcrew endured a very tedious and uncomfortable journey by rail, boat and truck from Asmara to Burg-el-Arab via Suez. The early months of 1942 at Burg-el-Arab were not a period of very demanding operational activity for the Squadron, now part of 201 Naval Cooperation Group, being engaged on convoy escort duty and anti submarine work with the now outdated Wellesleys. In March 1942 the Squadron moved to Kasfareet (107 MU) still with its Wellesleys but expecting conversion to Beaufort torpedo bombers as plans were developed to push the Afrika Korps out of North Africa. Early in September 1942 it was time to move on to Shandur, still in Egypt, with the Squadron having one flight equipped with torpedo carrying Beauforts under a new commanding officer, Squadron Leader Robert L B Carr. All was to change, as these Beauforts were to make a substantial contribution to the 8th Army's victory at the Battle of El Alamein on 2 November 1942.

As a torpedo bomber squadron a much more demanding role was looming ahead with the appointment of Wing Commander Richard A Sprague in October 1942 as the Commanding Officer. The Beaufort flight moved on detachment westward to Gianaclis, a forward landing ground close up to the El Alamein defence line and within range of Tobruk. Tobruk was the favoured port of entry for reinforcements and materials required by Rommel if he was going to have any chance to counter attack and break through into Egypt, having been halted at El Alamein. It was the responsibility of 201 Group to seek out and destroy all Axis convoys making for Tobruk with essential supplies, especially fuel for the Afrika Korps. Sailing from Taranto in the heel of Italy and able to shelter in German occupied Greece and Crete, before the final dash across the Mediterranean under heavy escort into Tobruk harbour, these convoys were a severe challenge to the RAF. All the enemy convoys trying to reach Tobruk during September and October 1942 were attacked and mostly destroyed by sustained strikes from the squadrons of 201 Group, despite the protection of destroyers and torpedo boats and rotating escorts from the Luftwaffe. Unfortunately, from June 1942 to March 1944 these successes were achieved at a high price in terms of lost aircraft along with their courageous and valuable crews. Early casualties were Pilot Officer Hooper and his Wellesley crew lost on 15 June 1942, with Warrant Officer Morse and his crew suffering the same fate.

The battle of El Alamein opened on 23 October. 47 Squadron with its Beaufort detachment was waiting at Gianaclis. There was no more important convoy for Rommel than that codenamed TT (Taranto to Tobruk). Comprising three supply ships escorted by four destroyers, this convoy managed to arrive undamaged within fifty miles of Tobruk on 26 October 1942. The prime targets in this convoy were the tanker 'Proserpina' of approximately 4800 tons and the ammunition/fuel carrier 'Tergestea' of nearly 6000 tons. The fuel and ammunition that these vessels were carrying was so vital to the Afrika Korps that it was later rumoured Rommel probably watched from the high cliffs above Tobruk as his ships tried to make harbour.

Flight Lieutenant Ronald Gee led a formation of eight Beauforts of 47 Squadron as part of a formation of twenty two aircraft dispatched on the morning of 26 October to destroy this convoy. The tanker 'Proserpina' was torpedoed and sunk by Pilot Officer Ralph V Manning of 47 Squadron. The ammunition ship the 'Tergestea' was torpedoed and sunk just outside Tobruk harbour later the same day by a formation of three Wellingtons from 38 Squadron led by Flight Lieutenant Albert L Wiggins. One Wellington crashed near Tobruk, the other two, although damaged by flak, managed to reach base safely. Only the smallest of the three supply ships, the 'Dora', reached Tobruk. Of the twenty two aircraft on the first assault that day on the convoy only sixteen made it back to base. For this exploit, Flight Lieutenant Wiggins received an immediate DSO and Flight Lieutenant Gee, the leader of the 47 Squadron formation, an immediate DFC.

Sadly from this operation two 47 Squadron Beaufort crews failed to return. The pilots, Flying Officer H J Davidson and Pilot Officer W Garrick, and their crews were reported 'missing believed killed'. The other aircraft in the formation of twenty two were five Bisleys of 15 (SAAF) Squadron, four Beaufighters of 252 Squadron and five Beaufighters of 272 Squadron. Two Beaufighters and two Bisleys were lost. 47 Squadron as part of 201 Group was now embarking upon a period of intense activity in the Mediterranean which was to last for the next sixteen months. There were to be several more examples of outstanding courage together with many casualties as the aircrew pressed home their attacks upon enemy shipping where ever it could be found.

For five months from September 1942 the main body of the squadron remained at Shandur, with the Beauforts flying from the forward landing ground at Gianaclis when scheduled to make torpedo attacks upon enemy shipping still trying to get into Tobruk, prior to its capture on 13 November 1942. During one sortie by three Beauforts of the squadron on 30 October Pilot Officer Frederick J Pile torpedoed and sank the German supply ship 'Ostia' of approximately 360 tons, as it was making for Tobruk along the coast from Benghazi. Back at Shandur the squadron were still flying some Wellesleys on anti submarine patrols and convoy escort in the Eastern Mediterranean, as the Afrika Korps retreated into Tunisia where all resistance ended on 12 May 1943.

On 4 November 1942 Flight Lieutenant Bill (Doc) Bamford, a native of Ireland, joined the squadron as medical officer. In all the squadron's vicissitudes over the next three years no officer was to play a greater part in keeping up the morale and fighting spirit of all ranks. The squadron, now equipped with only Beauforts and still based in the eastern Mediterranean, reverted to the rather mundane but very important role of convoy escort and submarine hunter. At Gambut and shortly after its capture from the Germans, Sergeant Ingram a navigator, was killed on 25 November by a booby trap. In December 1942 Wing Commander D E Bennett assumed command of the squadron from Wing Commander R A Sprague.

In March 1943 came a further move along the Mediterranean coast to Misurata in western Libya where convoy escort and anti submarine duties continued. It was here that the squadron prepared to service and fly the new Beaufighter TFX, an aircraft specially designed as a low level torpedo carrying twin engine fighter/bomber. In early June crews were flown to the Torpedo Training School at Shallufa on the Suez Canal for the conversion programme. The crew of four in a Beaufort was reduced to two for the Beaufighter. Many closely knit crews were broken up, but at least the Beaufighter was to prove to be a very versatile, sturdy and popular aircraft with the men who flew them. At Misurata Flying Officer Tony Norris joined the squadron as Intelligence Officer; like Bill Bamford the Medical Officer, he was to play a major role as mentor and friend to all the aircrew for the next two years.

Another period of intense activity was ahead, the squadron moving from Misurata on the Gulf of Sirte, to Protville ll, north west of Tunis as part of 328 Wing, arriving there on 18 June 1943. As Nick Colley, an LAC fitter of 'A' Flight, was to record in 1976, this was a road journey always referred to as the 'great ride up the desert', perched on the top of a three ton truck. In just six months the groundcrew travelled over 1500 miles from Shandur in Egypt to Protville near Tunis, and then virtually all the way back again in November to Libya. It was an endurance feat and experience they were to remember with pride. Nick was later to remark that with new torpedo Beaufighters to service 'we were now back in business'. To emphasise the challenges looming up, there was yet another change in Commanding Officer, with the appointment of Wing Commander Alistair M Taylor in May 1943. 328 Wing was made up to three Beaufighter squadrons, 39, 47 and 144 to be joined at Protville by Marauders, Baltimores and Wellingtons. Other aircraft also operated from Protville including USAAF fighters. All this activity was in preparation for the invasion of Sicily and the move into Southern Europe. The Beaufighter squadrons were ideally placed to attack any naval vessel trying to intercept the Sicilian invasion fleet. In the event there were to be many targets as the Germans and Italians endeavoured to keep supply lines open to Southern Italy, Sicily, Sardinia and Corsica.

The establishment needed to keep sixteen or so Beaufighters in the air was, excluding aircrew, approximately two hundred and eighty officers, NCOs and airmen. Most personnel were in specific trades i.e. Motor Transport, Maintenance, Equipment, Cooks, Gunners, Armourers, Nursing Orderlies, Clerks, Photographers, Wireless Operators,

Telephone Operators, Motor Cyclists and RAF Police. Maintenance included fitters-airframes and aero engines, instrument technicians, carpenters and electricians. Moving a squadron of two hundred and eighty men plus aircrew, plus the aircraft, plus all the equipment was an organisational feat of high order. Nothing had to be left behind. Grant Flook, an armourer on the squadron at this time, graphically describes how a movement order would be executed.

To quote from Grant's narrative: *'The Advance Party, the Main Party and the Rear Party were up at dawn, tents struck, breakfasted and paraded in full kit ready to move off as nominated. The Advance Party travelled up the coast road in about six three ton trucks including two of the open top type fitted with twin Lewis guns mounted on a tripod, a legacy from the redundant Wellesley aircraft. Around the tripod would be loaded all the equipment necessary to keep the aircraft flying from the forward base. On top of the equipment rode the fitters and armourers, described by them as 5th class travel. The officers and sergeants in charge were issued with side arms. Protection from thieves and robbers on the way was rather important.*

Arrival at these advanced destinations proved to be a rough and ready existence with water particularly in short supply. The Main Party following with the water bowser and around thirty three ton trucks, many with trailers, carrying Orderly Room, Photographic, Armament, sundry equipment, and tentage. Sixty ridge tents plus a marquee provided the shelter. One truck carried the most important item of all, namely the squadron piano 'acquired' from the Italians on the surrender of Asmara.'

LAC Syd Styles, an airframe fitter, grade ll, who joined the squadron at Kasfareet in March 1942, still recalls how the tents were always pitched into holes two feet down into the desert floor for better protection from dust storms. However, you could be caught out, as we were at Gambut, by a violent thunderstorm. With six men to a tent it was important to join a group that one could get on with. Any problems were sorted out by Flight Sergeant 'Pop' Lawson, a much respected pre-war entrant.

It is at Protville that my own story really begins. The survivors of the ordeals at Protville and later at El Adem and Gambut were to be my mentors when I took up my own flying duties in November 1943. July to November 1943 was to be one of the most traumatic periods in the squadron's history.

On 23 June the squadron suffered its first casualty after arriving at Protville. Pilot Officer I H Robertson and his navigator Pilot Officer W D Joy lost their lives during an attack on a German submarine hunter south of Naples. From Protville many successful sorties were mounted against a variety of enemy shipping moving between Sardinia, Corsica and down the west coast of Italy towards Sicily. Allied troops landed in Sicily on 10 July and rapidly advanced towards Palermo, which was captured on 23 July. On 11 July, leading six Beaufighters on an attack against two large merchant vessels escorted by a warship, Wing Commander Taylor's Beaufighter was shot down, both he and his navigator Flying Officer Frank Whitlock losing their lives. Both merchant vessels were hit by torpedoes in this attack, but the squadron had lost a much admired commanding officer. He was to be succeeded by a well liked pilot who first came to the squadron as a Flying Officer, now Squadron Leader J A (Jimmy) Lee-Evans, awarded the DFC in August. Promoted to Wing Commander and strongly supported by Squadron Leaders Geoff Powell and Ken Painter he kept the squadron at full stretch throughout July as they attacked and sank a wide assortment of merchant ships, always escorted by naval vessels who put up terrific barrages of flak. Sorties were usually formations of eight Beaufighters, four with torpedoes and four in an anti flak role. Two pilots shot down during these operations, Flying Officer Gordon Reneau and Pilot Officer Stewart Cowan who both ditched successfully, became prisoners of war, but both escaped with Gordon reaching Switzerland and Stewart regaining the Allied lines. Both these escapes were epic stories in themselves. Squadron Leader Ken Painter was not so lucky, being shot down on 18 September. He ditched successfully, but he and his navigator Flying Officer H T G Glen-Davison, endured the rest of the war in a German prison camp. It is worth recording that both Gordon Reneau and Ken Painter were awarded the DFC for their sterling work prior to capture. From late June to the end of September the squadron made a significant impact upon the German supply system attacking and damaging at least thirty large merchant ships and their escorts with the loss of sixteen aircraft from enemy action. Fortunately, seventeen of the crew members who ditched were rescued by high speed launch or became prisoners of war. By October, with the Allies advancing up the east coast of Italy, following the Salerno landings, and with the Germans out of Sardinia and Corsica there was a sharp decline in the squadron's area of operations. The squadron aircraft were moved to Sidi Amor, still in Tunisia, prior to redeployment.

After the surrender of Italy on 8 September 1943 and the ultimate success of the Salerno landing, there was a new challenge awaiting in the Eastern Mediterranean as British forces took over the islands of Cos, Leros and Samos in the eastern Aegean from the Italians. On 22 October the squadron moved from Tunisia to El Adem and then to Gambut. Gambut, to be the squadron's home for the next five months, was temporarily unserviceable due to heavy thunderstorms. Under the leadership of Lee-Evans they were soon ready to strike again at the German forces as they reacted to our occupation of Cos and the other islands. The British occupation of these islands posed a real threat to the German garrisons in Crete, Rhodes and Southern Greece. Could we maintain our newly won positions as the Germans prepared to challenge our recent successes?

On 5 November the squadron lost its second Commanding Officer within four months when Jimmy Lee-Evans ditched in Lavrion Bay, south east of Piraeus, after dropping his torpedo against three invasion ships destined for Leros. Lee-Evans, leading a formation of three torpedo carrying Beaufighters, with two Beaufighters from 603 Squadron in support, was hit by heavy and sustained flak. He managed to ditch successfully. Both the Wing Commander and his navigator Flight Lieutenant David Heden were picked up and became POWs. Another Beaufighter of 47 Squadron on this sortie flown by Flight Lieutenant T

C Graham with Flying Officer J H K Langdon as navigator was also hit by flak, ditched successfully after dropping its torpedo, the two crew becoming POWs.

The command of the squadron now fell to the next most senior officer, Squadron Leader Charles A Ogilvie who the very next day, 6 November, led four Beaufighters of 47 Squadron together with four Beaufighters of 603 Squadron on a strike by cannon fire on shipping off Paros in the Cyclades. Unfortunately Ogilvie, chased by Me109s, was forced down. He, along with his navigator, managing to evade capture by the Germans, was able to rejoin the squadron in December. On the same operation another 47 Squadron Beaufighter was shot down, with the pilot Flying Officer L Rossner and the navigator Sergeant H K Levy both killed. From the time of Ogilvie's loss until Wing Commander Filson-Young arrived to assume command of the squadron on 24 November, Flight Lieutenant Smith, a Canadian pilot, assumed the role of Acting Commanding Officer with operational flying coming under the control of the then CO of 603 Squadron, Squadron Leader Atkinson and later of Wing Commander J R H Lewis DFC.

With the loss of eight crews in fourteen days from all the operations in this period, the rather drastic step was taken on 13 November to reinforce 47 Squadron with seven crews from the Torpedo Training School at Shallufa on the Suez Canal. These reinforcements, led by Squadron Leader Stanley Muller-Rowland, were a mixture of 'tour expired' instructors and experienced trainees. Later that same day Muller-Rowland was shot down while leading a formation of seven Beaufighters as it attacked and chased a group of four Ju88s. Fortunately Muller-Rowland and his navigator were picked up from their dinghy by friendly fishermen, eventually making their way back to Shallufa. The reinforced squadron was led for the next few days, with great distinction, by Flight Lieutenant Lionel W Daffurn, Muller-Rowland's second in command at Shallufa, when the maximum effort was made, despite the continuing losses, in support of our troops defending their position on Leros from invading German forces. On 16 November Leros surrendered which was the day when Squadron Leader Geoff Powell was brought back from a well earned rest to lead six Beaufighters from 47 Squadron and two from 603 Squadron against a Siebell ferry carrying reinforcements to Leros. This operation, resulting in the loss of three more 47 Squadron Beaufighters and one 603 Squadron Beaufighter, is vividly recalled by Sergeant Pilot Bob Milne.

Bob summarises here those events in which he took part in his own words. *"After the loss of the CO, Wing Commander Jimmy Lee-Evans on 5 November and Squadron Leader Ogilvie on 6 November, two days later, on 8 November, six Beaufighters of 47 Squadron and six Beaufighters of 603 Squadron were despatched to attack an enemy convoy west of Cos. Three of 47 Squadron's Beaufighters carried torpedoes. The crews, of which I was one, were certainly rather fearful that they would be shot down. We were expecting to lose some, if not all, of our Torbeaus. I remember the ground staff waving us off - i.e. waving goodbye! On reaching the target area we encountered a terrible storm, at times the waves seemed higher than the plane and it was the first time that I had seen 'St Elmos Fire'. Then suddenly as we were coming out of the storm we sighted the ships. We attacked and a hit was observed on the leading ship. An Arado was shot down. Clearly they were not expecting Beaufighters to come out of a storm at sea. In the event all the Beaufighters returned to base."*

To continue with Bob's personal narrative: *"On 11 November we were briefed to attack shipping off Kalymnos and Cos but interception from fighters on Cos prevented us from locating the target as we were attacked by Me109s for twenty two minutes. On similar operations on 12 and 13 November three more Beaufighters of 47 Squadron were lost including Squadron Leader Stanley Muller-Rowland. Then on 16 November a Siebel Ferry carrying troops with an escort of two ships and fighter cover was located by reconnaissance west of Kalymnos. It was vital to prevent these forces reaching Leros. 47 Squadron had only five aircraft left, plus an old plane used for training. Only five crews of 47 were available to fly. Squadron Leader Geoff Powell had left the squadron as 'tour expired' but as he happened to be available, he was asked to return and lead this strike making up six 47 crews to man the six Beaufighters, including the training aircraft. Two 603 Beaus were added to the strike force. I flew the training aircraft 'E' for Edward. On approaching the target area we could see enemy aircraft circling the ships, 4 JU88s, 7 Arados and 6 Me109s. We managed to get to the target before the enemy saw us. We attacked with cannon and machine guns blowing up the ferry. The Me109s attacked, chasing us for 23 minutes. Three 47 Squadron Beaufighters were lost crewed by Flying Officer John Fletcher and Sergeant Jack Dale, Flying Officer Tony Bond and Sergeant Alfred Cottle, and Flying Officer Bill Thwaites and Flying Officer John Lovell. All were killed except Sergeant Alfred Cottle who was reported as 'safe', later awarded the MM for his exploits in evading capture. Sergeant Dale had joined the squadron the day before, barely having had enough time to unpack his kit. The surviving 47 Squadron pilots were Geoff Powell, Vic Borrowdale and Bob Milne together with their navigators. Powell received the DSO, his observer/ navigator Cyril Adams an immediate DFC, with Borrowdale and Milne together with Sergeant Craven of 603 Squadron awarded immediate DFMs. Leros fell that evening and this phase of the Aegean campaign came to an end. 47 Squadron had no serviceable aircraft and not many crews. Flight Lieutenant Smith was temporarily stood down. Flight Sergeants Heath and Wapshott were off sick and hopefully would soon be back on the squadron. This left Borrowdale and Milne as the only immediately available pilots*

Summarising, the Aegean/Leros Campaign as far as 47 Squadron was concerned it lasted 18 days during which time the sixteen crews were reduced to the five mentioned. All these losses occurred in the 12 days from 5 to 16 November. The squadron recovered quickly with an influx of new crews and planes, together with a new CO who was to prove to be a much admired leader. The Aegean campaign would continue with Leros just another enemy occupied island."

Bob Milne and his navigator Larry Lowman continued to serve in the squadron to the end of the Burma campaign; both were commissioned with Larry later being awarded a well earned DFC. Bob, awarded an immediate DFM after the Siebel ferry operation, quite inexplicably missed out on awards when he came to the end of his second tour in Burma.

It was not surprising that Tommy and I found a very depleted squadron without senior officers as we settled into Gambut. For the previous few weeks, prior to our arrival at El Adem on 20 November, squadron personnel had witnessed the events outlined, leading to the loss of the Dodecanese Islands of Cos, Leros and Samos, with bewilderment and sadness. The attempt to maintain our forces in the Dodecanese had, according to the official history, resulted in *"losses, among the combined anti shipping and night fighter forces of Beaufighters, at the fearful rate of fifty percent of all the Beaufighter squadrons"*. Operating at the extreme limit of their range and without single engine fighter support, the Royal Air Force was unable to obtain command of the air over our troops on the islands of Cos and Leros.

The operation to take over from the Italian garrisons on the islands of the Aegean had commenced on the 14 September. A few members of the British Special Forces landed on Cos and Leros and three days later on Samos. Reinforcements were brought in by Dakota to Cos and by destroyers to Leros and Samos. This was going to be the story of an 'island too far' as the Germans reacted with great vigour and determination to counter our occupation. Having the benefit of very short lines of communication from Crete and Rhodes, they soon launched a series of attacks by air and sea upon our forces in Cos, Leros and Samos invading Cos on the night of 2/3 October by paratroopers and eventually wresting all the islands back to their control by 16 November. Over three thousand British servicemen were captured and became prisoners of war. Others, after many hazardous adventures, managed to escape into Turkey and eventually find their way back to Egypt.

From 28 October to the surrender of the remaining British forces on Leros on 16 November the squadron was stretched to the limit, operating at maximum range in support of this toehold in the Dodecanese. In the space of nineteen days thirteen aircraft were lost with fifteen crew members killed, four became POWs and seven evaded capture, eventually returning to the squadron. This attrition rate of approximately 70% was clearly unsustainable, but says much for the courage and dedication of the aircrews involved. Taking the period from 23 June 1943 to 30 November 1943 as the squadron moved along the north African coast from Protville in Tunisia to Gambut in Libya thirty aircraft were lost by enemy action with thirty aircrew killed or missing. Heavy losses indeed over such a short period.

CHAPTER 7
THE AEGEAN: A FLAWED AND FORGOTTEN CAMPAIGN

It is necessary to look back a little to appreciate the tactical situation 47 Squadron were committed to as it moved to El Adem and then Gambut in October/November 1943. In January 1943 the Casablanca Conference considered capturing Rhodes and the Dodecanese islands. The garrisons were Italian and the exercise could be a useful diversion when the invasion of Sicily took place. Plans were drawn up for a full scale attack on Rhodes and Scarpanto (Karpathos) and then subsequently upon other islands in the Dodecanese - plans were complete by 2 May 1943. On four subsequent occasions a force was assembled and partially prepared to undertake the capture of Rhodes. The plan was further crystallised in August 1943 and given the code name 'Accolade'. The force would be assembled in and come from Cyprus. The date for the invasion of Rhodes was set for 1 September after the fall of Sicily. 201 (Naval Cooperation) Group (of which 47 Squadron was soon to be a part) would provide protection for all Allied shipping outside a forty mile range from Cyprus. The plan was that Cos was to be occupied first, followed by Leros and Samos, all to be organised and controlled from Castelrosso, a small island close to Turkey and in Allied hands. Cos is an island thirty miles long and seven miles wide with a population of some twenty thousand. Between 1 September and 18 September Cos, Leros, Samos, Symi, Stampalia and Ikaria were all taken by Allied troops. The Italian garrisons offered no resistance under the terms of the Armistice signed in Sicily on 3 September 1943. However, the Germans were expected to react strongly. In terms of air cover for our forces, Gambut in Libya was three hundred and eighty miles away with

Cyprus a little nearer, three hundred and fifty miles from Cos. The outcome was that the Germans invaded Cos on 3 October 1943, spearheaded by paratroops, and quickly overran the island by the following day. This operation by the Germans was code named Operation Polar Bear. Of the garrison of fifteen hundred men the Allies were only able to evacuate approximately one hundred to safety, the rest being either killed or taken prisoner. The Germans in the attack and occupation of Cos only lost eighty three men. One by one all the other islands occupied by the Allies were captured. Leros invaded on 12 November 1943 surrendered on 16 November 1943 but only after inflicting very severe losses on the invading force who suffered over eleven hundred killed out of three thousand invasion troops.

It is not the purpose of this narrative to tell the full story of this failure, as by 18 November, having evacuated Samos, it was back to square one with Cos, Leros and Samos now firmly in German hands. However, there is a lesson to be learnt here - that an indisputable pre-requisite of all successful sea-borne operations against defended coastlines is the establishment, if only temporarily, of air superiority. Despite the Allied preponderance of aircraft in the Mediterranean area, the Luftwaffe was able to establish local air supremacy long enough to allow their ground and sea forces sufficient freedom to invade and capture islands held by British troops. Operating at much greater distances from their bases in North Africa and Cyprus than the Germans in Greece and Crete, the air forces in the Middle East were not able to effectively challenge the local German dominance in the Aegean. Most of the Allied Forces were heavily engaged in the Italian campaign. They could afford little further aid to operations in the Aegean, which at an early stage was only seen as a diversion - so why did the Allies attempt it at all?

The decision to occupy these islands after the Italian surrender was at the very best a brave endeavour which failed because one of the cardinal principles in the deployment of front line aircraft was ignored. 47 Squadron and other Beaufighter squadrons of 201 (Naval Cooperation) Group were not designed to combat single engine fighters particularly in daylight. Without the benefit of a fighter escort they suffered the same fate at the hands of the Luftwaffe that overtook German bombers in the Battle of Britain. Many aircrews, trained at great expense, were lost through faulty 'Intelligence' and poor tactical understanding of the resources needed to capture and hold onto the Dodecanese Islands in 1943. We handed a quite unnecessary victory to the enemy, which was exploited to the full to bolster morale back in Germany. These islands were to remain in German hands until the end of the war.

The new Commanding Officer, Wing Commander Filson-Young DFC, posted from the UK, joined 47 Squadron on 24 November 1943. Coming from Coastal Command he had well over one hundred operational sorties to his credit on Sunderland Flying Boats and the torpedo Beaufighters of 254 Squadron, part of the celebrated North Coates Wing. By general consent of both aircrew and the long serving groundcrew, he was to prove to be the most outstanding commander of the squadron during World War 11. He served as Commanding Officer continuously, from November 1943 until tragically shot down and killed in Southern Burma on 15 May 1945. He was to lead the squadron with great distinction in two theatres of war over the next eighteen months. To quote Tony Norris (Flying Officer E T Norris at the time) the squadron's Intelligence Officer, *'Filson-Young's main characteristic was a determination to fulfil his duties and nothing else mattered so long as he achieved that end'*. He was not a dashing hero but had the remarkable quality of being able to lead without being a striking personality. He was a fair haired slightly built man sporting the traditional handlebar moustache, his rather diffident and shy manner hiding remarkable determination. He knew what had to be done as he overcame with great distinction all the difficulties associated with a squadron devastated by its recent losses. As recounted many years later by Nick Colley, the ground crew felt the losses keenly too, particularly when handing over the form 700 prior to take-off, for the pilot to check that all the pre flight procedures had been carried out. As the pilot added his signature and handed the form back, the men on the ground did wonder if this was to be the crew's last mission. Over a period of eighteen months, a squadron based overseas and constantly on the move was bound to have changing fortunes. Wing Commander Filson-Young led all the aircrew and the supporting team of officers and men of just over three hundred personnel, through periods of intense action in the Eastern Mediterranean, followed by frustration in Southern India and finally to the trauma of Burma. Again, as Nick Colley recalls, the new CO made his name and certainly earned the respect of the ground staff when he rescued several airmen from the clutches of the Royal Air Force Police - the 'SP's' - as they were having a last fling in Alexandria just prior to leaving for India. To the groundcrew he was often referred to as 'Flitgun' - a nickname which was widely used, but not in his hearing.

Three weeks after the arrival of the new Commanding Officer, on 11 December 1943 'A' Flight too had a new Officer Commanding, Flight Lieutenant L H Skinner, an ex flying instructor from the Canadian schools, soon to be made up to Squadron Leader and now starting his first operational tour. Having a moderately portly figure and a round humorous face with short curly hair, he was soon to be known, quite affectionately, as 'Porky Skinner'. The Commanding Officer of 'B' Flight was Major A R Pears, seconded from the SAAF, and a much more aloof figure than 'Porky'. He always had something of a military air about him, particularly as he, in his turn, sported a short clipped military-style moustache.

On 28 December the squadron aircrew were brought up to strength with the arrival of several Canadian pilots along with their English navigators, joining from the Torpedo Training School at Shallufa. Throughout the next few months, in North Africa and later in India and Burma, we never had available more than eight to ten crews in each flight which did impose some stress when maximum effort was called for. Among those joining at this time were Pilot Officer J E S Milroy and his navigator Sergeant C J Wright, Pilot Officer L E Gieselman and his navigator Sergeant A M Howard (always known as 'Foo' Howard), Flying Officer D R Stewart and his navigator Sergeant

T Cooney, together with Major A R Pears and his navigator Flight Sergeant O J Evans. All these crews were to follow the squadron into India and Burma. This mixed bag of aircrew was further supplemented in India by Flight Lieutenant Bill Hughes, a cheerful extrovert Australian pilot, who flew with Flying Officer John Kent, a navigator from the 'old country'. The Dominion crews were always a source of fun and inspiration. Filson-Young was to weld this group of UK, Irish, Australian, New Zealand, Canadian and South African personnel into a team exhibiting the highest standards of operational efficiency whatever the circumstances at the time.

Gambut under the authority of 235 Wing, 201 (Naval Cooperation) Group, home for the next four months, was a windswept airfield with rolled runways, not proof against heavy rain. Situated on the escarpment about twenty miles inland from the Mediterranean it suffered from frequent dust storms and could be rather cold after sundown during the winter months. Before every operational sortie the crew were briefed by the Commanding Officer or Flight Commander in the operations marquee. The targets to be attacked and the tactics to be employed were outlined on large scale maps. Details of flak, places to avoid and enemy aircraft dispositions came from the Intelligence Officer, followed by the Meteorological Officer on weather conditions, with call signs and radio frequencies from the Signals Officer. We had great respect for the squadron's Intelligence Officer, Flying Officer Tony Norris. With a dry sense of humour, always sceptical of the 'line shooter', he was very skilful in extracting the bare facts of an operation during de-briefing. As a teacher of Latin in his pre-war occupation, the logic of the Latin language must have been good training for interpreting our stories after an operational flight. Equally popular and respected was Flying Officer Harold Fishwick (always known as Joe) who, as an ex-RAF apprentice, was commissioned on the squadron as Signals Officer. He was another no-nonsense officer whose only interest was the care of his men in the Signals section and with giving all possible support to the aircrew. Harold, much to his credit, ultimately retired from the RAF as a Group Captain Mentioned in Dispatches and with the MBE.

GRT Willis Archives

*Above: January 1944, Gambut - eggs for 'V' cigarettes.
L to r Senussi Arab, Ken Thomas, Bob Willis and
Maurice Jones.*

*Below: 6 November 1943, Gambut B25 Mitchells
of the USAAF with 4 Beaufighters (3 with torpedoes).*

GRT Willis Archives

GRT Willis Archives

November 1943, Gambut. 'Airborne', squadron markings painted out.

The formation leader outlined the type of formation, with individual positions, together with the planned height and speed to fly. Other advice would be action to take if one was jumped by Me109s, including how or when to ditch a torpedo if in severe trouble. A torpedo ditched without proper cause would lead to a court of enquiry. As a crew Tommy and I were more worried about not putting up a black than being fearful of the enemy. As new boys we never had time to worry about the risks, the tasks were too absorbing. In the mess many theories were advanced on the avoiding action to take if attacked by single engine fighters. Fly as low as possible, literally just a few feet above the sea, then jink hard at the command of the navigator the moment before he estimated that the fighter had his 'bead' on you.

Probably because we got so psyched up flying at low level over the Mediterranean for long stretches, we usually slept for long hours after being debriefed and stood down. Some time later in Burma, one or two aircrew would arrive at a stage where they could not sleep, due to the climate and associated operational stress. Aircrew under stress, and at any one time it would only amount to one or two individuals, were quickly posted off the squadron under some pretext or other by a reasonably understanding Commanding Officer. Methods were found to move pilots or navigators away who did not appear up to the mark but these cases were very few, never discussed, and largely went unnoticed.

Returning to our personal story, Tommy and I had just one day to settle down at Gambut before we were airborne assimilating the squadron's current formation tactics during three practice flights. In the Sergeants Mess the talk was full of the story leading to the destruction of the Siebell ferry and the loss of three crews on that operation.

Feeling somewhat apprehensive, in the early morning of 26 November, we took off on our first operational mission, carrying a torpedo, in the company of three other torpedo Beaufighters from the squadron and three B25 Mitchells of 310 Bombardment Group USAAF. Possibly due to the lack of senior officers on the squadron, the briefing was short and to the point. Any mention that we were new to the squadron together with a few words of advice was noticeable by its absence. If shot down we would soon be forgotten. A supply ship sailing from Piraeus to Crete was the target. To our disappointment tinged with relief no sighting was made. The bird had flown, so it was back to base with our torpedo still in place. Even on this uneventful sortie one Beaufighter was lost, having turned back early with engine problems. No sign of the crew, Flying Officer F Gregory and Flying Officer J Wood, was ever seen despite a search of the area over the ensuing days. Ultimately they were posted as 'missing'.

Despite the rather primitive conditions on this dusty airfield, living with Tommy in a small ridge tent, fending for ourselves and getting fairly dirty due to lack of water, we both kept quite fit. With our makeshift beds, extra blankets and clean sheets washed by Libyan camp servants from time to time, we were remarkably comfortable. It was surprising how the well seasoned and travelled groundcrew looked after themselves through scrounging, acquiring and saving those little extras such as soap and toilet needs as they moved from place to place. The desert taught us a few lessons about German engineering skills, Within about one hundred yards of our tent was a crashed Ju87, the ubiquitous German dive bomber. We admired the quality of the German cockpit instruments in their brass mountings which appeared to be more reliable products than our own instruments in their flimsy plastic casings. Over fifty years later we still respect German engineering skills. Frequent visitors to our lines were the Senussi Arabs looking to exchange their eggs for our 'V' cigarettes (RAF issue). Being non-smokers the eggs as a supplement to our diet were more than welcome. It was all rather amusing as no-one ever knew for certain who manufactured 'V' cigarettes. The airmen purported to believe that they were made from camel dung. The quality of a 'Woodbine' was certainly missed by the smokers.

Tactics changed in December as we largely discarded our torpedoes. For the next few months most operational flying by the squadron consisted in attacking small cargo ships and caiques in the ports and harbours of the Cyclades and Dodecanese Islands. When we found any caiques of cargo-carrying size, which were usually holed up during the day in well defended harbours, the Beaufighters attacked with cannon fire, supplemented by 100 pound bombs in the target area. These operations could be quite hazardous, demanding an element of surprise through low flying tactics, although pretty intense and accurate return fire from the ground was the usual experience. Additionally, light or heavy anti-aircraft fire was also to be expected from Crete, Rhodes, Cos and Leros if one flew too close. Other tasks could be escort duty for destroyers of the Royal Navy, or convoy escort. However, the main objective was to disrupt the supply chain from Greece to the German garrisons on Crete and the other major islands they occupied in the Eastern Mediterranean.

On 1 December, as part of a formation of six Beaufighters, we experienced our second operational sweep led by Flying Officer Arthur Unwin, searching for supply caiques sailing between the islands or hiding in the many small harbours or inlets. Flying as low as possible we rounded the western end of Crete on the outward journey, north to the Cyclades, to Melos and Naxos and then back south between Scarpanto and Rhodes to head across the open sea to base. This was our second mission without any tangible result. By good fortune we were being run in for the action to come.

On 4 December with a similar formation of four Beaufighters the long awaited action came as we sighted four Arado 196, single engine float planes, circling at about five hundred feet over the sea, near the island of Kinaros to the west of Leros. With a crew of two and armament fore and aft the Arado 196 is quite a manoeuvrable aircraft, very useful in island waters as an escort for transport aircraft or for small ships plying between the islands.

Now for maximum concentration, safety catch off, gun sight in place, all rather exhilarating. The first Arado I attacked was stationary on the water. It had apparently landed on the sea with engine failure with its three companion Arados circling overhead. I strafed the aircraft on the water with cannon. Arthur Unwin, as leader of the formation, was concerned that we would be jumped by Me109s. He circled above ready to give warning if the dreaded 109s appeared. Arthur explained later at de-briefing that he thought the Arado on the sea might be a decoy designed to get us into difficulty and here was I having a go! The Arado on the sea was an easy target. Through the gun sight I could see the 'plane breaking up with one of the crew clambering onto a float as it sank. After this first success I made to attack another Arado still circling overhead. Climbing at full throttle I made a quarter turn attack.

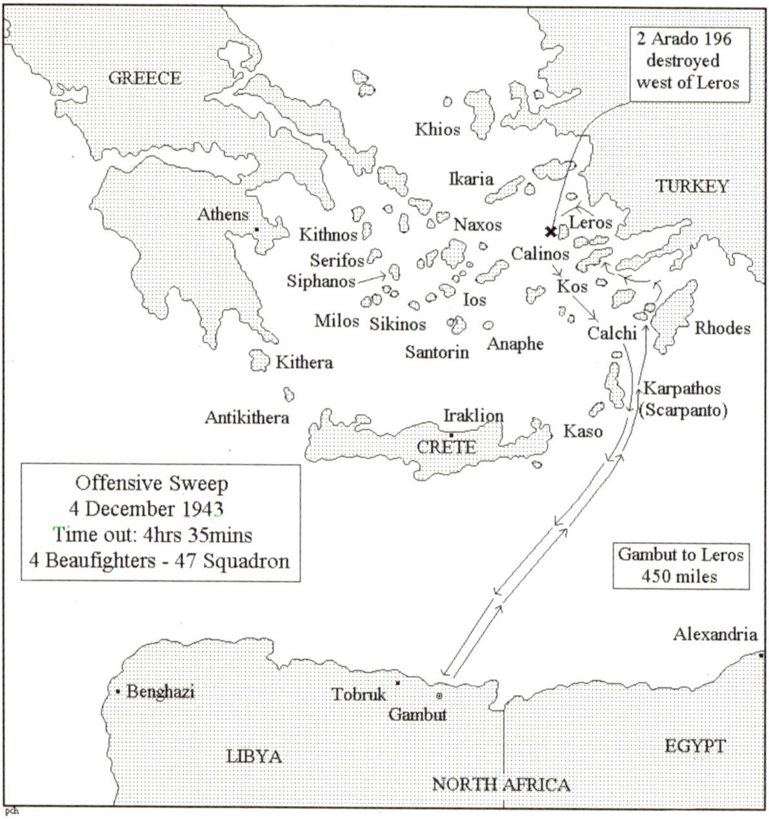

I shot off the support of one of his floats which, as it was hanging down, made the aircraft unflyable. It went down and hit the sea with a big splash. As it was going down the rear gunner was still firing at us, well wide of the mark, but we did admire his courage. So I was credited with those two aircraft. The rest of the formation, concerned at our nearness to German airfields on Crete and the possibility of Me109s making a quick appearance did not engage the other Arados for long, but they did strafe a high speed motor launch which came into view. These events did have a later personal reaction when I thought of the Arado crew trapped and unable to escape as we bore down with cannon blazing. I could not help thinking about the families of the men I probably killed.

In the present squadron headquarters at Lyneham there resides a large wooden propeller taken from a crashed Italian bomber. Inscribed on this propeller, as a battle honour, are the two Arado 196 destroyed on 4 December 1943, the Heinkel 115 destroyed later and of course the Siebel Ferry success. Most of the notable achievements of the squadron in World War ll are highlighted on this propeller, recording the destruction of many enemy ships and aircraft.

On 7 December Flying Officer Nicol and Warrant Officer Ball of 'B' Flight failed to return from a shipping sweep and were posted 'missing'. We hardly knew them.

After another uneventful sweep on 10 December with a formation of six Beaufighters north of Crete we had better luck on 14 December with another formation of four Beaufighters, this time led by Flying Officer J Edwards. South of Stampalia we sighted a Heinkel 115 flying low over the sea escorted by four Arado 196. The Heinkel 115 is a large twin engined seaplane with a crew of three, similar in size to a Handley Page Hampden. It was used as a troop carrier or supply aircraft to the various German island garrisons. Whilst two Beaufighters of our formation were paying attention to the escorting Arados I attacked this large seaplane in formation with another Beaufighter, flown by Sergeant

Ken Thomas. I could see my cannon fire sparking as it hit the wings of the Heinkel. About twenty feet of the port wing of the Heinkel came off, it was in real trouble. Concentrating too hard in my eagerness to finish the job I came in too close to the enemy aircraft, forcing me to fly over it to avoid a mid-air collision. We were an easy target to the Heinkel rear gunner who hit us and set us on fire. Turning and looking out I saw the Heinkel splash into the sea, as confirmed by other members of the formation. The downed Heinkel was credited to my score. With our aircraft full of smoke thoughts were quickly concentrated on survival. The Heinkel rear gunner had shot off the tip of our starboard wing and ignited the verey cartridges stored in the rear of the aircraft.

The verey cartridges, which produce a bright magnesium flare, gave off a tremendous cloud of white smoke containing magnesium powder. The whole aircraft was full of choking smoke. The instrument panel was blotted out by the magnesium deposit. Through the smoke I could not even see the horizon or any of the instruments. It appeared impossible to fly the aircraft. Tommy had evacuated his position at the rear. All his navigation equipment and navigation table were burnt out, but he had very courageously beaten out the flames, despite the heat, preventing any further damage to the aircraft. My immediate reaction was to jettison the cockpit roof with a view to baling out. We would have to go through the roof as the best option to get out whilst still airborne.

In the Beaufighter some instructors advised that the easier option was to turn the aircraft upside down to get out safely. The alternative was to go through the escape hatch in the floor of the aircraft. Either way it was considered rather difficult to bale out of a Beaufighter, particularly when you also had a dinghy pack attached to your parachute. I did not even think about the hazards, but jettisoning the roof canopy brought in an immediate rush of air completely clearing the cockpit of smoke. Instinctively I rubbed the magnesium deposit off the instrument panel and the windscreen. The aircraft was still more or less straight and level with both engines functioning normally. This was an all metal aircraft where the fire, prevented by Tommy from spreading, burnt itself out in the tail end. Fortunately there were no fuel lines in this section to feed the flames. Without our cockpit roof the noise of inrushing air made communication on the inter-com impossible. By hand signal I indicated we would fly south until the coast of North Africa was sighted. We were just alright for fuel. Approximately two hours later the North African coast came into view. Tommy indicated our location on the map. Following the coast I made course for Gambut. I had become aware that the elevator was partially damaged due to its lack of response from the controls. With the wheels and flaps in good order I was able to land without any real problem, helped by Gambut having a very long landing strip, enabling me to bring the aircraft down to ground level on a very shallow glide path. We had been in the air for five and a quarter hours. As we climbed out Flying Officer Edwards, the leader of our original formation, was waiting at the foot of the exit hatch. All he said to me was, 'Oh, we thought you had 'bought' it!' That was a typical greeting, as we went off to be debriefed. The rest of the formation had already reported to Tony Norris of our possible demise, as we disappeared over the horizon with smoke pouring from our aircraft. We soon discovered that shooting down a Heinkel, or the Arados ten days previously attracted little comment. It was taken as just part of the day's work. Later that same day Tommy and I examined our damaged Beaufighter in the maintenance section. The heat from the fire had been so intense that the aluminium stringers in the rear section which make up the aircraft frame, and which contain a series of holes to keep the weight down, had partially melted and run into each other.

From December 1943 to March 1944, besides its very active daytime role, the squadron also made a few night sorties in support of the Navy on anti submarine patrols or the Special Boat Squadron activities. These Special Forces were very active during our time at Gambut attacking many of the islands under the cover of darkness, destroying caiques and taking the odd prisoner. Islands attacked included Calchi, Stampalia, Lisso, Nistro, Simi, Patmos, Leskli, Cos and Calinos, all in our own patrol area. I was reminded of the NCO I had met earlier in 1943, on the US troopship 'Mariposa', who had been engaged on this type of operation. Night sorties by Beaufighters from Gambut gave support for these operations by patrolling over Heraklion, the main airfield on Crete, or other specified areas, to deter any E Boats or enemy air activity which could impede clandestine operations. This type of sortie appeared to be reasonably successful without much enemy interference. Taking part in one such operation on 9 March 1944 Tony Norris as Intelligence Officer outlined the purpose of the mission and why it was necessary to patrol over a certain area. Given vectors off the island of Crete we had to keep the aircraft within a pre determined sector. If we saw any enemy activity we fired a red verey light. Any Allied vessel engaged in clandestine infiltration into Crete would be warned of the danger of being spotted. Our mission proved to be uneventful.

On 10 December I sent Joan a Christmas Greetings Telegram. I was receiving an Air Letter from Joan every week which was only taking around fourteen days to arrive. Most of my letters emphasised how well Tommy and I were keeping with numerous references to the countless flies and the occasional dust storm when visibility on the airfield was down to zero.

Christmas Day 1943 arrived. The squadron stood down for a rest, providing the opportunity for all ranks to enjoy a good Christmas dinner. The cooks excelled themselves with the menu for the Sergeants' Mess comprising Tomato Soup, Hors d'oeuvres, Turkey, Pork or Poultry with seasoning, Potatoes - creamed and roast, Cauliflower, Brussels Sprouts, Bread and Apple Sauces, Christmas Pudding with Brandy Sauce, Fruit and Nuts, Mince Pies, Biscuits and Cheese, Coffee - black or white, Cigars. As was the custom, the officers and sergeants waited on the groundcrew in their dining marquee, with us helping to bring the Christmas fare across from the cook-house. Thankfully, there was no dust storm that day. What followed in subsequent days was considerably more modest.

December closed on a quiet note after the stresses of the previous months. After Christmas, together with several new arrivals, training concentrated on air to ground firing, formation flights and night circuits and landings.

From 2 to 17 January 1944 Tommy and I were despatched on a refresher course to No.5 ME Torpedo School at Shallufa, flying down from Gambut in a Wellington bomber. The course provided more training on torpedo tactics against enemy shipping, with a particular emphasis upon night operations. Several units of the Eastern Mediterranean fleet took part in these exercises, including the capital ships of the 1st Battle Squadron, HMS 'Renown', HMS 'Valiant' and HMS 'Queen Elizabeth'. There were several very experienced instructors at this school including Squadron Leader Stanley R Muller Rowland DFC, now back at Shallufa after being shot down when leading a 47 Squadron strike on 13 November 1943.

By January 1944 there were very few large ships left in the Mediterranean which justified a torpedo attack. Perhaps, unknown to us, we were being prepared for action against the large Japanese fleet based in Singapore. During these sixteen days at Shallufa no time was lost. Seven practice torpedo attacks were made at night and three similar attacks during the day. Eleven ships of the Royal Navy in the Suez area were involved. Practice night attacks were made under the illumination of the moon or by the alternative method on moonless nights of illuminating the target by flares released from supporting Wellingtons, to provide a silhouette of the target ship. My last night exercise on 15 January 1945 was with Stanley Muller-Rowland flying the aircraft with myself observing the tactics as I stood behind the pilot in the aircraft well.

The plan on these exercises was for a formation of four Beaufighters to mount a simulated torpedo strike against the 1st Battle Squadron exercising in the Gulf of Suez. As the torpedo Beaufighters approached the capital ships flares dropped behind the ships by two Wellington bombers illuminated the target. The flares, as they hovered in the sky, allowed us to see the silhouettes of HMS 'Renown', HMS 'Valiant' and HMS 'Queen Elizabeth' enabling us to position ourselves to launch a dummy runner torpedo against the best positioned target ship. Torpedo Beaufighters carrying out these exercises carried F24 cameras to assess results and to assist in deciding the best tactics to use against capital ships. In view of the intense AA fire expected from capital ships, night attacks were deemed at the time to have the most chance of success. Either way it would be a hazardous mission. This consideration was certainly to the fore when the squadron was later based outside Madras on permanent standby for any possible incursion by the Japanese Navy. Extensive reports and photographs of these exercises were submitted to 201(Naval Cooperation) Group and 203 Group Headquarters, emphasising their value not only to the RAF aircrew involved, but also to the participating naval vessels in deciding the most appropriate evading action required to thwart torpedo bombers.

By 1941 all three brothers of the famous MacRobert Scottish family had lost their lives as flyers. There were also three Muller Rowland brothers in the RAF, Eric, Stanley and John, all flying Beaufighters. Eric was lost in June 1944 whilst with 144 Squadron. Stanley disappeared on a night sortie from North Coates in Lincolnshire on 3 October 1944 flying with 236 squadron. It is a sharp reminder of the sacrifices made by so many families when sons joined the aircrew ranks in World War ll, with the last Muller Rowland brother John, losing his life as a test pilot for De Havillands in 1950. All the Muller Rowlands were very special and a great tribute to the RAF. Like all aircrew Tommy and I had our duty to do. We were much in awe of those, like the Muller Rowlands, who appeared to have no fear and were always hungry to meet the enemy.

Back to Gambut. Our first sortie on returning from Shallufa was on 23 January 1944 as part of a formation of six Beaufighters led by Flying Officer Arthur Unwin for a daylight attack on Rhodes harbour. The old crusader fort adjoining the harbour housed the German garrison. Each aircraft carrying two 100lb bombs. The fear of interception by Me109s, possibly based on any of the three German airfields on Rhodes, decided a strategy of approaching Rhodes at sea level from Turkish waters. 201 Group gave permission to fly for a short while over Turkish territory, despite the fact that Turkey was a non-combatant. We did succeed in the element of surprise climbing up off the sea and over the cliffs, to one thousand feet to position ourselves for a bombing run on the old fort. The bombs from my aircraft overshot and landed in the sea. These cliffs adjacent to the harbour are now, over fifty years later, covered with holiday hotels. The whole operation was really quite futile. As any tourist knows the walls of this medieval crusader fort are around two metres thick. Our one hundred pound bombs made little impact. The attack on Rhodes was followed by a strafing run on the caiques and stores in Cos harbour. There was intense light and heavy flak from both Cos and Rhodes. On Cos caiques moored against the harbour jetty were hit and damaged. The mission was completed without any aircraft suffering serious damage. Tommy with his hand held F24 camera took photographs of Calchi and Cos harbours.

Our seventh operation on 28 January, in a formation of three Beaufighters, was uneventful as we swept around Santorin, Sikinos and Melos, to the north of Crete, failing to find any targets. Despite the marginally lower level of activity since November the squadron lost five crews on operations during December and January, events which we hardly noticed. With the squadron split into two separate flights, 'A' and 'B', with mixed crews of officers and sergeants in separate messes, it was only when a close friend failed to return that the loss sank in. For the sake of morale, aircrew losses were never dwelt on in briefings or announced to squadron personnel in any official form. We had no time to worry. If we were not out on operations, air tests or training flights, we were cooking on our battered primus, writing letters, playing in some sport, or just sleeping.

Casualties did arise from a wide variety of causes. It could be an engine failure, having to leave the formation and unable to maintain height, ditching. If a straggler, there was always the chance of being picked off by an opposing aircraft. As in all theatres some losses were never explained. Another hazard, which we were well aware of, was the possibility of flying into the sea when at minimum height to avoid radar detection. Continuous low flying, with the bright Mediterranean sun on the water, could have a hypnotic effect with a subsequent unfortunate result if the pilot lost concentration. Our greatest fear was to meet an Me109, which in skilful hands would always have the capacity to destroy a Beaufighter. This fate befell Warrant Officer Roger Barrett and Flight Sergeant William Fairfield who were shot down by Me109s on 3 January whilst on a sweep of eight Beaufighters led by Wing Commander Filson-Young.

Another formation of four Beaufighters from 47 Squadron had better fortune on the same day, sinking the German motor lighter 'Seerose' at

Mykonos. On 30 January, as part of a force of six torpedo aircraft and two anti flak aircraft of 47 Squadron escorted by six Beaufighters from 603 Squadron, Flight Sergeants Melling and Davies were shot down by ack-ack fire as they attacked a two thousand ton merchant vessel at Melos. Fortunately they ditched successfully and became POWs. Not so fortunate were Flying Officer D Hume and Flight Sergeant E Pegram whose Beaufighter was lost on 22 January with only the navigator Flight Sergeant Pegram surviving.

Operational flying was not the only hazard we faced. On 29 January 1944 I took off in Beaufighter 'T'5171, with LAC Johnny Bull as a passenger but with no navigator, to carry out a little practice bombing on a wrecked freighter beached on the coast, west of Tobruk. Just after completing the second run over the wreck there was a loud bang and the port engine seized up. I was only about four hundred feet above sea level. The port propeller failed to feather; it was turning a little with a very loud noise coming from the engine. Pushing the throttle on the starboard engine through the 'gate' I managed to stop the aircraft from losing any more height. Due to noise, communication with my passenger, who had come for the flying experience, was impossible. The only sensible action was to make a wheels up landing on the escarpment or ditch in the sea. It was impossible for the aircraft to gain sufficient height for a return to base. With an unfeathered propeller and with maximum power on the one engine, the aircraft was losing height. Coupled with the difficulty in maintaining control due to severe torque, and with the starboard engine under strain, I was anxious to find a suitable spot on which to execute a crash landing. Fortunately our practice bombs had already gone. The coast was about two miles away. The incident happened immediately after flying over the target wreck and heading out to sea. With difficulty I turned the aircraft towards the coast. We cleared the escarpment with about two hundred feet to spare. The desert floor was cut up with numerous waddies (dry river beds) and strewn with rocks. With the starboard engine still at full power we descended onto a relatively clear patch ahead. With wheels up we

Left: 29 January 1944, forced landing by Bob Willis in Beaufighter T5171 'T' in the Libyan desert.

GRT Willis Archives

Below: January 1944, a casualty used for practice bombing off the Libyan coast, west of Tobruk.

GRT Willis Archives

GRT Willis Archives

30 January 1944, the rescue party: back l to r, Curly Wallace, Johnny Bull, F/O Holdstock, Bob Willis, Jock Mackay (M/T driver); front F/O Arthur Unwin 2nd left and several Senussi Arabs.

GRT Willis Archives

Above: 1 December 1943, Beaufighter LX910, offensive sweep, Milos north of Crete. Note Beaufighter low over the coast.

Below: 14 december 1943, Beaufighter JM410, offensive sweep, Amorgos Island west of Cos.

GRT Willis Archives

GRT Willis Archives

December 1943, Gambut, Sid Appleton and Bill Powell - a JU87 ends its days in the desert.

GRT Willis Archives

Above: January 1944, strike at Kalamata, southern Greece from Berka, Libya.

Below: 23 January 1944, Beaufighter LX997, Calchi Harbour at Halki west of Rhodes (on the skyline) bomb on quayside.

GRT Willis Archives

GRT Willis Archives

Above: 22 January 1944, Beaufighter 'M' LX997 leaving Cos Harbour after photo reconnaisance.

Below left: 23 January 1944, Beaufighter 'M' operational sweep, Calchi Harbour.
Below right: 1 February 1944, looking for shipping at Port Maltesana, Naxos.

GRT Willis Archives

GRT Willis Archives

touched down and slid to a halt. It was a good crash landing, more by luck than judgement as we contemplated the rough terrain around us. Both propellers were bent back but no other visible damage apart from a badly scored and dented airframe as it hit the ground at around one hundred and twenty miles per hour. A very relieved Johnny Bull and I climbed out and viewed the scene. We were in the middle of a deserted and barren landscape. There was nothing to do until we sighted a search aircraft which would come looking for us. Just before dark a squadron Beaufighter flew over. We fired a red Verey cartridge. The pilot came over low as we waved. We knew he would report back that we appeared OK. We slept as best we could in the aircraft. Dawn came and outside were three Senussi Arabs, plus camel, who spoke no English but gave us hard boiled eggs to eat. They were dressed in Italian military uniforms, the origin of which was not hard to guess. Late that afternoon the rescue party arrived in a three ton lorry led by our old friend Arthur Unwin. With him was the Squadron Engineering Officer, Flying Officer Holdstock. It was quickly established that the main crank shaft in the port engine had fractured between the two banks of cylinders. The oil sump was chock full of chewed up metal. The guns were taken out with all the ammunition and together with the radio and any loose equipment loaded onto the lorry. The fuel tanks were drained leaving the aircraft abandoned on the desert floor. Just to make our day our rescue party, returning to base as darkness was falling, had to be careful to check map references due to the presence of minefields off the marked tracks. Much to my surprise following this rather minor non operational incident, I was given a Commendatory Endorsement in my log book for 'executing with skill' the forced landing just described, by the authority of the Air Officer Commanding the Eastern Mediterranean. The Adjutant jokingly told me that they had difficulty in manufacturing the green ink for the endorsement.

Fifteen days later, on 13 February 1944, Arthur Unwin and his navigator Flight Sergeant Ken Farmer were killed by ground fire as they attacked caiques at Hydra. Arthur (his first name was Joseph but he was always known as Arthur) had been an inspiration to the squadron over its period of exceptionally heavy losses, when over half of the aircrew strength was lost in the few weeks immediately before Tommy and I arrived. Arthur's loss was keenly felt, he having welcomed us to the squadron on our first day and then rescued us from our forced landing in the desert.

February came in with us taking part in two early operations, one a convoy escort (Code name PAPER) on 3 February, the other a formation of three aircraft taking off from Berka on 4 February. Berka, west of Tobruk used as an advanced landing ground, enabled us to search for targets as far north as Naxos in the Cyclades. Both of these two sorties proved to be uneventful. On 7 February, with Wing Commander Filson-Young leading our formation of six Beaufighters, we struck at Khios harbour, expecting to find a large merchant vessel which reconnaissance had reported. Carrying two 100lb bombs, each aircraft bombed and strafed either the merchant vessel, which was of about 1,000 tons, or the many caiques moored against the north east jetty. Later reconnaissance reported at least six caiques sunk. As we broke away after our first attack, much to my surprise I saw large red crosses on the side of the merchant ship. I broke RT silence and called up the leader with the message 'Hospital Ship'. Filson-Young broke off the action and we returned to base. Apparently it was a Swedish hospital ship, rumoured to be giving some support to the Germans. The ship escaped serious damage, with the British Government making suitable apologies to the Swedish authorities. What is certain, we weren't told when we took off from Gambut that the target had red crosses displayed. The reconnaissance aircraft, unless it flew very low, probably never saw the red crosses on the side of the ship's hull as it lay in Khios harbour.

Locating ships, used by the enemy to supply the islands of the Eastern Mediterranean, was far from easy. Apart from accurate flak from the designated target, Me109s had a free hand if they intercepted the Beaufighters, as our area of operation was far removed from any possible single engine fighter support. We aircrew, as just a small part of the extensive operational activity by 201 Group found it difficult to appreciate the full strategic plan and tactics applied in this theatre of war. The Germans now occupied all the islands of the Aegean. For them it was to become a wasting asset as we relentlessly harried their supply routes. Over these months four Beaufighter squadrons, supplemented by Mitchells, Marauders, Baltimores and Venturas based at Gambut, were deployed against the Germans on Crete, Rhodes and the Dodecanese Islands. Two of the Beaufighter squadrons, 227 and 252, were based at Berka in Libya and in Cyprus with the other two Beaufighter squadrons, 47 and 603, at Gambut. 47 Squadron was the only squadron equipped with torpedoes and with aircrew trained to use them against enemy shipping. By the beginning of 1944 very few targets remained which could be attacked using torpedoes.

An opportunity to deny the Germans the use of one of their few remaining ships in the Eastern Mediterranean was seized upon very successfully, following a sighting by a Baltimore of the 13th Hellenic Squadron on a reconnaissance flight. On 22 February 1944 Wing Commander Filson-Young led a formation of eighteen Beaufighters, including six carrying torpedoes and with two anti-flak Beaufighters, all the latter from 47 Squadron, against a five thousand three hundred and forty three ton merchant vessel, the SS Livenza sailing from Piraeus, bound for Candia harbour in Crete. The 47 Squadron aircraft supported by eight Beaufighters of 227 Squadron, including five equipped with rockets and two Beaufighters of 603 Squadron, flew at low level around the west side of Crete which, coming out of the sun, could provide an element of surprise. Approaching the target from the eastern tip of Crete, four Mitchells (B25s) of the 340th Bombardment Group were deployed to draw away from the target some of the escorting German aircraft. Despite an escort of Ju88s, six Me109s and six Arado 196s the tactics succeeded brilliantly. The Livenza was sunk, probably by a torpedo, with one of the escorting destroyers severely damaged. Three Beaufighter crews of 227 Squadron and one Mitchell crew were lost, counterbalanced by the shooting down of two Me109s and two Arados. This operation was a well executed tactical success, but we were sorry to learn that Flight Sergeant Sid Appleton and his navigator Flight

Sergeant Jack Fenton, old friends at Gambut, recently transferred from 47 Squadron to 227 Squadron were both killed. For this success and his leadership of the squadron, Filson-Young was awarded a bar to his DFC.

On 25 February, Flying Officer R S Euler together with his navigator Flight Sergeant C A Boffin were shot down by flak as they attacked a caique and schooner off Scarpanto. Following a successful ditching both crew members were rescued by a British destroyer. Another casualty of the squadron at this time was Sergeant Ted Daden and his navigator, Sergeant Ron Meredith, who failed to return from their mission. They ditched successfully and subsequently returned to the squadron.

Flying Beaufighter LX951 on the morning of 28th February when, searching for the crew of a Wellington ditched to the south of Crete, we were fortunate enough to sight the dinghy containing the six Wellington crew members. We were able to divert a destroyer to the scene to effect a rescue. Tommy took the usual photographs before returning to base.

Settled into Gambut our tent soon became the kitchen for many 'fry ups' of what ever we could beg or borrow from the units around us. We usually had at least two extra guests for supper. In a letter to Joan of 26 January 1944, I described the menu, cooked on the primus stove, as two fried eggs, baked beans, toast and hot malted milk for each person. The primus, second hand, came from Alexandria, the fuel was kerosene used on the airfield in landing flares supplemented by a little 100 octane aircraft fuel to eke it out. This rather lethal mixture made the primus smoke so badly that the inside of the tent canvas required a regular brush down to remove the smoke stalactites. On another evening I noted that we had toast, tongue, beans and fish paste for supper with Californian sliced peaches for dessert, courtesy of the USAAF stationed on the airfield. Water came up by a small tanker (a 'water bowser') from the delta. The water supply from local wells in Tobruk was, we understood, contaminated with salt by the retreating German forces. Toilet facilities were 'hole in the ground' and buckets, but with reasonable washing facilities, using old tin containers, we coped quite well.

By the end of 1943 the UK had been at war for over four years. 235 Wing part of 201 (Naval Cooperation) Group under the command of Air Vice-Marshal T A Langford-Sainsbury was a good example of the Allied cooperation now in place to achieve victory as soon as possible. Supporting the Beaufighters at Gambut we had 24 Squadron of the South African Air Force, flying American Marauders, B25s (Mitchells) of 310 Bombardment Group USAAF, Hudsons of 459 Squadron RAF, and Baltimores of the 13th Hellenic Squadron. Gambut certainly demonstrated how aircraft from different squadrons could work together in a mutually supportive role. We followed with much interest the offensive activities of the B25s whose tactics of close formation at high level were their defence against the Me109s. Additionally we soon came to respect the American and the South African Air Force commitment and determination to reach their designated targets.

At their well organised base camp on the perimeter of the airfield the standard of amenities for American Air Force personnel was superior in many respects to ours. The relaxed informality of the American aircrew and the supporting ground staff was most refreshing. They enjoyed the luxury of heated tents (it could be cold at night), a very wide variety of food, a mobile cinema, an aircrew tour which lasted only three months and then it was back home to America. However, neither they nor the South Africans flinched at flying long distance missions in daylight over the whole Eastern Mediterranean. There were no long range allied fighters to give protection from German fighters when over the target, although the Beaufighters were used in a variety of supporting roles as far as their range would allow. Sweeps of four to six Beaufighters across the Dodecanese were frequently designed to divert attention from B25 or Marauder sorties, whilst at the same time searching for enemy shipping bringing supplies from Piraeus to Crete, Rhodes and the other occupied islands.

In this partnership we as aircrew enjoyed most cordial relations with the American aircrew who showed great generosity towards us in many small matters. 'Come to the cinema, share our food', was a frequent invitation taken up with enthusiasm. They could always supply us with plenty of freshly baked bread which spread with American 'Olio' margarine was a welcome supplement to our rations. With one of the frequent sand storms starting to blow, I still recall the kindness of one American airman who gave me his torch so that I could find the way back to our lines, after an evening at their open air cinema.

The South African aircrew of 24 Squadron (SAAF), flying from Gambut in their Marauders, suffered severe casualties as they engaged in high level bombing missions over Greece and the Aegean. We often counted them out and counted them back, if we were not flying ourselves. On 6 March 1944 four Marauders were shot down out of a formation of six attacking shipping in Scala Bay, Santorin. They were jumped on by nine Me109s and three FW190s. The cost to the enemy was three Me109s and one FW190 destroyed with two Me109s damaged. On and off for the next two years or so we would scan the horizon awaiting the return of aircrews hoping that casualties would be few. Commanders responsible to achieve results by deploying aircrew on operational missions had an expendable asset at their disposal. However, to give credit to the Air Council, commanding officers were instructed that for our type of operation one hundred and fifty hours was the maximum. On this first tour I was made tour expired after only seventy nine hours. The tour would probably have been twice as long if the posting to India had not arisen in March 1944.

Compared to the thousands of servicemen who had fought over this desert terrain before us, our comforts were luxury indeed. No doubt we were pretty adaptable. Flying out from the UK we were given no idea what to expect if and when we were posted to an operational squadron. On the completion of our training to drop torpedoes or to fire rockets we had little idea where our skills would best be employed. Gambut was a true desert airfield, all tented and without permanent buildings, ultimately to be abandoned as the significance of the Germans on Crete and in the Dodecanese declined. Any serviceman who has served in Libya will testify that the desert is a dirty place. There were no baths and only very makeshift showers. Desert sand sticks to your skin and gets in your hair. On more than one occasion a severe sandstorm reduced visibility on the airfield to nil. The priority was to make sure that the tent was well pegged down and closed up. A sandstorm could well be followed by a severe thunderstorm entailing ditch digging and more clearing up after it passed over.

Missing the 'Livenza' operation of 22 February, it was our good fortune to be on leave in Alexandria. All Royal Air Force aircrew had free access to the Royal Navy's Alexandria Fleet Club where a hot bath and a hair cut helped to make you feel civilised again. Writing to Joan on 16 February from Alexandria, as Tommy and I enjoyed ten days leave, I extolled on the luxury of eating out, shopping and doing nothing in particular. We were to share this pleasure again, when we moved down to LG91, at Amyria, as we prepared to fly to India at the end of March 1944. These were occasions we were not likely to forget for the sheer feeling of cleanliness and well being it gave. With good quarters and clean cotton sheets on the beds in an RAF leave hostel, Alexandria was a very attractive city after the desert squalor.

We made the most of the opportunity to explore. There was a feeling of history as we walked down the extensive and wide sea front, which had witnessed Nelson's victory over the French fleet in 1798. There was much to see as we shopped in the wide boulevards laid out by the French, or viewed the Roman archaeological sites including 'Pompey's Pillar' dedicated to the Roman Emperor Diocletian. It was reputed that British sailors had dined on the top. Perhaps we knew in our bones that we were but two of the many millions who for thousands of years had moved through the countries of the Eastern Mediterranean leaving behind something of their culture. We were to witness the best in personal sacrifices and the worst in attitudes to the indigenous population. It was not uncommon for an army in transit to show a lack of respect for the local inhabitants and their culture. Some members of the Allied forces were no exception. An example was soon to hand as we witnessed a heated argument one evening between an Australian airman and a horse drawn 'gharrie' driver over the level of fare. The climax came as the 'gharrie' driver was felled to the ground by a blow to the head from his prospective Australian customer, who plucked the kerosene lamp from its bracket on the side of the 'gharrie' for use as the offensive weapon. We were not the military police. Tommy and I, climbing into our own 'gharrie' to be driven back to our lodgings, quickly said to our driver "drive on". We were not in England so self-preservation and the avoidance of a squalid conflict ruled our actions.

Returning from leave there was no time to be bored as we settled down once again in our small ridge tent. There were always letters to write, books to read of which we had a small selection, and sport to enjoy, especially football and volleyball. Volleyball, requiring no specially prepared ground, was played nearly every day. The Sergeants mess, a large marquee with its battered piano, a survivor of many squadron moves, encouraged much convivial company around the inevitable bar, all presided over by the senior NCO, Warrant Officer 'Smudge' Smith. Tony Norris always maintained that on being instructed by the Adjutant to assemble all and sundry prior to one of the squadron's many moves Warrant Officer Smith retorted, "We have 'All sir, but we do not have a Sundry."

We followed the progress of the Fifth and Eighth Army in Italy together with the success of the Russians in driving the Germans back from Moscow and Leningrad from the various newspapers and magazines which came to hand. 'Parade', a black and white picture magazine published by GHQ, Middle East Forces in Cairo, was a popular publication, giving much home news and coverage of the Middle East and the war in general. Intelligence reports, which we were able to read on the deployment of the Luftwaffe, were remarkably detailed and interesting. For example the night spots, some of dubious reputation, frequented by Luftwaffe personnel on leave in Rome were published, causing some amusement. We had no idea that the Bletchley Park code breakers were responsible.

GRT Willis Archives

1 February 1944, Beaufighter 'E' attacking a boom across the entrance to Port Maltesana, Naxos, Cyclades.

GRT Willis Archives

Above: 7 February 1944, shipping on fire in Khios Harbour.

Left: 7 February 1944, Beaufighter 'H' strafing shipping in Khios Harbour.

GRT Willis Archives

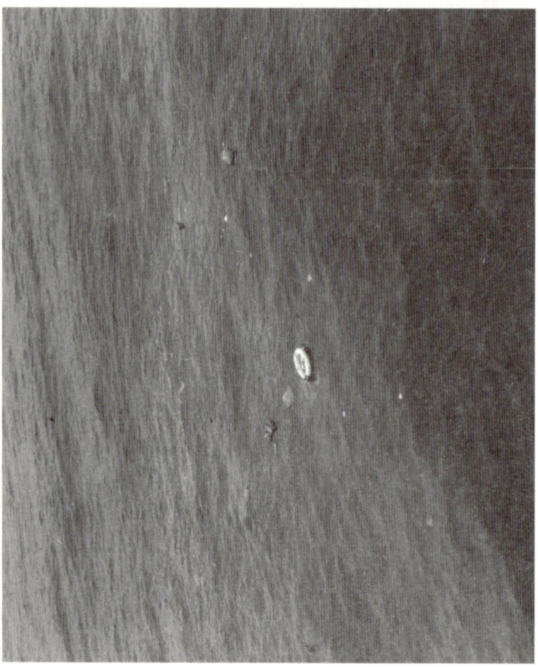

GRT Willis Archives

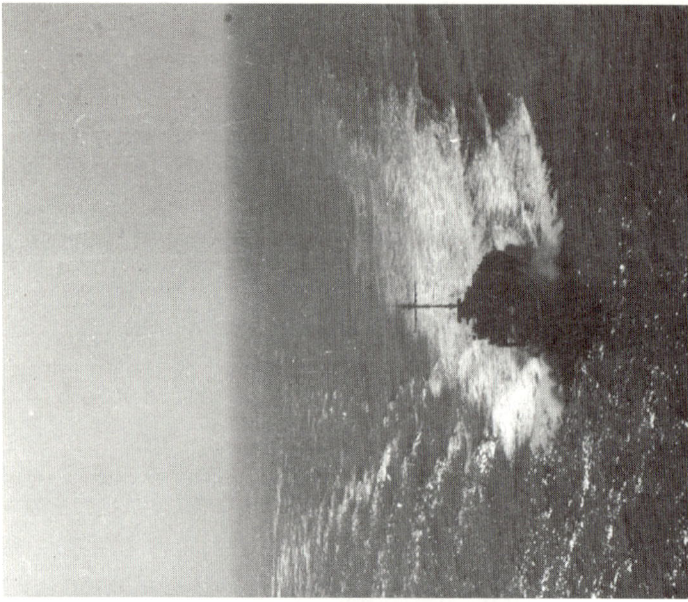

GRT Willis Archives

28 February 1944, survivors found from a ditched Wellington scramble into a dinghy.

Right: 28 February 1944, a destroyer alerted to the rescue by Beaufighter LX951.

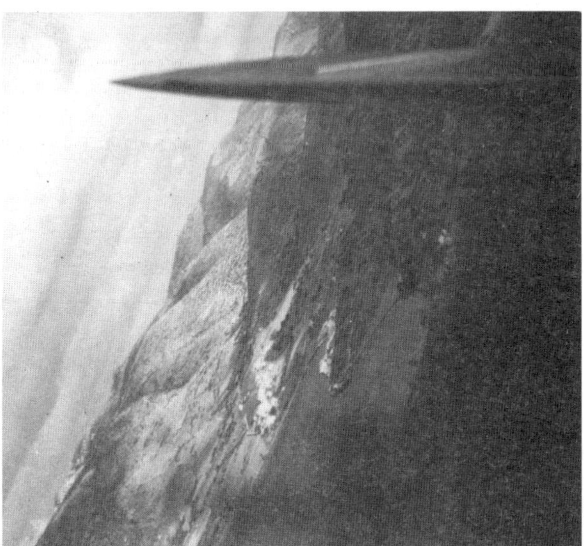

GRT Willis Archives

GRT Willis Archives

Left: 6 March 1944, Beaufighter 'C' LZ234, offensive sweep over Scarpanto (Karpathos) east of Crete.

Right: 12 March 1944, Beaufighter 'K', shipping strike in Naxos Harbour.

As March 1944 came in the squadron continued to fly an assortment of missions which varied from attacks on defended harbours in the Dodecanese targeting the supply caiques to the German garrisons, or to less dangerous convoy escort duties and naval cooperation patrols. Usually formations of four to six aircraft were involved. Invariably attacks on defended harbours took place in daylight when the cannon fire from the Beaufighter was usually accurate and effective.

March was our final month at Gambut. With worthwhile targets proving more difficult to find, we just hoped that the fiasco experienced in trying to bomb the old crusader fort on Rhodes would be remembered. On our first sortie in the month on the morning of the 4th, with a formation of four Beaufighters, we had a good look at Leros and its harbours. For our pains we drew much light and heavy ack-ack, but found no targets. We had better luck on 6 March when with a formation of six Beaufighters, led by Squadron Leader Skinner, we strafed four Arado 196 float planes drawn up on the beach in Pigadia harbour at Scarpanto, north east of Crete. One of the Arados caught fire but seeing two unidentified aircraft overhead we beat a hasty retreat. Despite the considerable ack-ack all aircraft returned safely. Subsequent reconnaissance confirmed three Arados damaged. There were, at that time, two German satellite airfields on Scarpanto and three on Rhodes, besides the main German fighter base at Heraklion. Once a mission was completed there was no point in hanging around. In any case, we were reminded of the danger of interception as we flew through the Kaso Straits at low level, with the German radar masts clearly visible on the south east cliffs of Crete. The enemy certainly knew we were around. Having destroyed three enemy aircraft, and participated in the probable destruction of three more, I was not anxious to meet any Me109s. Our last sortie over the Mediterranean was on 12 March with a formation of four Beaufighters led by Flying Officer Bill Bailey. This sortie was a sweep at maximum range to the harbour at Naxos where we attacked with cannon two large caiques and a 300 ton schooner inflicting much damage. Despite some intense ground fire from Naxos all aircraft returned safely.

Four months in the Libyan desert was now coming to an end. At least we had survived. Pilots and navigators, all who naturally wanted to stay alive, soon learnt how to reduce the risks, but luck also had to be on your side. Careful pre-flight preparation and constant practice in air-to-ground firing, bombing, evasion tactics and low flying in formation over the sea certainly improved one's chances. As already noted, the glare of the sun on a calm sea made it quite difficult to judge height when flying at low level to avoid radar detection. More than one accident, with the inevitable fatal consequences, was incurred by such misjudgement. Filson-Young took every opportunity to maintain a continuous training programme, all designed to raise the standard of our operational activities.

CHAPTER 8
INDIA: THE JAPANESE NAVY - A THREAT?

On 13 March, the day after my last operational flight, the squadron stood down pending the move to India. We were to be an essential element in the defence of Southern India or Ceylon against any attack by the Japanese navy. By early March 1944 three divisions of the Japanese Army, all under the overall command of General Mutaguchi, a force of approximately 100,000 men, had been assembled in the Manipur and Naga Hills in preparation for a break out into India. The assault proper started on 15 March with the objective of overrunning Imphal and Kohima the main allied supply bases from which the reconquest of Burma by the 14th Army would start. General Mutaguchi signalled to the High Command in Tokyo that he was embarking on 'the march to Delhi'. Facing many setbacks in the Pacific at the hands of the Americans, Tojo, the Japanese Premier, was very anxious to announce a major success. He was to be disappointed.

A large Japanese naval force had assembled in the early months of 1944 at Singapore, comprising seven old Battleships, two Fleet Carriers, six Heavy Cruisers, two Light Cruisers and eighteen Destroyers. The presence of a torpedo squadron in Southern India would act as a strong deterrent against any possible foray across the Bay of Bengal planned as a diversion to stretch further the defence of India already under severe pressure in Northern Burma. Perhaps our intelligence could have been better as it turned out that the Japanese naval forces in Singapore were not very battle inclined but were licking their wounds and resting after several maulings by the Americans in the Pacific.

Married aircrew of the squadron, who had completed their operational tour, were given the option to stay in the Middle East pending eventual repatriation to the UK. We lost our long serving engineering officer Flight Lieutenant Holdstock and welcomed Flying Officer M R V (Mike) Mackay, a graduate of Trinity College, Dublin, a true Irishman but a great friend he proved to be to all the aircrew over the next two years. Unattached aircrew, such as Tommy and I, even though we had completed one operational tour, were expected to go with the squadron to India. We were quite happy to comply, although I was sorry to leave Gambut despite the sand and the flies. The other squadrons, particularly the Americans with their B25s (Mitchells), had always been very hospitable. It had been a privilege to be on operations with them.

To prepare for the move to India the squadron moved to LG91 at Amyria on the edge of the delta, close to Alexandria. Tommy and I travelled in the back of an army truck from Gambut to LG91 - a most uncomfortable ride. Driving through the old defences of El Alamein, past the abandoned and broken tanks and trucks, on a rutted and very bumpy road, we reflected on that important victory against Rommel, won only seventeen months before. Coming to the Nile delta we drove through several villages with their whitewashed, flat roofed, and huddled dwellings and semi-naked children playing in the sun, hardly able to keep the flies out of their eyes. Trachoma appeared to be endemic. This was rural poverty, sad to see. The Senussi Arabs were kings in comparison.

LG91, sometimes referred to as Amyria South, was a desolate dusty base used as a transit airfield close to the coast railway running from Alexandria to Mersa Matruh. We had lost our bed and the personal tent we enjoyed at Gambut. Making sure we didn't lose sight of our kit, it was ground sheet and blankets on the floor in a dirty ragged marquee set aside for transit personnel. The good news was that we were to ferry one of the squadron's sixteen aircraft all the way to India. During a couple of trips into Alexandria we seized the opportunity to stock up with supplies to make our stay in India and possibly later into Burma a little more amenable. Previously in Cairo we had each purchased a large tin trunk into which were packed books - for me H G Wells, Aldous

Huxley and Bertrand Russell - serious reading indeed, plus soap, razor blades, toilet paper, stationery, ink, and plenty of clean stockings. Tommy acquired quite a collection of jazz records, including Glen Miller, Joe Loss, Anne Shelton and the Andrews Sisters, knowing that one of the navigators was taking over a gramophone. Other kit went into a large leather suitcase, plus primus stove, and a new camp bed with extra blankets and sheets. Most of this kit stayed with us until the day I found myself, some sixteen months later, in the Grand Hotel, Calcutta on the way back to the UK.

March 20 and 21 were taken up air testing our aircraft NE285 'G' in preparation for the flight out. I was able to write home and most importantly to Joan who was continuing to write every week. My letters could only say that I was moving on to India and that future letters should be addressed to 47 Squadron, Royal Air Force, India Command. No further details of our activities could be given. Letters were coming through regularly from Mother and my sister Maisie. Father seldom wrote. He had never been a letter writer. Joan's letters were always looked forward to and opened first.

To return to LG91. Tommy and I were briefed on 26 March 1944 to fly to an airfield outside Karachi, India and then onto a maintenance unit at Allahabad on the river Ganges. The first leg of the flight to Karachi involved a re-fuelling stop at Habbanya (Iraq) near Baghdad with an overnight stay in a modest Baghdad hotel. This first leg was conducted in a loose formation of six squadron Beaufighters, taking us over the town of Suez, the odour from which we could smell at eight thousand feet, and then across the Sinai and the Syrian Desert to Habbanya. Flight time was four hours and twenty minutes. From Habbanya our formation was down to five aircraft, one having been left behind for repair. Navigation was comparatively easy, with clear skies and good visibility. We just map read from one visual point to the next. On the first leg the briefing was simple and to the point, 'follow the oil pipeline across the Syrian desert to Baghdad'. The next leg, to the island state of Bahrein, half way down the Persian Gulf, took just three hours and twenty minutes. Flying down the Persian Gulf at eight thousand feet, it was essential to wear our RAF issue sunglasses - the glare from the sea was blinding without some form of eye protection. At this time Bahrein was a posting for RAF personnel which lasted just three months due to the extreme heat and humidity - no air conditioning and all accommodation tented. After landing at Bahrein, and waiting until the cool of the evening, Tommy and I walked down to see the small jetty and modest oil terminal which the island boasted at that time. None of us imagined or dreamt of the dramatic changes which were to come to this island state in the Persian Gulf.

After one hour into the last leg to Karachi we were obliged to effect an emergency landing at a small RAF strip near Jask in Persia (Iran), a country which was officially neutral at the time. We had an oil pump failure on the port engine, indicated by an immediate drop in oil pressure. Fortunately, we were close enough to this emergency landing ground before the oil pressure failed completely. Before we left LG91 we had been briefed on the location of emergency landing grounds along the route. This landing ground was a barren two thousand yard strip on the coast, manned by a very small RAF team, comprising a sergeant, two airmen and a radio. They lived in a small hut located in semi-desert and very isolated, apart from a few visits by the local inhabitants from the small town of Jask a few miles away on the coast. RAF Bahrein, in response to a radio call, dispatched a Wellington the next day, 29 March, with a replacement oil pump. The sergeant, an experienced fitter, who had earlier diagnosed what was wrong, soon replaced the pump with the assistance of his small team. Despite the isolation, this small party of RAF personnel, who were available to assist any aircraft passing their way, enjoyed a relaxing life away from RAF disciplines. A weekly visit by a Wellington from Bahrein brought in mail and supplies. Most of their time was spent cooking, sunbathing or in the sea which provided excellent surfing. We enjoyed the surfing too for the two days of our stay.

Landing at RAF Karachi on 30 March 1944, four days after leaving Egypt, we dumped our kit in tented accommodation near the Sergeants

Mess. It would be six days before we were given the all clear to fly on to Allahabad. Arriving in Karachi we were tired and hungry; food in transit camps was never of the best. To hitch a lift into Karachi to obtain a good meal was first priority. Chinese restaurants were reputed to be the only safe eating places to avoid 'gippy' tummy. This was a rule we stuck to. The mixed grill we ordered tasted like food from heaven after the corned beef, bread and margarine at LG91. On 5 April we took off for the RAF Maintenance Unit at Allahabad. Here the aircraft would be modified for Far East conditions. Staying in tented accommodation on the airfield at Allahabad, a holy city, for a couple of days before entraining to Madras, we were able to mingle with the thousands of Indians crowding the banks washing, cooking and bathing in the holy waters of the River Ganges. It was quite an experience watching under a hot, cloudless sky, the crowds and the buzz of activity, as people lived out their lives on the banks of this holy river.

On 10 April we completed the journey by train to Madras travelling second class in reasonable comfort. On the train we were to hear those memorable words so familiar to all servicemen in India 'Cha-wallah sahib, cha-wallah'. The essential brew offered was most welcome as we perspired in the hot humid air. Cha was supplemented by 'Egg banjo, sahib' heralding egg rolls at four annas or so. Thus we learnt our first words of Urdu. The big problem on trains was always the 'loo', never a very savoury place. A personal and plentiful supply of soap and toilet paper was essential.

A train journey across the central plains of India must be as good a way as any to see some of this vast country in all its variety. Stopping for water or passengers the track swarmed with bodies scrabbling for coal which fell from the engine's tender or jostling with hawkers and their rich assortment of strange and sumptuous looking food stuffs. Naked children and wizened old men in dirty white dhotis performed their daily ablutions as they splashed on the track in the railway company's water supply. Through the bars on the carriage window there was always the outstretched hand of a beggar, only to be withdrawn as the train moved on. We rattled on to Madras through towns, villages, forest and the never ending paddy and maize fields. In the open country kites and vultures wheeled overhead in a cloudless sky. Dogs and cattle, all looking half starved, wandered around at will, as we watched daily life from the train on this long three day journey.

Central Station, Madras was a scene of utter confusion. Directed to sit outside the station by the Troop Movement Officer we retrieved our kit, still all in one piece, and contemplated the jostling mass of brown bodies all around us. The road was dusty, the afternoon sun bore down, as we sweated and waited watching the cheerful crowds swirling around the station, shouting and grimacing with mouths stained red with betel juice. As darkness fell we piled into a three ton truck to be greeted at RAF Cholaveram by the deafening sound of thousands of crickets as we humped our kit to the sergeants mess, our home for the next six months. Cholaveram was an all weather airfield a few miles to the south west of Madras. Twelve of the squadron's Beaufighters had arrived before us at the end of March. As 47 Squadron moved into Cholaveram 45 Squadron moved out to convert from their American Vengeance light bombers to Mosquitos. We were to catch up with 45 Squadron in northern Assam in due course.

In the meantime the main body of the squadron had sailed from Port Said through the Suez Canal and then on to Bombay. Here they entrained for Madras, arriving at Cholaveram on 20 April 1944. It was to be another three weeks before the squadron equipment arrived from the Middle East. As part of 172 Wing of 225 Group we were joined at the end of March by 27 Squadron, commanded by Wing Commander J B Nicholson VC. 27 Squadron was 'on rest' after eighteen months of operations over the Arakan and central Burma with their Beaufighters. They brought to Cholaveram seventeen of these aircraft. From April through to September six torpedo carrying Beaufighters of 47 Squadron were kept at instant readiness, together with an equal number of 27 Squadron Beaufighters, designated to fly with us in an anti-flak role. The two squadrons would be a formidable anti-shipping strike force.

As the months went by it became apparent that the Japanese fleet in Singapore had no intention of testing Allied air strength in Southern India or Ceylon, unless there was a substantial breakthrough by the Japanese Army out of Burma into India proper.

Cholaveram was an airfield bulldozed out of paddy fields, originally planned as a training and rest airfield, with all accommodation in standard Indian bamboo 'bashas' furnished with Indian charpoys - quite comfortable beds of wooden frames and hessian rope mattresses. Of a similar construction were the mess halls with the added luxury of overhead 'punkas', large bamboo flaps hanging from the ceiling, pulled back and forth by 'punka wallahs' to stir the humid air, adding a little to our 'comfort'. Lighting was by hurricane lamps or Tilley pressure lamps. Outside, in the evening, the crickets were always lively and noisy. It was advisable to keep covered up once darkness fell. Mosquito nets over the beds were essential with anti-malaria Mepacrine pills the order of the day. Life at Cholaveram, if you could cope with the high humidity, was pleasant but rather boring with not enough demanding activity, apart from the training exercises designed to keep us on our toes. We were also to learn that when the south west monsoon hit us with heavy storms, buildings could be severely damaged, with roofs particularly vulnerable. A welcome diversion, as we speculated on the future, were visits by the RAF Roadshow and the ENSA concert party. These shows always went down well.

During April and May 1944, adjusting for our new role, we carried out combined exercises with the Royal Navy performing simulated torpedo attacks over the Bay of Bengal, off the coast of Madras, with HMS 'Penn', HMAS 'Nizam' and HMS 'Siam' taking part. Further training involved formation flying, cross country navigation and air-to-ground firing at the local range plus some night flying in cooperation with naval ships and flare dropping Liberators. There was every incentive to make the training programme as varied as possible, designed to meet any eventuality from a most resourceful enemy. Future tasks could well be intruder missions over hostile jungle territory, an environment far removed from our Eastern Mediterranean experiences. However, the lack of real action against the Japanese forces was very frustrating as we waited for a more positive role to play. Early warning facilities and fighter control were based at Vizagapatam on the east coast half way between Madras and Calcutta. The defence of East India depended upon Medium Bomber, Light Bomber and Fighter Squadrons based in the Calcutta area along with 27 and 47 Squadrons and other units in the Madras area. Quite close to Cholaveram, at Red Hill Lake, a squadron of Catalina Flying Boats was stationed. Their duties were convoy protection and reconnaissance, also being part of 225 Group. St Thomas' Mount, another airfield a few miles to the west of Madras, held detachments of RAF and USAAF Liberators, also on stand-by in defence of southern India and Ceylon. Further afield, Strategic Air Force Heavy Bombers of the USAAF were on stand-by in Bengal.

Through March and April 1944 the 14th Army fought a bitter battle to stem the Japanese advance over the Chin Hills to the Imphal plain and to Kohima, which if captured would have opened the way onto the plains of Assam and East Bengal. Down at Cholaveram we were only faintly aware of the dire struggle taking place in north eastern India close to the border with Burma. On 8 July 1944 the Japanese 15th Army under General Mutaguchi had to admit defeat and commenced a general retreat from the area around Imphal and Kohima. Much has been written about the heroism displayed by the defenders of Imphal and Kohima between March and July 1944. Twenty squadrons of 221 Group flying Hurricanes, Spitfires, Vengeances and Beaufighters claimed thirty three enemy aircraft destroyed plus twenty two probables and sixty one damaged during this period. On our arrival over Burma the following January we in 47 Squadron were to reap the benefit of this sterling performance as we enjoyed complete air supremacy.

With the Allies in Paris on 25 August 1944 and the Japanese decisively defeated in Northern Burma final victory was forecast in Europe to be some time in mid 1945 and in the Far East hopefully by early 1946. What was certain was that the Japanese army, repulsed at Imphal and

Kohima, was going to fight every inch of the way as they tried to regroup in the plains of central Burma, which in 1945 was to be 47 Squadron's opportunity.

Apart from keeping the aircrews up to operational efficiency the squadron was having to give attention to the ambitions and anxieties of its personnel. Many were writing home hoping that they would not be at a disadvantage in the job market as they awaited their turn for repatriation. Boredom after the daily duty was the greatest enemy. Doc Bamford, as sports officer, made tremendous efforts to encourage an intensive sports programme. There were no pubs, clubs or home leave. Off-duty facilities for all ranks left a lot to be desired.

Apart from the immediate wartime tasks, government ministers were beginning to recognise the need to assist service personnel to adjust to a peacetime role and to understand post war policies such as, employment rights, the Beveridge Report, a proposed post war comprehensive medical service and various political solutions to post-war problems. In the not too distant future another General Election would be called in which the service vote could prove to be quite decisive. With the squadron having to find personnel to lead discussions on these subjects Tommy and I were dispatched on 16 July to attend a five day discussion group course at 225 Group Headquarters in Bangalore. At the same time we attended a commissioning board having been recommended by our CO. To fulfil these appointments we flew Beaufighter NE268 for a major service check to Yelahanka, a maintenance unit on the outskirts of Bangalore. Bangalore, a pleasant town, four thousand feet above sea level and well away from the heat and humidity of Madras, was very popular as a rest and holiday location. Writing to Joan on 27 July I remarked that we were accommodated in a first class hotel run on 'American' lines prior to attending the commissioning board of three senior officers chaired by Wing Commander W R Beaman. Trousers were pressed, shoes were cleaned and buttons polished. We must have satisfied the board as our commissions were dated to be effective just seven days later.

Confirmation had to come from the Air Ministry in London followed by the appropriate documentation to Group Headquarters. We were not to know the result for three months. The discussion group course led by Flight Lieutenant Bigg, 225 Group Education Officer, gave us some insight into the very different world most of us would face on return to civilian life. Back to Cholaveram on 21 July ferrying Beaufighter NE301.

Still concerned that boredom and frustration could be a problem, the CO asked Tommy and myself to organise educational activities for all the squadron personnel. Facilities were made available through leaflets to encourage correspondence courses and contact with all levels of the educational establishments back in the UK. We had pamphlets entitled 'Current Affairs' and 'The British Way and Purpose', available to all ranks. We did believe that political parties of all persuasions were anxious to lay the foundations of a more caring and fair society which would see abolished for ever the poverty, mass unemployment and misery of the 1930s. Over fifty years later, I can only say that much still remains to be done. Far away from the UK, it was not easy to maintain interest in these issues as we pursued our flying training programme and waited for a more active role. As involvement in the education programmes was entirely voluntary, take up was only modest. Tommy and I, together with other aircrew officers and NCOs, supported discussion groups and meetings for all ranks, usually held in the Airman's Mess. We debated a wide range of topics ranging from current affairs to religious and political issues. More popular were sessions of classical and jazz music, with Glen Miller, Tommy Dorsey, Artie Shaw and Benny Goodman always in demand. A concerted effort, much to the credit of the squadron, was made to assist all who sought help as they considered re-adjustment to civilian life. An abrupt end came to most of this activity when, at the end of September 1944, our role as a torpedo bomber squadron was terminated and exchanged for a fighter bomber role on Mosquitos, for ultimate deployment over Burma. Why, we asked, the sudden decision to convert the squadron to Mosquitos?

GRT Willis Archives

The author reflects at Cholaveram, Madras, June 1944.

Left: June 1944, Cholaveram, Madras, Maurice Jones and Bob Willis.

Below: Keeping cool, Maurice Jones and the author with our indispensable bearer, Cholaveram, Madras, June 1944.

GRT Willis Archives

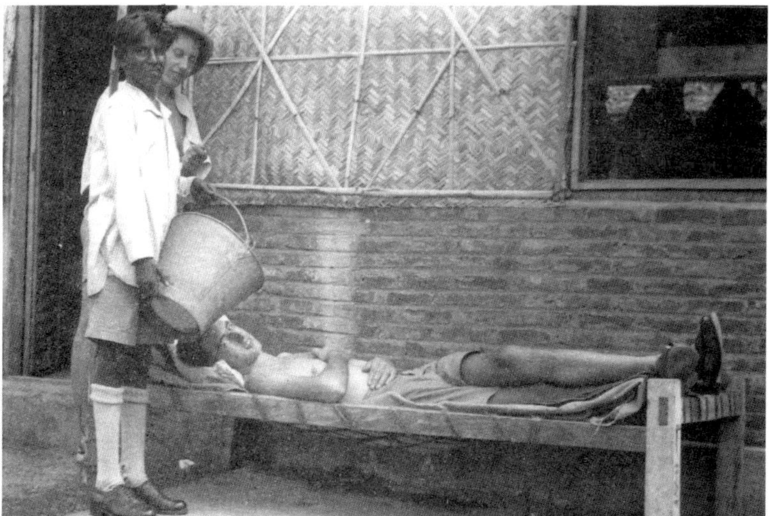

GRT Willis Archives

June 1944, Cholaveram, Madras, the sergeant's mess. Bob Willis 2nd right, back row. Centre W/C Filson-Young.

GRT Willis Archives

GRT Willis Archives

Above: 15 January 1944, HMS Renown, Gulf of Suez.

Left: Ranchi, Jimmy Gibson and Pete Rostance plus two bearers.

How had we all coped with the heat, humidity and frustration of waiting at Cholaveram?

To answer these questions it was interesting to note that letters sent home by the groundcrew in many cases reflected their over-riding wish to see the war over, as we junior officers pursued our censorship duties on the squadron. Letters to Joan centred upon the humidity, the mosquitoes, sport including cricket, and the hospitality offered on various afternoons by the English ladies, mostly retired, and many widowed, living in pleasant bungalows in the English quarter of Madras. Writing on 24 June I described the evening scene from the sergeant's mess: "Outside the mess the lights can be seen over the airmen's quarters, it is 9pm, the mosquito nets are down, and the gramophone is playing some popular jazz. There is a new moon with the stars bright in a cloudless sky, a faint breeze, and if you stand still you can hear the crickets chirping away. The palm trees on the edge of the camp are silhouetted against the dark purple sky. Jack, the mess barman, is leaning on the counter as all his customers have faded away to appreciate the breeze outside on the veranda. On the bar is a large piece of corned beef and a loaf. It's a bit extra we get for supper." I could have added that also on the bar was the jar of Mepacrine tablets usually downed with a large gin and orange.

From June to the end of September we were afflicted by severe monsoon storms bringing torrential rain, followed by several days of clear moonlit nights until the next storm came over. Writing again on the 5 July I described how the base was flooded one evening by a violent thunderstorm. "It rained so heavily that all the paddy fields around were turned into shallow lakes. The rain poured through the roof of our basha just missing my charpoy. Fortunately this storm passed over after a couple of hours leaving the atmosphere considerably cooler." A month before on 3 June the station had suffered such severe storm damage that fifty three buildings required urgent repairs, to be followed by another storm on 10 July destroying and damaging many more buildings. Again on 8 August the rain was so heavy, flooding many of the airmen's quarters, that the Station Commander decreed that rum be issued to all airmen on the station.

Cholaveram may have been a 'rest' station but it was far from ideal. Despite the heavy monsoon rains the Station Commander, Wing Commander W A L Davis DFC, was having to complain to Group Headquarters at the lack of pumps necessary to maintain the domestic water supply. In January 1945 Wing Commander Davis was still reporting to Group that, 'the standard of health is quite high considering the disgraceful state of affairs as regards drainage, fly proofing, and sanitation generally. These points have been brought to your notice on repeated occasions since April 1944 but under the present system of works services the Station Commander is powerless to do anything more than complain. Morale remains high and in general the airmen are contented' Perhaps morale remained high as we didn't expect anything better. Maintaining good health was very much a personal effort in adapting to the conditions and taking all the sensible precautions which were available. Just keeping prickly heat at bay was a daily chore requiring the liberal use of talcum powder.

In November 1943 Rear Admiral Lord Louis Mountbatten (later Admiral of the Fleet, the Earl Mountbatten of Burma) was appointed Supreme Allied Commander, South East Asia Command, with a brief to develop a strategy which would ultimately drive the Japanese out of their South East Asia conquests. From late 1943 and throughout early 1944 plans were drawn up and constantly modified, in light of the resources available, for seaborne invasions of Rangoon and Malaya (Operation DRACULA). The Japanese naval threat to India may have disappeared, but we were still very much a torpedo squadron and an essential element in all this planning. Consequently, July 1944 saw the squadron earmarked for further naval cooperation training, based at Vavuniya airfield in northern Ceylon.

On 25 July 1944, with Tommy as navigator, I flew Beaufighter LX906 to Vavuniya as part of a detachment of eight squadron Beaufighters for torpedo attack training in liaison with the Royal Navy. Preparations were now under way for RAF and RN torpedo squadrons to work together in support of the offensive action planned against Japanese forces in the Andaman Islands and the Dutch East Indies (Operations BUCCANEER and CULVERIN). Our training reflected this need. During late July and early August 1944 the squadron detachment held several joint exercises with the Royal Navy and Mark Vlll Spitfires based at China Bay, an all weather airfield on the east coast of Ceylon. These exercises, involving HMS 'Ceylon', HMS 'Unicorn', HMS 'Cumberland' and HMS 'Indomitable', were mounted both by day and night. Tommy and I participated in six dummy runner torpedo sorties, five by day and one by night, against these naval vessels. Results were analysed through cameras fitted to the aircraft. We were joined in these activities by 22 Squadron Beaufighters and also by 815 Squadron of the Fleet Air Arm flying Barracudas, a torpedo dropping aircraft.

Training with the Navy off the coast of Ceylon employing evasion tactics with locally based Spitfires was not without its hazards. On 2 August whilst engaged in one of these exercises, a 47 Squadron Beaufighter collided with another Beaufighter. The pilot Flying Officer Macklem was killed, his navigator fortunately escaped with minor injuries but a passenger in the aircraft, Corporal Best was severely injured. The other Beaufighter landed safely. On 28 August during a formation exercise, Flight Lieutenant A J Smith and Warrant Officer L Grimshaw, long serving squadron members, were killed in another mid-air collision. Again the other aircraft involved managed to land safely. These accidents were sharp reminders that training to be realistic also carried its degree of risk.

In addition to these naval cooperation exercises, simulated torpedo attack exercises using a Link Trainer were conducted at No.3 Torpedo Refresher School based at Ratmalana airfield near Colombo. For visiting RAF aircrew accommodation at Ratmalana, where I spent two days on the Link Trainer, was very primitive. Never to be forgotten were the dreadful latrines and the hot humid conditions. What a relief it was to leave! The Link Trainer was mounted in the centre of a dome shaped room painted to simulate the sea, horizon and sky. The trainee, shut inside the Link Trainer, was required to employ all his instrument flying skills to attack the projected target ship moving along the horizon. Relying entirely upon the blind flying instruments in the cockpit, the trainee had to approach the target at the correct angle to the bow and 'fire' the torpedo when within range, and with the 'aircraft' straight and level at the right speed and height. All that was missing was ack-ack. A hit would depend on whether the course and speed of the target had been correctly assessed, evasive action allowed for and with the attacking 'aircraft' at the correct height, speed and angle of approach. At least these exercises in the Link Trainer kept our instrument flying skills up to scratch, which would prove to be essential when flying through cloud and rain in monsoon conditions.

Letters to Joan briefly referred to Ceylon as "an interesting place, real jungle and swamps, rain every day, with Colombo full of rickshaw wallahs and scrupulously clean Chinese restaurants." By September 1944 India Command considered that the threat from a possible Japanese attack on Eastern India was now negligible. The Americans were making good progress in the Pacific with the capture of Guam on 27 July. So while our training in Ceylon in cooperation with the Royal Navy continued, plans were being completed to redeploy the squadron in a more immediate and active role. The revised deployment was not to be in support of the Navy, amphibious assault plans having to be deferred yet again due to lack of resources, particularly landing craft. All was to change; we had to retrain yet again, this time to give support to the 14th Army in its drive from the north to get the Japanese out of Burma. The planners decided that we convert from Beaufighters to Mosquitos before assuming active operations over the Burmese mountains and jungles.

Returning from Ceylon on 7 August, activity on the squadron had fallen to a low ebb although, as yet, we did not know what our future activities would be. Apart from a little night flying on radar and WT exercises I did very little of real consequence for the next fourteen days.

It was quite a relief to be granted fourteen days leave on 26 August to escape from the humidity of the coastal area. In letters to Joan I commented on "the most frightening racket kicked up by seemingly hundreds of bull frogs, all croaking in unison after each monsoon storm". I described what a welcome change it was to have a break away from a bustling Indian city with "its pavements and roads crowded with a mass of humanity, all barefoot amidst the clanging of crowded trams, the hooting of ancient taxis, the cries of bicycle rickshaw wallahs, the pleading of beggars and the shouts of pedlars". Tommy and I teamed up with our aircrew colleagues, Flight Sergeants Bill Powell and Maurice Jones with our destination an established hill station at Ootacamund seven thousand feet up in the Nilgiri Hills, over two hundred miles to the west of Madras. A day's journey by train, first class to avoid the hazards of native travel in open carriages on wooden benches, brought us to the Nilgiri Hills. The train was crowded but at least everybody appeared good humoured. 'We are all poor so let's make the best of it' appeared, at least to us, to be the prevailing mood. We completed the last three thousand feet climb to Ootacamund by a narrow gauge funicular railway. We could have been in the Swiss Alps. The scenery was quite stunning and a great change from the coastal plain. We had a splendid fourteen days in the home of a Miss St. Pourçain, a retired teacher, who regularly provided full board for eight to ten airmen at a time in her large bungalow, 'Tiverton' on Coonoor Road. We had a very comfortable and relaxing time, cycling through the picturesque valleys which reminded me of the Lake District back home. We played tennis, read or just enjoyed a drink and a gossip in the cool night air. Our hostess, who will be remembered by many airmen, insisted we called her 'Flo'. She even arranged for Tommy and me to have three days away in Mysore and Bangalore. We were welcomed at the Maharajah's Palace and gardens in Mysore and did a little shopping in the bazaars of Bangalore. Two weeks were soon over as we returned to Cholaveram feeling refreshed from the change of scenery and climate.

At the end of August the squadron's detachments had all returned from

Ceylon, able to report a success of over 75% hits by dummy torpedo runs during the naval cooperation exercises over China Bay. Routine training started again with cross country flights and air to ground firing over the range. We hardly realised it at the time but this was the end of a chapter. In the six months stationed near Madras, a city with a long history associated with the British Raj, squadron members saw just a little of Indian life. The main Post Office in Madras, with its 'writers' and general bustle of activity, always fascinated us. The city had a wide variety of shops, including a varied selection of bookshops, craft shops and Chinese restaurants which we frequented from time to time. If tired of walking there was always the ever present cycle rickshaw or a taxi back to the airfield. Particularly memorable were the fine sea front government buildings with their distinctive Victorian architecture. I was reminded of the dedication of the many expatriates working in the Indian Civil Service as District Commissioners or lesser ranks, who had given their lives to India, often to die before their time of malaria. Filson-Young, as Squadron Commander, much preferred a 30cwt pick up truck to a car. The weekly foray into town by aircrew led by Filson-Young and packed into this vehicle was always a high spirited affair. When a Canadian pilot decided that the pitch of the electric overhead fans in one down town restaurant required physical amendment the proprietor was not amused. A hasty retreat was effected. If a more sedate English life style was sought the Connemara Hotel proved popular.

As we travelled the country by truck to the firing range, through villages and past the paddy fields, it was so peaceful. We were intruders with the war far away. The sun was high in the sky as the kites and vultures circled overhead and we enjoyed seeing a little of the real India. On the station the airmen were entertained by the usual collection of itinerant traders. Of never failing interest was the snake charmer, together with his dancing cobra. Further entertainment was enjoyed as a small Indian woman was placed in a wicker basket by her male companion and the lid closed over her. A sword was then passed through the basket from all sides and from the top, with the sound of the sword hitting the ground being quite impressive. Out steps the woman and a few more airmen part with a few 'accas', as a price for the entertainment.

British servicemen can be equally enterprising. Cholaveram was a large open base, virtually unfenced, onto which would wander that animal sacred to the Hindu, the village cow. Safety had to come first, apart from the protection of the animal, so a compound was put in place adjacent to the control tower in the centre of the airfield. The RAF Regiment personnel guarding the airfield rounded up the stray animals and impounded them. The airmen in the control tower enjoyed a small income from Nallur village, adjoining the airfield, as the village head man paid a modest price for their release provided he took them back to the village from whence they came. As far as the officers were concerned it was rumoured that they employed a snake catcher together with a mongoose. Tony, the Intelligence Officer, always maintained that the place was cobra infested. We in the Sergeants Mess didn't worry so much.

On 15 September, along with 27 Squadron, we were drawn up on parade to mark the anniversary of the Battle of Britain. Shortly afterwards the CO announced that the squadron was to be deployed in Burma, but first we were to be equipped with the faster Mosquito instead of the Beaufighter. To the end of August 1944 the flying training programme had reflected our role as a torpedo bomber squadron. Our future role was to be in support of the 14th Army. We were surprised and delighted. Lord Louis Mountbatten, the Supreme Commander, had been unable to obtain the substantial numbers of landing craft necessary to support a large amphibious offensive. The plan had been to capture Rangoon in late 1944 from the sea (Operation DRACULA) and to make assaults further south and east. The priority now had to be the destruction of the Japanese Army in Burma through a sustained frontal assault from the north, particularly down the Chindwin and Irrawaddy river valleys. This policy was endorsed by the Chiefs of Staff in November 1944 and code named Operation 'CAPITAL'. The 14th Army, advancing over the Manipur and Naga Hills on the north west border of Burma, was already moving south east, preparing to cross the Chindwin River one hundred miles north west of Mandalay. These forces were totally supplied from the air by RAF and USAAF DC3 Dakotas and C46 Commandos. Artillery to support the ground forces would largely have to come from RAF strike squadrons. The sooner 47 Squadron was deployed the better.

The squadron prepared to leave Cholaveram at the end of September 1944, with all personnel looking forward to making a more positive contribution to the war against Japan. We had been on continuous standby since April 1944 against a supposed threatened incursion by the Japanese Navy. Our destination was Yelahanka, a newly constructed airfield, close to Bangalore, and home to 1672 Conversion Unit. Here we would receive familiarisation training on the Mosquito Fighter Bomber Mark Vl, leaving our Beaufighters behind at Yelahanka. At last, with the prospect of flying one of the fastest aircraft in the RAF at the time, real action was promised.

On 5 October tragedy overtook the last flight out from Cholaveram, destination Yelahanka. I watched from the 'A' Flight buildings of bamboo and thatch as Flying Officer Roy Euler flew his Beaufighter down the runway at virtually zero feet towards us. He pulled up aiming to skim over the roof tops, misjudged the forward momentum of his aircraft and hit the roof of the building just behind me with his tail section. A huge crash, a ball of flame and another well trained pilot was lost. A squadron detachment attended a very dignified funeral service in the Anglican Cathedral of Madras. On 8 October there was a concert in the station cinema by the 'Gang Show' which was a great success - despite tragedy, life had to go on. In the meantime, 27 Squadron had left Cholaveram on 18 September with their Beaufighters bound for the Special Low Attack Instruction School at Ranchi, in Bihar State. Here rocket rails were fitted under the wings of their aircraft in place of the six machine guns.

Following losses through training accidents, sickness or other reasons, several replacement aircrew joined the squadron to bring our establishment back to between eighteen and twenty crews. One such replacement, posted to the squadron from the Torpedo Attack Training School at Shallufa on the Suez Canal, was Flight Sergeant Jimmy Gibson and his navigator Flight Sergeant Peter Rostance. They were flown by Sunderland Flying Boat from Egypt to Karachi, completing the journey to Cholaveram by train. Jimmy recalled that at their briefing before leaving Egypt it was assumed that on joining 47 Squadron they would be engaged in immediate action against Japanese naval forces. As he later remarked 'I was rather relieved to learn on arrival that instead of hazardous operations the squadron was about to convert to Mosquitos'. Jimmy and his navigator Peter were to remain on active service with the squadron until VJ Day, to be followed with further operations against Indonesian Nationalist forces in Java. Jimmy completed several operational sorties in Java during late 1945 and early 1946, in addition to his operations with the squadron over Burma. We were to become lifelong friends. To his old squadron colleagues he is always remembered as the football team captain in India and Burma. Unfortunately, for Jimmy's RAF record, he suffered a broken elbow playing for the squadron football team, followed by hospitalization in Calcutta thus missing some of the action which was to come later.

In the second week of October 1944 the squadron with all its equipment entrained for Yelahanka, the base for No.1672 Conversion Unit. We were lucky to leave when we did as a cyclone hit the base on 25/26 October causing extensive damage, with many buildings collapsing. Fortunately there were no serious injuries. Tommy and I, together with Jimmy Gibson and Pete Rostance, made the journey from Madras to Bangalore by train, crowded as usual with more passengers than there were seats provided. Other aircrew flew the serviceable Beaufighters to Yelahanka, about fourteen in number. Looking back at our six months stay in Cholaveram, it had at least provided a varied and interesting period of flying, as well as the necessary rest period due after our activities in the Eastern Mediterranean. In particular, I was pleased that Tommy and I had made some contribution to the discussions on the future world scene we hoped for after the defeat of Germany and Japan. Perhaps we did help a little to keep boredom at bay.

As we settled down at Yelahanka we had few illusions that operations against the Japanese, particularly if captured or severely injured following a crash in enemy territory, would be any less hazardous than operations in Europe. Briefing and training commenced without delay as we prepared for our new role, this time without torpedoes and with a new and faster aircraft. My instructor was a jovial and relaxed Flight Lieutenant from Australia, Bill Hughes, later to join the squadron and become a firm friend. The characteristics of the Mosquito were explained to pilots by reference to the aircraft handbook (The Pilots Notes) and by demonstration in the air, the trainee pilot occupying the navigator's seat. There was no dual control aircraft available. The Mosquito FBVI was a fighter bomber used for intruder duties, equipped with four 20mm guns and fours .303 machine guns. Originally considered as a high speed reconnaissance aircraft able to outperform in speed any fighter aircraft, it was soon devolved as a fighter bomber. Powered by two Rolls Royce Merlin 23 engines, it was at least 60mph faster than the Beaufighter. Of nearly total wooden construction, as a beautifully streamlined monoplane, it was much loved by the aircrew who flew it.

On 11 October, after two short demonstrations, each of twenty minutes, in Mosquito HX945, I went 'solo' with Tommy in the navigator's seat. As the pilot, I was back in the left hand seat for the first time since leaving the UK, Tommy sitting alongside, slightly set back. I completed the pre-flight checks, signed the Form 700, checked the controls, started up and waved 'chocks away'. Taxiing out to the end of the runway, lining up, applying the brakes and then giving the engines a final boost to clear the spark plugs was just routine. The propeller constant speed units were in fully fine pitch, outer fuel tanks engaged, and with 15° of flap and a little forward trim we were ready to go. Push the throttle forward, check any swing to port and down the runway you go to reach take-off speed of 125mph. Much to our surprise the starboard engine failed just as we were lifting off the ground. There was a loud crack with the starboard propeller milling around and failing to feather. The starboard engine was still functioning but not driving the propeller. There was no time to speculate. We just had to keep airborne. We just scraped over the airfield buildings ahead. Tommy called down the intercom with some anxiety 'Bob, for God's sake hold it!' With the wheels and flaps still down I engaged maximum power on the port engine the moment the starboard engine failed. I had my right leg locked stiff on the rudder bar to contain the torque created. Despite activating the feathering button again, the starboard propeller continued to rotate causing extra drag. Climbing slowly I was then able to raise the wheels and flaps and, by making a very wide circuit, reach sufficient height to effect a single engine landing. The landing was OK, but it was immediately obvious that the brakes were faulty. As the aircraft ran off the end of the runway a hedge and then the main Yelahanka to Bangalore road loomed ahead. Without effective brakes I swung the aircraft round in a ground loop to halt further progress. The undercarriage collapsed. As the aircraft, now partly through the hedge and over the road, swung round a propeller caught a male Indian civilian riding in the back of a truck as it drove past the airfield. Switching off the ignition, I scrambled out of the cockpit as fast as possible. I could hear the cries of the injured Indian. One of his arms appeared to be severed. There was much blood as we applied a makeshift tourniquet torn from his cotton shirt. To our relief he was quickly in the care of a British Army ambulance team, part of a military convoy travelling on the road at the same time. At the best of times single engine landings are tricky - this is more so when you have never flown the type of aircraft before. In a subsequent court of inquiry on 16 October, chaired by Squadron Leader Skinner, I was cleared of any fault, it being confirmed that the brakes were indeed faulty. The constant speed unit and the drive shaft to the starboard engine had fractured on take-off, also making it impossible to feather the propeller and reduce drag. It spoke well of the Mosquito that I was able to get it into the air at all. I have always regretted, despite the faulty brakes, not being able to bring the aircraft successfully to a halt at the end of the runway. Many years later, I met Stan Watts, the duty driver for the aircrew, who was on standby when the accident happened. He recalled watching the landing, with the aircraft failing to slow as much as it should as it went down the runway. 'Through a hedge and then it disappeared' he recalled, adding that the groundcrew thought we had done rather well, especially in attending to the injured civilian.

Our training programme was not without other incidents. Both Flying Officer Benison and Flight Sergeant Palmer of the squadron had their undercarriages collapse after a heavy landing, and Pilot Officer René, Provost overshot the runway on a night landing. Fortunately there were no aircrew injuries. On 26 October 110 Squadron arrived, also for conversion to Mosquitos. They were to join us some months later in Burma.

Running parallel to the conversion programme from Beaufighters to Mosquitos during October/November 1944, were ground lectures covering the environmental and operational problems expected to be encountered over Burma. Apart from hearing how to cope with the climatic conditions, the need for extra care when flying during the monsoon season was emphasised. The basic rule was to keep out of storm clouds in all circumstances. If trapped by impenetrable cloud quite possibly the only course of action would be to fly below the cloud base, if at all feasible, even if it meant going down to one hundred feet or less over the sea. Always turn away or go round storm clouds which being black, thick and full of turbulence, could rise to twenty five thousand feet or more. You entered a monsoon storm cloud at your peril as a complete loss of control would be the probable result. Writing to Joan on the evening of 22 October by the dim light of a hurricane lamp I remarked on the recent stormy weather arriving with the south west monsoon.

Our lectures again left us in no doubt of the attitude of the enemy towards aircrew who fell into their hands. We were fully aware that the prospect of surviving a crash in enemy territory, if you were injured, could be very slim indeed. In those circumstances you would probably suffer a most distressing and painful death. Despite the dangers, briefing officers usually had some hair-raising and often humorous survival story to relate just to keep our spirits up. To many a Japanese soldier to die fighting for his country and Emperor was a great privilege. For him it was more honourable to die in battle than be captured. For any aircrew captured there would be no sympathy shown to the seriously injured. Those who surrendered and were uninjured faced the prospect of prolonged and hostile interrogation. Possible torture, including the threat of execution followed by forced marches and cruel prison camp conditions, was the general experience. Personal survival kits together with a bush knife and a .38 Smith and Wesson revolver were issued to all aircrew engaged in operational flying. Bush knives or jungle knives with a folding 16" blade were in quite short supply, although they could be very useful if walking back through the jungle. Some crews also acquired 9" commando knives but through all our sorties the only protection Tommy and I had was our .38 revolvers together with a clip of bullets. We were given some confidence that it was possible to survive and walk back after a crash in enemy territory, which several airmen achieved. With luck, one could be rescued by friendly natives or Force 136 patrols operating behind the Japanese lines. Carried on our person in a small flat plastic box was the survival kit containing local currency, water purification tablets, messages in the local language to encourage assistance (a 'goolie chit' similar to the one carried in North Africa), a silk map of the area, bandages, a fishing hook and line, a hard biscuit, a tube of condensed milk and a small tube of morphine incorporating a sharp quill to provide the means of injection. The morphine injected would alleviate the pain following a severe injury from a crash in the jungle or mountains and perhaps give a little time to decide on an appropriate form of action. One alternative could be a swift end from a bullet from the Smith and Wesson .38 revolver. My navigator Tommy, who had a warped sense of humour over these possibilities, acquired two surplus Smith and Wesson revolvers recovered from crashed aircraft as souvenirs. Many years later after he died, they were handed in by his wife Ethel to the police during an arms amnesty. Although no questions were asked at the time a few eyebrows were raised. And of course we never forgot to have our water bottles full before take-off.

We had some information about the harsh conditions in Changi prison in Singapore and in the large POW compound in Rangoon. The conditions in which POWs were held were said to be very rough indeed. 'Stone walls do not a prison make' was a booklet distributed to encourage and guide escapees. If we knew what to expect, survival would be more likely. Later in Burma, as we came within range of the Burma to Siam railway, we were to remember the many British and Indian lives lost in its building. Reconnaissance often reported that damage inflicted from the air to this railway had been repaired surprisingly quickly, no doubt by British and Indian POWs employed as forced labour. Despite the very real sufferings of the POWs held by the Japanese we certainly didn't dwell on these grim possibilities. We just took each day as it came along avoiding fruitless speculation.

A few weeks later before moving up to Assam for our first operations, the aircrew attended a lecture by a Major who had served with General Wingate and the Chindits in northern Burma. We were given a vivid description of the achievements of the Chindits operating as a Long Range Penetration group in Japanese held territory during 1943 and in the early months of 1944. Bad weather had claimed the life of General Orde Wingate on 24 March 1944 when the USAAF B25 Mitchell taking him out of Imphal crashed an hour later in the Manipur Hills. There were no survivors. Wingate had demonstrated very forcibly that the British soldier, properly trained to understand and cope with jungle conditions, was more than a match for opposing Japanese forces. Wingate was one of the many senior officers in both the 14th Army and in the Royal Air Force who were determined to reverse the defeats in Burma and Malaya of previous years. He had proved to be a very charismatic leader who in a signal to his forces before moving into the Burmese jungle said, "Our aim is to make possible a government of this world in which all men can live at peace and with equal opportunities." Inspiring sentiments which have proved very difficult to implement. We also received an update on the present overall position of the British and Japanese ground forces, without giving too much detail in case we were captured.

Early in December 1944 the Chindwin River, east of the Manipur Hills, was crossed from Kalewa, bringing the 14th Army to the edge of the Burma central plain. They had advanced more than one hundred miles over jungle covered mountains from the killing fields of Imphal. The over-riding message we absorbed, from lectures and briefings, was that the British forces had to be just as ruthless and determined as the Japanese if they were to succeed in achieving the total defeat of the enemy. The war in Burma, now in its fifth year, was going to continue to be a hard slog through all weather conditions with no let up from the monsoon. There was a determined desire in the whole Burma theatre to finish the job and put the personal privations and horrors of war over mountains and jungle behind. But first we had to defeat a very determined foe who would show us little mercy if we relaxed our efforts. On 23 October Tommy and I heard from the Adjutant that our commissions were through, back-dated to 24 July. We moved across to the officers' mess where we were given a warm welcome by our Canadian, Australian, Irish and UK colleagues, with drinks all round on us. There was never to be a dull moment with this mixed bunch. However, we did not notice much improvement in living conditions. Surprisingly the Indian tailor on the station was able to provide a 'best blue' uniform for immediate wear. It turned out to be of better quality and fit than a duplicate I acquired at a well known establishment in London a year later.

I completed twelve training flights at Yelahanka when suddenly, at the end of October, we were deprived of our Mosquitos. Apparently they had structural problems and were not safe to fly. On 15 November, following the grounding of all our aircraft, I flew Mosquito HX 943 to Kanchrapara, a maintenance unit north of Calcutta. The flight was at a pre-determined speed, with instructions to make no violent manoeuvre but just deliver the aircraft safely. Provided the aircraft arrived in one piece it could be repaired and modified. How great was the risk to the aircrew in flying the aircraft was never spelled out. As a reward on arrival at Kanchrapara, we were given a few days leave in Calcutta. We had first class accommodation indulging in a little sight seeing and shopping for the usual luxuries such as razor blades, toilet soap and books as we walked down Chowringhee, one of the main shopping thoroughfares. The street bustle and confusion was a never-ending source of interest. It was then back to Bangalore by train, in first class accommodation as usually reserved for officers.

During November 1944 every Mosquito in the Far East had to be inspected and if necessary repaired before it could be flown on operations. We were unaware that a signal was sent to the UK in October expressing alarm at three fatal accidents to the Mosquitos of 45 Squadron, which it was considered were caused by structural failure. These three accidents had arisen from aircraft losing a section of wing resulting in the loss of valuable and experienced aircrew. From May 1944 to October 1944 there were five accidents to Mosquitos in India/ Burma which were put down to structural failure. In May 1944 Wing Commander Stumm the CO of 45 Squadron and his navigator Flight Lieutenant McKerrachen were killed at Amarda Road airfield when the aircraft broke up on a practice run. On 13 September Flying Officer W C Tuproll and Flight Sergeant V A Ball of 82 Squadron were killed when their Mosquito crashed when making practice attacks on another aircraft. On 10 October Flight Lieutenant Campbell and Flight Lieutenant Rimmel of 143 RSU were killed when their aircraft crashed near Bishnupur. On 20 October Flying Officer Al Parker (RNZAF) and Flying Officer M D Randall (RAF) of 82 Squadron crashed when half a wing came off at practice on the Random Range. The same day Squadron Leader Edwards of 45 Squadron crashed at Kumbhirgram, his aircraft breaking up as he came in to land. It became rather obvious that apart from the climatic conditions with the monsoon weather and the hot sun, some other factor was having an adverse effect upon the aircraft structure.

These accidents brought Major Geoffrey de Havilland to India with other experts on 24 November 1944 to assess the problem. The faults were diagnosed as being a combination of the climatic conditions and a manufacturing deficiency affecting the main spar in a particular batch of aircraft built by Standard Motors at Canley. However, similar faults were later found in aircraft built in Canada and by de Havilland at Hatfield. On inspection the standards of gluing in the manufacture of some main wing spars left much to be desired resulting in the failure of the spar scarf joints to bond effectively. Unless all the surfaces of the scarf joints matched exactly giving a properly glued bond, the main spar carrying the wing would be fatally weakened, particularly if the glue itself was suspect. All parts made with casein glues were destroyed but formaldehyde glue proved to be satisfactory. Weather conditions could cause unsuitable glue to crack and the plywood skin to lift off the wing spars due to shrinking and imperfect manufacture. An extra inspection hatch was installed on all Mosquitos in the Far East theatre to ensure that the main wing spar could be inspected thoroughly during the standard maintenance programme. Additionally, European style camouflage paint was removed to be replaced with silver paint designed to reflect the sun and avoid a heat build up inside the airframe.

Research on these problems of manufacture was carried out in Canada, sponsored by the Canadian Institute of Strategic Studies, and published by Dr A R Molozzi in 1997. Canadian scientists with ready access to a wide variety of woods did much to improve the quality of manufacture of the Mosquito, particularly to enhance the durability of the wood veneers and to find the most appropriate glue suitable for all conditions. Later research undertaken in the UK indicated that accidents classified as ‘loss of control’ were three times more frequent on Mosquitos than any other type of twin engine aircraft. The problem of serviceability of the Mosquito in the Far East was never fully resolved.

After thorough inspection and appropriate modifications Mosquitos trickled back into squadron service from February 1945. The engineering and servicing echelon under Mike Mackay carried out rigorous inspections on all Mosquitos as they arrived back on the squadron. This was very necessary to maintain the confidence of the aircrew in this fine aeroplane. Over the following months Mike became quite agitated over the problem, instigating additional inspections to those laid down. He came to reject many Mosquito arrivals which on inspection were below standard, requiring repairs or modifications. Mike's commitment was such that no instance of airframe failure in flight befell the squadron for the whole period it flew the Mosquito on operations. Our establishment was supposed to be twenty aircraft with a minimum of sixteen. With some variation this minimum number was the average strength over the months ahead. Mike made constant pleas to HQ in striving to keep up this number.

The doubts over the air worthiness of the Mosquito in Burma were quite a blow coming just before our scheduled move to Ranchi, the Special Low Attack Instruction School (SLAIS), in Bihar State. Moving to Ranchi in early December we reverted to Beaufighters just three weeks after losing our Mosquitos. Here we underwent the same ground attack training that 27 Squadron had undergone in September. Re-established with Beaufighters there followed four weeks of intensive army support training together with low level cross country exercises. Much emphasis was placed upon rocket and 20mm cannon firing over at the Random Range. For practice firing over the range four rails, each carrying a twenty five pound high explosive rocket, were fitted under each wing in place of the six machine guns.

Ranchi was a well equipped station with an all weather runway and several permanent buildings. The overall facilities were quite an improvement on Cholaveram. Situated a good one thousand feet above sea level and nearly two hundred miles from the coast it enjoyed quite a reasonable climate without humidity, but it could be cold at night. Our only real concern was the prevalence of black kites - large carrion eating birds, with a wingspan of up to four feet, always referred to as 'shite hawks'. Coming into contact with one of these birds on take-off or landing could have very unpleasant consequences. Kites were particularly adept at removing a meal from your plate as you left the kitchen area on the way to the mess. A few months later in May 1945 one of these birds hit the Beaufighter of Wing Commander T P A Bradley DSO DFC, CO of 27 Squadron, when coming in to land, resulting in both the Wing Commander and his navigator Pilot Officer Holmes losing their lives. Tommy and I had now been with the squadron for over twelve months as we were prepared for our second operational tour in quite a different environment. For the past year most of our experience and training had been associated with low flying over the sea. To fly over mountains with a hostile jungle beneath was a different kettle of fish. An interesting diversion, which I enjoyed, was flying the squadron Harvard or the Auster on ferry or range duties from time to time.

In a letter to Joan from Ranchi, sport particularly football, featured prominently. Playing for the officers' and sergeants' team on Christmas Eve in the final of the 1944 Squadron Inter-Section Football Cup, against the Signals Section, I acquired a small 'losers' cup. We lost 3-2 supported by a 'capacity crowd' as virtually the whole squadron cheered their side on. The small 'losers' cup, still a proud possession, was presented by the CO to all the team members. I also had a shot at hockey against the Gurkhas but we were no match for their bare-footed skills. Despite preoccupation with sport, I did remember to send Joan a Christmas card acquired when on leave in Calcutta.

Christmas Day and Boxing Day were rest days with the squadron stood down and when most of our stock of beer was happily consumed. As was the usual custom the officers and sergeants joined with all ranks to be sure there was a good Christmas dinner. By some miracle the cooks provided turkey, Christmas pudding and mince pies complemented by free beer and cigarettes! On Boxing Day the RAF played the Army at soccer. In front of a large cheering crowd the Army won 4 - 0.

After this Christmas dinner, at the instigation of Flight Lieutenant Sid Parker and encouraged by the CO, Tommy and I along with four more officers, Sid Parker, Philip Henman who had been a rancher in Argentina, Jacomb Hood and Rene Provost, were encouraged to look for a suitable animal in the jungle to extend the Christmas feasting. With the squadron shooting brake, two spotlamps, three rifles and a hamper of turkey and ham sandwiches we drove out into the bush in the late afternoon. There was no particular skill required. As darkness fell the anticipated target was a deer or antelope roaming in the undergrowth. Attracted by the spot light sweeping the ground in front of us it would be an easy target. And so it happened. Ahead, at the side of the track two large soft eyes turned towards us. Sid Parker lifted his rifle, took aim, and we had a very large roan antelope of five to six hundred pounds to take back. It was so large and heavy it took us one and a half hours to lift it into the truck. Our trophy proved to be excellent fare, much enjoyed by all ranks for the few days immediately after Christmas. Perhaps we should speculate at our arrogance in driving out into the jungle and shooting the first large animal that came in sight. The British in India had been thus engaged for over two hundred years.

Originally deployed as a bomber squadron and then converting to a torpedo strike squadron, we were again facing the need to adapt to new operational tasks. Since May 1940 the squadron had moved from Khartoum in the Sudan to Eritrea, across North Africa, on to India and were now preparing to change to a ground attack Army support squadron using cannon, bombs and rockets. In the process we had converted from Wellesleys to Beauforts to Beaufighters to Mosquitos and then back again to Beaufighters It had been a long and frustrating wait in Southern India hoping to make some effective contribution towards the defeat of the Japanese. Nobody felt this frustration more keenly than the CO. The CO and Flight Commanders, apart from keeping up the morale of the whole squadron, had to contend with applications for repatriation back to the UK from personnel who were difficult to replace. Several had been overseas for four years or more. Nick Colley recalls the joy there was around when the boat home was announced to those who had been with the squadron since its days in Southern Sudan and Eritrea. They were the unsung heroes who kept us flying, often in the most difficult conditions, without the comfort of any home leave. Mike Mackay, as engineering officer, never forgot how well his men coped

GRT Willis Archives

December 1944, 47 Squadron 1st Eleven, Ranchi. Back l to r: Ronnie Isbell, Ferguson, M Jones, J Gibson (Capt). Middle l to r: Frank Henderson, Ron Watson, Bill Powell. Front l to r: Sheff Birkenhead, Jock Laing, Dusty Miller, Titch Fry, Bob Barrett.

GRT Willis Archives

Above: Christmas Day 1944, Ranchi, Bihar State, India, Officers' Mess. The author far left 2nd row, partly obscured. Back row, centre S/L Skinner, W/C Filson-Young, Major Pears.

Below: A shooting expedition for a second Christmas dinner, 26 December 1944. From left Tommy Thompson, Pip Henman, Bob Willis, Rene Provost, Sid Parker, Jake Jacomb Hood.

GRT Willis Archives

GRT Willis Archives

Above: Christmas 1944, Ranchi, Bihar, India. Squadron Leader Skinner and Major Pears (SAAF).

Below: Christmas 1944, Ranchi, Bihar, India. The 'Erks' relax.

GRT Willis Archives

GRT Willis Archives

Christmas 1944, Ranchi. Tommy Thompson and Bob Willis with John the bearer and squadron mascot.

GRT Willis Archives

December 1944, Ranchi. Jimmy Gibson and Pete Rostance.

with all the aircraft and servicing changes. Years later we can still say well done and many thanks.

On New Year's day 1945 came confirmation of the squadron's move to Northern Assam for a very active role in support of the 14th Army as it drove south towards Mandalay. This role would continue without a break until VJ Day over seven months later. When the signal came through on 17 January 1945 from HQ Air Command South East Asia, that our first operational tour and rest period were completed, Tommy and I were aware that our greatest personal challenges lay ahead. In many ways the censorship of letters and being far away from home was a blessing, as Joan and the folks back home would not worry too much. The only hint I gave of any underlying anxiety was in a letter to Joan on 26 November simply saying "Ops can be a bit worrying at times". My parents were not to know I was even flying over Burma until an article appeared in the local newspaper, released by the Ministry of Information, from a war correspondent who interviewed us in April 1945.

CHAPTER 9
TARGET: MANDALAY

On 10 January 1945 sixteen Beaufighters of 47 Squadron moved up to Kumbhirgram in Northern Assam from Ranchi. Kumbhirgram was an airfield close to the railhead at Silchar, with the rather forbidding mountains separating Assam from Burma only ten miles distant. Here we joined 45 and 82 Squadrons of 908 Wing, to form a long range striking force as part of 221 Group commanded by Air Vice-Marshal S F (Stanley) Vincent DFC, AFC, a veteran of World War l and the Battle of Britain. Vincent had a command in Java when the war against Japan commenced. After command and staff responsibilities in Australia and New Zealand and with much experience of Japanese tactics, he had been AOC 221 Group since 17 February 1944. Directing the squadrons of 221 Group he played a major part in the defeat of the Japanese 15th, 31st and 33rd Divisions at Kohima and Imphal, part of the Japanese 15th Army. At the time the Air Commander South East Asia was Air Marshall Sir Guy Garrod KCB, OBE, MC, DFC, to be succeeded in February 1945 by Air Chief Marshall Sir Keith Park, KCB, OBE, MC, DFC. After the many months of training on torpedo Beaufighters and the frustrations of Cholaveram, coupled with the intensive training at Ranchi, we were more than ready to resume day and night operations against the Japanese army. These forces retreating down the valleys of the Chindwin and Irrawaddy from the Manipur and Chin Hills were expected to make a strong stand at Mandalay.

From Ranchi to Kumbhirgram, not being assigned an aircraft to fly, Tommy and I made the journey with the main squadron party by train to the south of Dacca and then across the Ganges Delta by paddle steamer to Chandpur and then by train to Silchar. The scenery south of

Dacca, was more lake than river as the ferry steadily steamed past vast collections of house boats, providing a precarious existence in a landscape of more water than dry land. I managed some interesting photographs, the ferry crossing taking some eight hours. The journey from Chandpur involved one night in a four berth sleeper shared with three junior Indian Army officers. I was the only RAF occupant of this compartment. During the night one of the officers left the train at an intermediate station. Unknown to me, as I was asleep, he took my best shoes and left behind a very worn out pair which fortunately were my size. At least I did not arrive at the squadron barefoot.

What was the position, vis a vis the struggle for Burma, as we prepared for operations from Kumbhirgram in January 1945? 47 Squadron had come upon the scene as the 14th Army was making every effort to break the will of the enemy to stand fast. We were fresh aircrew ready to play a vital role in the disruption of the supply chain to the retreating Japanese forces. The squadron started operations on 20 January 1945 still equipped with Beaufighters, alongside 45 and 82 Squadrons who were back with Mosquito Mark VI FBs. It was to be the end of February 1945 before we had our Mosquitos back. Flying with our colleagues from 45 and 82 Squadrons gossip in the mess soon alerted us to the fatal accidents which had affected 45 Squadron in 1944. Doubtless there was concern at the highest level that aircrew did not lose confidence in flying Mosquitos. Officially the only message ever given to us was that all precautions were being taken to watch for any structural problems which could arise from the weather conditions. At the time, we certainly didn't worry a great deal, having much confidence in the squadron's servicing personnel, particularly in Flight Lieutenant Mike Mackay, our Irish engineering officer. He was a great guy, very competent and never afraid to demand the greatest possible support from the powers above.

As part of 908 Wing we were quickly deployed in a supporting role to XXXIII Corps of the 14th Army which was driving down the Chindwin River towards Mandalay, having just captured Yeu and Shwebo seventy and fifty miles north of Mandalay. These two areas contained important airfields now denied to the Japanese. 5 Division of XXXIII Corps was poised to advance to the south west of Mandalay, to effect a crossing of the Irrawaddy and then swing to the south of Mandalay, hopefully to cut off the line of retreat by the enemy still fighting to the north. In the months ahead the squadron was to play a full part, albeit at some cost, in supporting these strategic objectives, through the constant harassment from the air of the retreating enemy, as the 14th Army pressed on towards Rangoon and ultimate victory. Sad to say, the folks back home knew little of these endeavours with most news coverage preoccupied with the Yalta conference and the Allied advance into Europe from the west, together with the Russian victories in the east. War correspondents did interview aircrew at Kumbhirgram, followed by articles in the local press back home. Burma was given poor coverage by the national media, contributing to the general feelings of a forgotten army and airforce.

We were soon to realise that the advance of the 14th Army and the movement forward of any Royal Air Force units into Burma depended entirely upon there being sufficient Dakotas (DC3s) and Commando aircraft (C-46) to maintain supplies to the advancing forces. Allied air supremacy was total, largely thanks to the losses inflicted on the Japanese Air Force by Hurricanes and Spitfires over the Arakan, Kohima and Imphal earlier in 1944. Tribute has to be paid to the squadrons of RAF and USAAF who were to keep those vital supplies going no matter what the weather conditions.

Kumbhirgram was an all weather airfield, surrounded by jungle, built in the apex of the Manipur Hills rising up from the flat plain and paddy fields to between six thousand and nine thousand feet, with tea plantations on the lower slopes. These formidable mountains stretched one hundred and twenty miles eastwards to the upper Burmese lowlands and the mighty Chindwin River. Squadron aircrew became very fearful of these mountains knowing that if they lost radio contact with base it could be very difficult to descend safely to the airfield in bad weather, without a position and course to steer from ground control. We were to discover the hard way how hazardous getting into Kumbhirgram would prove to be, particularly during our night operations. The race was on to capture Mandalay and then drive south to Rangoon before the monsoon broke in May.

As aircrew, it was quite difficult for us to envisage the conditions the Army was having to endure as we flew our sorties. Flying into Kumbhirgram from the south west, across the plains of Bengal, over the extensive landscape of emerald green paddy fields with clumps of palm trees and scattered villages stretching to the horizon, war and the Japanese seemed far away. As the Manipur Hills come into view the green foothills merge into the mountain tops often covered in cloud or haze. As we later flew over these hills, we looked down upon a green blanket of many different shades dipping into undulating valleys, all of which looked so calm and beautiful but containing a deep and virtually impenetrable jungle with very few roads or trackways. It was an environment that offered little opportunity for a successful forced landing by any aircraft in difficulty. It was a hazard that all aircrew over the years in Burma had to take in their stride.

We were back with our much loved and sturdy Beaufighters, although they too had their problems. Whilst climbing to over ten thousand feet over the Manipur and Chin Hills into central Burma all Beaufighter pilots carefully checked the oil pressure and looked at both engine cowlings to be sure that there were no telltale oil leaks. At night the Aldis (signalling) lamp was used for this purpose. An engine failure the wrong side of the mountains at best meant a forced landing in enemy territory and, if at night, probably a fatal crash. This anxiety was only eased as emergency airfields became available on the Burma side of the Manipur and Chin Hills as the 14th Army drove down the Chindwin towards Mandalay.

Still being in India, living conditions at Kumbhirgram were quite reasonable. Accommodation was similar to that endured at Cholaveram, with permanent quarters and messes for all ranks constructed from brick, bamboo and rattan. Water was heavily chlorinated and taken with salt tablets as a precaution against dehydration. Some potassium permanganate was also introduced into the washing water as a disinfectant; thus the term much used - 'pinki parni'. By this time we had taken on a yellow oriental pallor from the daily anti-malaria dose of Mepacrine tablets. Personal hygiene was always a priority as after the risk of malaria came dysentery which both Tommy and I managed to avoid throughout our time in Assam and Burma. One great asset on the station, much appreciated by everybody, was the cinema, which showed quite up to date films.

As at Cholaveram, the squadron had to be mindful that all its personnel needed to consider their future when returned to civilian life, now that ultimate victory was on the horizon. Tommy, following his previous discussion group duties was appointed Squadron Education Officer, hoping to encourage the take-up of further education and training by all ranks, particularly through correspondence courses. Many leaflets on current affairs together with copies of the Manchester Guardian, Economist and New Statesman came from Headquarters to encourage these activities. The overriding wish for most personnel was to finish the job in Burma, thus bringing forward the day when they could hope to return home. There were still many personnel who had been with the squadron for over three years. Home beckoned to them very strongly. As we censored the mail we were left in no doubt that the government's information and policy over the matter of repatriation was felt to be woefully inadequate. Whether true or false, home based personnel appeared to have a better chance in landing a good job on demobilisation than those in far away lands. There were still bitter memories of the 1930s depression years. Despite these thoughts and the seeming disadvantage of being far from home, morale on the squadron was always very high. No doubt Filson-Young's leadership was a key factor.

After the capture of Mandalay (Operation CAPITAL) on 20 March 1945 the push to remove the Japanese from central Burma was on in earnest. 221 Group of eighteen squadrons comprising Hurricanes, Spitfires,

Thunderbolts, Beaufighters and Mosquitos, was deployed to give direct support to XXXIII Corps and to IV Corps of the 14th Army. It was essential to reach Rangoon before the monsoon rains came to slow down or even halt any advance. To a large degree these squadrons were the artillery component of the advancing divisions. Complete air supremacy was maintained over Japanese held airfields, which could pose a threat, putting them under constant attack and surveillance. Our role in 47 Squadron over the next few months was a mixture of direct army support and sustained attack upon Japanese lines of communication. The enemy were very skilled at hiding their movements during daylight hours. The Mosquitos and Beaufighters of 908 Wing were ideal to harry Japanese forces as they moved under the cover of darkness. 47 squadron were to achieve considerable success in these night intruder operations, despite the very difficult terrain.

On 23 January, early in the morning, Tommy and I took off on our first operation over the Burma front, crossing the Chin Hills and then down the Irrawaddy River to Myingyan, a riverside township of around one hundred thousand inhabitants about two hundred and forty miles from Kumbhirgram. We were part of a formation of four Beaufighters led by Squadron Leader L H Skinner, the 'A' Flight commander. In the same formation was Bill Powell and his navigator Maurice Jones. The four of us were still together after our early days with the squadron at Gambut. On this first sortie we achieved very little apart from strafing a thirty foot sampan on the Irrawaddy well over the bomb line. Pre-flight briefing had indicated that any boat of a reasonable size on the river was a fair target as it would be in use as a Japanese supply vessel. The bomb line was an established line on our maps, amended from day to day, indicating the division between friend and foe. We were forbidden to remove the safety catch on our weaponry until over the bomb line.

This first operation over Japanese held territory was quite an anti climax to what we expected. It was daylight, clear weather and no sign of enemy activity. We were to learn the hard way how deceptive this apparent calm could be. The anxieties attending the pre flight briefings prior to an operation over Burma were to become much more pronounced and tense than during our Eastern Mediterranean experience. A sudden dash to the nearest bush as an impromptu toilet was not an unusual experience prior to take-off on some mission which appeared to be a little hazardous. A salutary reminder of these hazards was the issue of the .38 Smith and Wesson revolver with its clip of bullets together with the 'escape kit'. It was most unlikely that, in the event of a successful bale out or forced landing in enemy territory, there would be recourse to a dignified surrender or treatment in a field hospital.

A comprehensive briefing for all aircrew taking part in each operational sortie was given by the Commanding Officer, or senior officer leading the day's sorties, plus the Intelligence Officer, the Signal's Officer, the Meteorological Officer and on occasions the Army Liaison Officer. Preparation for each sortie needed to be carefully organised. Maps were studied, bomb lines and radio call signs noted, together with the probable weather pattern and the latest intelligence information on enemy movements memorised. Most sorties by the squadron were of maximum range and duration which made it essential for the navigator to have a comprehensive flight plan with the main target, alternative targets and emergency landing grounds marked on his map, having already calculated the distance, time and probable fuel consumption. A five hour flight in a Beaufighter could take us over four hundred miles into enemy territory which always looked strange, empty and inhospitable. Before take-off each crew member collected a parachute on which, as said before, the pilot literally sat, the parachute being compressed into the pilot's bucket seat. If flying over the sea Mae Wests (inflatable life jackets) were worn with the pilot sitting on a dinghy pack, containing a compressed air bottle. The dinghy pack, attached to the parachute, made a rather uncomfortable ride. Into the pockets of our flying overalls went the emergency pack. I still had sewn into the collar of my battledress a rubber encased hacksaw together with 'compass' fly buttons on the trousers. I couldn't imagine that they would be of much use in a Japanese jail. They were just reminders of our time in the Eastern Mediterranean.

All sorties from Kumbhirgram necessitated flying over the Manipur and Chin Hills which ran approximately north/south on the border between India and Burma. The tallest mountain was Mount Victoria, at just over ten thousand feet. Aircrew flying Mosquitos had the benefit of an oxygen supply through the oxygen masks attached to their flying helmets, together with an integrated microphone for internal voice communication and VHF communication to base. Oxygen was mostly used on night operations being switched on at take-off, and always when climbing up over cloud to fourteen thousand feet or more. If left until we had climbed to say twelve thousand feet it would be possible to forget the need for oxygen and lose control. For specific targets it was usually felt desirable to reach the target area just after day break, hopefully taking advantage of at least some measure of surprise and also having the best of the weather before thunderstorms could build up. At least we enjoyed the most spectacular sunrises with brilliant red skies over the mountains. Back with the familiar Beaufighters it was going to be another month before I again took a Mosquito into the air. A snag with the return to Beaufighters was that they did not carry the oxygen facilities which the Mosquitos had. Crossing over the mountains without oxygen limited our height to around ten thousand feet.

Three days later, on 26 January 1945, came our second sortie of the tour with another formation of four Beaufighters led by Wing Commander Filson-Young. This operation was serious business, in support of the assault on the defences of Mandalay. XXXIII Corps of the 14th Army had the Japanese forces in full retreat to the north and west of Mandalay. The 2nd Division had captured Shwebo, an ancient Burmese capital, on 7 January, with the 20th Indian Division as far as Monywa on the Irrawaddy, fifty miles to the west of Mandalay. The plan was for the 2nd Division to advance on Mandalay from the north and the 20th Division to advance on Mandalay from the west and south. Also in support was the 19th Indian Division moving down the west side of the Irrawaddy aiming to cut off Japanese forces retreating to the east. In the event all three divisions were involved in the capture of

Mandalay. If we were to give effective close support to these advances, both then and later, navigators had to be very sure that they knew when we were over Japanese held territory, i.e. past the 'bomb line'.

The target on this day was described as a large factory building on the Irrawaddy waterfront at Mandalay. The building was suspected to be an enemy supply centre and transit area for retreating Japanese forces. The attack was to be by rocket firing Beaufighters - eight sixty pound high explosive rockets from each aircraft. It was approximately three hundred miles to the target from our base in Northern Assam. We rose at 4.00am, had breakfast followed by last minute briefing in the operations room where all the maps and positions were laid out. After collecting our kit including parachutes, maps, revolvers and emergency packs it was out to the aircraft by jeep for take-off about 6.30am. All four aircraft on this particular sortie had been air tested and armed the evening before. At the same time we were briefed on target details with the use of aerial photographs and army intelligence reports. Tommy, as navigator, collected the appropriate maps, F24 camera, recorded the radio frequencies and call signs and had a brief chat with the lead navigator, Flight Lieutenant O'D McGlory. The CO indicated the type of formation we were to fly in. Navigation lights were switched on to ensure that we did not lose touch with each other as the dawn broke. Besides the CO and the Squadron Navigation Officer in the lead Beaufighter, Tommy and I were accompanied by two other aircraft flown by Flight Lieutenant Bill Hughes, an Australian and Flight Lieutenant Al Scott, a Canadian.

After crossing the Chin Hills with dawn breaking, the formation approached the target from due west, flying at ground level to avoid detection until the last possible moment. It was then a quick climb to two thousand feet, lining up the target as the aircraft was put into a shallow dive, then firing the rockets at a range of about eight hundred yards. As Bill Hughes remarked later, you are a 'sitting duck for ack-ack' prior to firing the rockets. The consolidated sorties report for that day submitted by Tony Norris as Squadron Intelligence Officer, confirmed that all thirty two rockets from the four aircraft hit the target area. The time difference between the first rocket and the last was only a matter of seconds. Thirty two 60lb high explosive rockets hit the target sending much smoke and debris up into the air. Bill Hughes in the last aircraft in the formation reported debris falling all around his aircraft. John Kent, Bill Hughes' navigator, reported 'flak' as we broke away with a sharp turn to port over the Irrawaddy, but no hits were sustained. All the aircraft took photographs of the target area which we hoped were useful to the army in evaluating Japanese defences. The CO then led the formation south west at low level looking for enemy movement but without sighting any targets, returning to base three hours and twenty minutes after take-off satisfied that a standard type mission had proceeded smoothly without loss.

In all such operations each crew taking part had a slightly different story to tell. It is interesting to read Bill Hughes' description of his participation in the foregoing attack on Mandalay which I reproduce here as he recorded in 1989.

'As an Australian pilot I was posted to 47 Squadron RAF in November 1944 (the only Australian on the squadron) and after completing a low level attack course at Ranchi the squadron moved to Kumbhirgram, Assam in January 1945 to commence operations against the Japanese.

The Beaufighter, a twin engine aircraft was equipped to carry 8 x 60lb HE or 8 x 25lb AP rocket projectiles and 4 x 20mm cannon all operated by the pilot. A navigator made up the crew of two and the aircraft had a range of over 1,000 miles to and from base operating at low level. The 8 x 60lb HE rockets when fired simultaneously were reputed to be the equivalent of a broadside of a light cruiser.

One sortie, memorable for me, took place on 26 January 1945 when 4 Beaufighters from the squadron were detailed to attack a large factory on the bank of the Irrawaddy at Mandalay. This was my fourth operation on the squadron and as it was considered a big and important target there was some excitement at the briefing. The factory was believed to be an enemy supply centre which also housed many Japanese. The plan was for each aircraft to make one run into the target in line astern firing in turn the 8 HE rockets simultaneously. We took off in the early morning darkness with a strictly timed schedule and complete radio silence to arrive at the target at first light. The Squadron Commanding Officer, Wing Commander W Filson-Young, DFC led and I, with John Kent as my navigator, was No.2 in the formation.

Unfortunately, my aircraft was sluggish and both engines were overheating on the climb up to about 12,000ft to clear the Chin Hills. I had to throttle back to keep the engine temps. down and so lagged behind the formation. The small recognition lights of the other aircraft soon disappeared into the darkness. When the formation reduced power to cruising speed we eventually caught them, still with high temperatures on the gauges. Later the formation increased speed to arrive at the target on time and again we could not maintain station. At this time I had vivid thoughts that I would be attacking solo after the 'hornets nest' had been stirred. When we reached the target area to execute a straight run in over the Irrawaddy from a height of 2,000feet we were lagging a bad fourth in the group.

I watched the other three aircraft fire their rockets, all of which hit the target and we were still lumbering in. In the excitement, and after firing my rockets I made the cardinal error of watching them enter the building, but with a quick reaction executed a 'screaming' steep turn out over the Irrawaddy at about 50 feet above the water. My navigator who had the rear seat looking aft, was shouting 'flak' but all I could see were parts of the building splashing in the water around us. Miraculously, we flew through it without incurring any damage to the aircraft or ourselves. All I wanted to do then was to get back to base, but the CO who had other ideas took us on a 'sector recce' along the Irrawaddy south west of Mandalay prior to returning.

We were lucky that the aircraft got us there and back safely and that I had seen all 32 rockets go into the target. It was rather incongruous that on landing at base we declared the aircraft unserviceable. By way of explanation our method of firing rockets was to dive at a 10° angle from 2,000ft releasing at about 800 yards from the target, speed 220 knots. This enabled the pilot to make a steep turn in time to clear the target area, missing most of the blast. The dangerous part about rocket attack at low level was that on the run in from 2,000ft the aircraft had to be perfectly level with no slip or skid to ensure that the rockets maintained a straight course to the target. A sitting duck for ack-ack! To this day I continue to wonder what effect, if any, this raid had on the Japanese defence of Mandalay'.

Log Book Entry

Date	**Aircraft**	**Number**
26.1.45	Beaufighter X	KW394 'B'
Pilot	**Navigator**	**Hours**
F/Lt Hughes	F/O Kent	3.20

Duty, including remarks:
Pranged factory on bank of Irrawaddy west of Mandalay with RP 8 x 60lb heads. Rhubarb SW of Mandalay.

The squadron had made a good start in its introduction to the Burma Theatre. The Air Officer Commanding 221 Group, Air Vice-Marshal Vincent, had taken a special interest in this particular Mandalay waterfront target, having briefed the Squadron Commanding Officer and planned the attack with the use of rockets at a special 221 Group HQ meeting early in the evening before the subsequent briefing by the CO of the crews who were to take part. In the meantime the 19th Indian

Division had established the first bridgehead over the Irrawaddy forty miles to the north of Mandalay at Singu/Kyaukmyaung.

Three days after the Mandalay target on 29 January, Tommy and I undertook our third operational sortie as a night intruder patrol over the Singu bridgehead, the object being to prevent the opening up of artillery fire from fifty two heavy guns brought together by the Japanese to hold back and restrict the use of this crossing by the 19th Indian Division. These guns had been continuously attacked during daylight by bombers and fighter bombers from other squadrons in 221 Group. The sky was clear as we came over the Chin Hills in Beaufighter NV505 at around 10,000 feet. On this particular mission, besides patrolling the river crossing area, we also made a circuit to the east and south of Mandalay without any targets coming to our attention in the dark. Completing this sortie by dropping leaflets over the patrol area we returned to base completing 6 hours and 10 minutes flight time. Other Beaufighters from the squadron maintained the patrol for the rest of the night. As the Japanese guns remained silent all night at least the main objective was achieved. From the Japanese viewpoint, the best time for the movement of guns or transport was when the sky was clear and a full or nearly full moon gave sufficient light to facilitate movement along the roads or tracks without the use of headlamps. Unless enemy transport showed headlights it was very difficult to spot them from the air during night patrols. We were soon to learn how skilled they were in concealing their transport and movements, particularly during the daylight hours. Both by day and night it was to prove quite difficult to catch the enemy out in the open especially if there was jungle or forest at the side of the highway into which a hasty retreat from our prying eyes could be made.

By the end of January we had settled down quite well at Kumbhirgram. The station cinema occasionally doubled as a concert hall. It was a full house when we enjoyed a visit from Gracie Fields accompanied by her husband Monty Banks. As was to be expected, the show they put on was enthusiastically acclaimed. However, we were not to forget that it was still flies in the daytime and mosquitoes after sunset. Fortunately, we were not too far away from the Assam Tea Plantations where much needed rest locations, with a cooler climate in the hills, were available. We were to be grateful for the very generous hospitality from many of the tea planters who opened up their homes, providing a change and rest to many squadron personnel.

Since leaving the UK in October 1943 I had been writing regularly to Joan, now a nurse at Edinburgh Royal Infirmary. From that October day to my return to the UK some twenty one months later letters between us continued to be at least once a week, despite the fact that we had never met. Letters did refer to the stress of flying missions to maximum range and the tiredness which resulted. Apart from the attractions of the bar in the mess, relaxation was a mixture of listening on the gramophone to some classical music or Glen Miller, Tommy Dorsey and their contemporaries or perhaps playing pontoon, whist, poker or bridge together with reading and writing letters home. Aircrew were generally a high spirited bunch of fellows. However, the climate, and the rather shy character of the CO rather tempered any thoughts of wild parties. Filson-Young had a reputation for posting away any 'wild cards'. In any case, there was nowhere to go off the station to have parties out of sight of higher authority. As a diversion, a little shooting with 12 bore shot guns against pigeons was indulged in from time to time. For junior officers there was always the daily chore of glancing through the airmen's mail as a censor. Much criticism of the proposed demobilisation plans in this mail was a clear indication as to which party most of the airmen would vote for in the pending general election. Generally airmen were looking for new leaders to provide a better country to live in than many had experienced in the 1930s. Considering that a large number of the groundcrew had been away from home for three years or more, morale remained remarkably high, with great feelings of loyalty towards the squadron and its contribution to 221 Group.

Despite high temperatures, monsoon rains and variable rations, Tommy and I maintained good health throughout our period of operations over

Burma. At Kumbhirgram we had comfortable beds, (a 'charpoy'), complete with a mosquito net, with cotton sheets washed weekly by the 'dhobi wallahs' with much pounding. We also enjoyed the luxury of an enrolled follower or 'bearer', a native Indian, usually shared with one or two other aircrew. Our 'bearer' John looked after us right royally, ensuring that a 'dhobi wallah' also washed and pressed our clothes, even keeping our uniforms in good order with sharp creases in the trousers. Payments to our bearers were very modest, well within our resources. Toilet facilities were primitive but OK, comprising holes in the ground ten to twenty feet down, dug by Indian labourers, with flies kept under control by liberal doses of DDT or, if necessary, high octane fuel. However, there was a plentiful supply of cold running water with showers. We shaved every day.

All changed to much more primitive conditions when we moved to Kinmagon, a captured Japanese airfield south west of Mandalay in May 1945. At Kinmagon it was a case of looking after oneself in a small ridge tent for two plus camp bed, canvas wash stand, Tilley lamp and a few minor luxuries usually begged, borrowed or scrounged. However, even on the Burma plain camp followers were there, particularly useful to do the washing and drying of shirts, shorts and underwear in or around a nearby chaung (river bed). The climate both in Assam and Burma drained us of energy, but the Doc continued to make sure that there was always plenty of activity on the ground to keep us fit and occupied. Football, rugby and hand ball were always a priority, with inter section games and contests with our neighbours, 45 and 82 Squadrons. Our maximum indulgence as a crew would be the evening gin and orange, taken as a long drink, with which we washed down the daily Mepacrine anti-malaria pill. In any case, Doc Bamford, with his inimitable streak of Irish humour, was very good at keeping an eye on us. The climatic conditions certainly restricted the desire for high jinks in the mess. Anyway, it was not easy to get up a head of steam with beer always in short supply - one bottle of Australian lager per man per month - perhaps! 'Carruse' Indian Gin was more readily available, but no substitute for a pint! We were aware that the campaigns in Europe were nearing their successful climax, but these events seemed far away. We were still striving to defeat the Japanese in Burma as quickly and decisively as possible.

During the early months of 1945, as the war in Europe drew to a successful conclusion, many of the aircrew in Burma, including myself, couldn't wait for the devastation and destruction of Burmese towns and villages to end. It was no fun flying over the inhospitable mountains as we continued to wage war far from home, knowing how risky it all was and how sad was the death of friends and colleagues, many in unknown graves. There was no glamour and no real wish to record or remember the many operations in which we participated. My camera stayed in its case with the urge to take any photographs completely gone. Each loss of a crew was just a sad event, and so tragic for the families back home. For everybody concerned, whether in the army or the airforce, Burma appeared to be a comparatively poor and under developed country. We from the west really had no business to be there at all, apart from the imperative need to drive out the Japanese, who should not have been there in the first place. Who was going to rebuild this country in the years ahead, now being fought over so bitterly? As we now know, a high price is still being paid by the people of Burma for a war they did not seek.

Several unique factors bore upon aircrew operating in this theatre, particularly when flying at low level, seeking military targets by day and night. The terrain was generally hostile with low hills and scrub in the central plain, running into thick jungle and high mountains to the west, north and east. The enemy was adept at the hidden deployment of small arms anti-aircraft fire. Often there was no warning that hostile fire was imminent as tracer fire was little used. The first intimation of enemy response to our activities was usually a bang on the aircraft from a 'hit'. Tactics over this difficult terrain were a mixture of low level flying at around one hundred feet or alternatively at over two thousand feet to avoid small arms fire. The Japanese were also adept at stretching wires across rivers or narrow valleys which if struck would be the end of another crew. The rule was to always cross a river at right angles if flying low, never to fly along it. The greatest enemy of all was the weather, which became progressively worse as the monsoon came into full swing from May onwards. In monsoon conditions tremendous efforts had to be made to avoid abortive sorties, but going around and under storm clouds was never an easy task.

From January to VJ Day, for over seven months, the squadron never let up on the task of giving maximum support to our advancing troops, determined to reach and capture Rangoon before the monsoon made roads virtually impassable. Tommy and I concentrated as hard as we could to reduce the risk of fatal consequences to ourselves, particularly due to adverse weather conditions. A priority had to be comprehensive pre-flight planning and preparation. Even as we carried out our operational tasks as competently as possible, we were well aware that luck and our faith had to be on our side. This was the background to the absolute maximum effort by the squadron over the next three months, which culminated in the capture of Rangoon on 1 May 1945, followed by the drive south and east of that city as we harassed a stubborn but defeated enemy retreating into Thailand and southern Burma.

Unlike a UK RAF station, airfields close to the front line in India/Burma often lacked good communication systems, with W/T (wireless telegraphy) equipment housed in temporary structures or in marquees. This was particularly true of Kumbhirgram, our base until the end of April 1945, which relied to a large extent upon the W/T installation at Sylhet seventy miles to the west. Over one hundred miles from the airfield all contact with base whether by VHF or R1154 and T1155 W/T equipment would be lost. Unless we had plenty of spare fuel, a QDM (course to steer) from Sylhet was not much use either. Navigation was a mixture of Dead Reckoning, visual sightings and a large element of luck. The variable weather and monsoon conditions did not lend themselves to reliable communication between aircraft and base. Long distance sorties meant that for most of the time you were entirely on your own.

Our first experience of communication failure was soon to hand on the night of 2 February 1945 with Tommy and myself in Beaufighter 'H' NV563. This was a night intruder patrol over the Heho group of airfields one hundred miles south east of Mandalay, with the object of attacking any enemy aircraft seen to be taking off or landing when the use of some form of airfield lighting would be essential. These airfields were near the railhead at Taunggyi in the Southern Shan State of eastern Burma, situated in a secluded valley surrounded by mountainous country with peaks up to seven thousand feet. It was not an easy area to patrol in the dark especially with the moon obscured by cloud. Four aircraft were scheduled for this particular night patrol, relieving one another over the target area. Squadron Leader Skinner was the leader for the night. Who goes first? The Squadron Leader produced four matchsticks of varying length. He drew the shortest and took off first at 16.20 on this February night in 1945. I was to take-off next at 18.30, setting a south-easterly course and climbing to around ten thousand feet over the Manipur Hills. At around 19.30 when about twenty miles south of Monywa, over the River Chindwin, a 'Mayday' call came over our VHF transmitter/receiver. We recognised the voice as that of Squadron Leader Skinner. There was only one call which just said 'Hello Mayday'. We responded by calling back using Skinner's call sign 'Stayput 32'. There was no response. No other aircraft or base heard this 'Mayday' call. We arrived over the target area at 20.10. Just before our arrival we spotted what appeared to be a single engine aircraft well above us flying north at about ten thousand feet. We only spotted this aircraft as the cockpit light was on. Subsequently intelligence believed it was a Japanese Tojo. This was the only aircraft and activity we saw that rather dark night with the moon mostly obscured by cloud. We had to rely entirely on visual sighting to catch any activity. Radar available in Europe was not for us. Tommy continued to keep radio watch hoping to hear from the 'Mayday' caller. Unfortunately, it was not to be. Squadron Leader Skinner's aircraft was reported crashed and burnt out later the next day just south of Shwebo. How was such an experienced crew lost? Squadron Leader Skinner and Warrant Officer Laing, his navigator, were a very competent crew. Perhaps the most likely explanation was engine failure, or did the Tojo spotted flying over us play a part? We will never know.

Five days later on 7 February, in Beaufighter NV505, we were part of a similar staggered night patrol laid on over the 19th Division's Singu/Kyaukmyaung bridgehead on the Irrawaddy east of Shwebo, forty miles north of Mandalay. We were last here on the night of 29 January. The patrol also extended south down the Irrawaddy to Madaya. We had the usual briefings with the designated time over the patrol area defined. To assist us in keeping awake we were issued with a Benzedrine tablet as a mild stimulant. Neither Tommy nor I felt that it made any difference in our ability to keep awake. We were the first to take-off leaving Kumbhirgram at 17.00 hours and arriving over the bridgehead at around 18.45. It was a dark night with the moon again obscured by heavy cloud. Coming out of Madaya heading south on the road towards Mandalay we spotted several vehicles with lights on in convoy. We were not to know at the time, but the Japanese were pulling out, having failed to halt the 19th Division crossing the Irrawaddy. Making sure we were well over the bomb line we attacked in a shallow dive lining up on the road and firing the four 20mm cannon, hitting eight vehicles, one of which burst into flames. There was no other activity to be seen that night. Immediately after our first attack, apart from the burning vehicle, no lights were visible. There were too many low hills in the vicinity to make a low level search feasible in the very dark conditions. We then took a northerly course setting off for base at the designated time. As was usual practice we checked our fuel reserves against our expected time of arrival over base. Both Tommy and I then realised that it was going to be a close run thing as fuel consumption had been greater than anticipated. We had taken off with six hundred and twenty four gallons of fuel, stored in six wing tanks including two long range tanks. The inner tanks on the Beaufighter were always engaged for take-off after which the pilot switched to the outer supply. If very short of fuel one could run the outer tanks dry before switching over to the inner tanks. The pilot knew when the outer tanks were bone dry as the engines stopped. It was always a very nervous experience, especially in the dark. However, this is what was decided later that night, although at the back of our minds we wondered if a possible air lock would prevent the inner tanks coming in when switching over from the outer tanks.

We climbed up to ten thousand feet and set course for base. At about an estimated half an hour's flying time from base we called up by VHF to flying control for a weather report and a QDM (course to steer). There was no reply. We continued to try to make contact but received no response. It was all up to us, trusting that Tommy's navigation was spot on. Some time before we had switched from outer tanks to inner tanks when the fuel gauge indicated outer tanks empty with both engines still running. Now was the time to run the outer tanks really dry. We switched back to outer tanks, the fuel gauge moved past zero and then an engine stopped. Tommy made an unprintable exclamation and we held our breath as we switched back to the inner tank. No problem, the engine started and we breathed a sigh of relief. We repeated the exercise successfully with the other engine a few minutes later. At least we knew that the outer tanks had been drained to the last drop. These night patrols were scheduled to last nearly six hours which meant removing the .303 Browning machine guns to allow the fitting of the two extra long range tanks. Later on Beaufighters operating from bases inside Burma had the machine guns re-installed thus reducing the sorties to approximately four hours duration.

We were now on inner tanks only, expecting to be over base with approximately twenty minutes fuel in hand. We were at ten thousand feet, flying over solid cloud. How could we descend through cloud over base when we had no radio contact with an airfield surrounded on three sides by mountains over six thousand feet in height and only a few miles from the airfield? We could not risk it. Around 2330 Tommy estimated that we were now directly over the airfield. Had I flown a precise course on his direction and was his navigation accurate? We had to believe in both. We had the stars above but no means of obtaining a fix - or time to work one out. There was just solid cloud below, hiding those forbidding mountains to the north, east and south of Kumbhirgram. A course was set which we estimated would take us westward down the valley towards Silchar. We silently prayed for a break in the clouds. We knew that if we flew too far from Kumbhirgram we would not have enough fuel to return. The only alternative would be to bale out, it being far too risky to descend through cloud with mountains close by. Baling out from a Beaufighter was through a hatch behind the pilot's seat and in the dark would be far from easy. I just prayed! Then as all seemed lost, and some fifteen minutes after turning towards Silchar, through a small gap in the cloud which had suddenly appeared, we spotted a flashing beacon below. An immediate and steep diving turn was made through the cloud gap before we lost the light.

Height was reduced rapidly as we were already down to about seven thousand feet along the course which we estimated was over lower ground. The light we had spotted was a flashing beacon mounted on an RAF lorry. These beacons were dispersed down the valley to give navigational assistance to the literally hundreds of aircraft supporting our forces on the other side of the Manipur and Chin Hills. We were now below the cloud base and away from the mountains. Tommy quickly established the identity of the beacon from the pattern of flashes it was emitting. Pinpointing the location on his map, I was given a course for base. Again we tried to call up flying control with no response forthcoming. It was then a question of watching the fuel gauges on the inner tanks move closer and closer to zero, with about fifteen minutes to go before we could attempt a landing.

The airfield lights came into view. I called up control hoping they were hearing us and despite receiving no reply requested that the runway be clear as we were without fuel and coming straight in to land. Base got closer and closer, the fuel gauges were now at zero. How much fuel had we? Fuel gauges were notoriously inaccurate when near zero. The undercarriage and flaps were down. The runway lights were fortunately just about straight ahead, so with landing lights on, we both held our breath and silently prayed. On touch down all I could say, which was heard in flying control as our VHF transmitter was still switched to the transmitting position, was the heartfelt 'Thank Christ', which graphically reflected the tension we had been under. Flying control had been receiving our transmissions but faulty equipment in the aircraft had prevented us receiving their responses. We were able to taxi off the runway - just - and then stopped, no fuel left to go any further. Certainly a close run thing.

This whole night exercise turned out to be a disaster for the squadron. Of the four aircraft which took part on this particular patrol over the 19th Division's Irrawaddy bridgehead, the last two Beaufighters to go out did not return. Two more experienced crews and personal friends were killed, namely Warrant Officer Ted Daden, a pilot, and his navigator Warrant Officer Bill Lorrains together with Warrant Officer Ken Thomas, with whom we flew on operations in the Eastern Mediterranean, and his navigator Warrant Officer Tommy Bashford. The other aircraft on this night mission flown by Flying Officer Sid Parker and Warrant Officer D McKenzie was out five hours and twenty five minutes as opposed to our six hours and seven minutes. However, Sid Parker was able to maintain communication with flying control and land safely despite the dense cloud over the airfield. Ken Thomas' Beaufighter was later found crashed five miles north west of the Imphal airstrip, which presumably he was trying to reach. Perhaps he had the same experience as ourselves, short of fuel, and not being able to get above the dense cloud over the Chin Hills. He possibly decided to try the Imphal strip as an emergency landing despite it being surrounded by very mountainous country. Ken Thomas and Tommy Bashford are both remembered on the War Graves memorial at Imphal. Ted Daden and Bill Lorrains were posted as missing. These losses were attributed to the severe weather conditions which prevented any further flights by the squadron over the mountains for the next two days. The night's disaster highlighted the difficulty aircrews had in communicating with flying control when in difficulty. It was also known at the time that our VHF equipment could be unreliable. There is no record of any communication from either of the two aircraft who failed to return. On this one night, in giving protection to the ground forces, we lost two valuable crews and nearly a third, namely ourselves, not to mention the loss of Squadron Leader Skinner and Warrant Officer Laing in very similar circumstances five days before.

After this experience we were given a brief rest. I flew the squadron's communication aircraft, an Oxford, just a few days later to Imphal. This was a daylight flight to collect a Sister Macdonald from Imphal and bring her back to Kumbhirgram An easy mission taking just forty minutes each way.

On 16 February, nine days after the Irrawaddy bridgehead experience, we were back on a long daylight sortie of nearly five hours. This mission was to photograph Toungoo airfield, from the lowest possible level, to provide valuable intelligence in support of the advancing 5th Division of IV Corps. Toungoo is over two hundred miles south of Mandalay on the main railway line and half way to Rangoon. With its two all-weather airfields and as a major Japanese supply base it was expected to be heavily defended against the advancing IV Corps. This would be a major prize following the capture of Mandalay, which was completed on 12 March. Toungoo was a large town of over fifty thousand inhabitants, adjacent to the twin-strip airfield developed by the Japanese during 1944. This airfield had been a frequent target for the strategic bombers of ACSEAC over the preceding months. In the company of another Beaufighter we flew at low level down the railway running south from Mandalay. There was no action until we arrived over the airfield making two photographic runs at one hundred feet, for the benefit of our navigators' hand held cameras. Also operated was the F24 nose camera. We were hit by light ack-ack, fortunately suffering no material damage. In fact, we were unaware of any hits on our Beaufighter until pointed out to us on return to base. The flight back to Kumbhirgram was north following the railway to Pyinmana then north west, across tree covered low hills to another large town, Minbu, of over fifty thousand inhabitants, on the west bank of the Irrawaddy. Here we located our secondary target, a factory on the outskirts of Minbu fronting onto the Irrawaddy which had been identified by Special Forces as a Japanese assembly point and supply base. The two Beaufighters strafed both the factory and a convoy of loaded bullock carts in the vicinity with 20 mm cannon fire. Bullock carts were much used by Japanese troops to move ammunition and other supplies. Fuel for the motorised transport of the retreating Japanese forces was in exceptionally short supply. Allied attrition had played its part. The attack on the factory and the bullock carts did not appear to show much result from the air. However, 221 Group at this time received many signals of appreciation from IV Corps for the softening up and destruction of Japanese supply facilities.

On 18 February we were briefed to fly another night sortie to the south and west of Mandalay. As was the usual drill, we checked both engines of Beaufighter KW382, by Aldis lamp for possible oil leaks before completing the crossing of the Chin Mountains. This time we were out of luck. The port engine showed substantial oil streaks back from the engine nacelle and over the top surface of the wing. We immediately set course for the nearest emergency airfield. There was still a little daylight left as we landed at Tamu, an old Hurricane base, captured the previous October after the relief of Imphal. Tamu, now an emergency airfield, was guarded by the Royal Air Force Regiment. We had an oil pump failure. Flight Lieutenant Al Scott came over from Kumbhirgram the next day to ferry us back to base, leaving our aircraft behind. Our vigilance had avoided a single engine emergency landing later that night which would have been very difficult.

Two days later on 20 February 1945 we were briefed for another night sortie or 'Rhubarb'. 'Rhubarbs' were seek out and destroy missions along lines of communication, railways, roads and rivers, without any pre-determined or specified targets. We patrolled the area east of the Irrawaddy in support of 17th Division, who on 14 February had forced

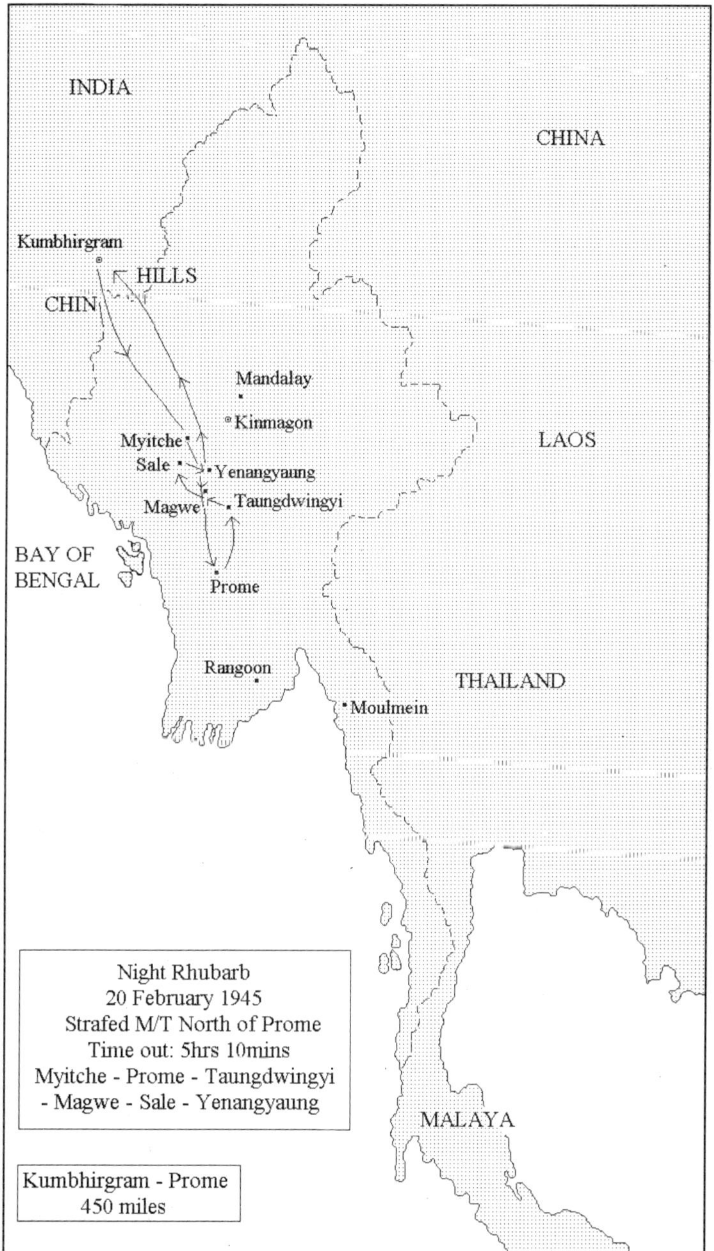
INDIA
CHINA
Kumbhirgram
HILLS
CHIN
Mandalay
Kinmagon
Myitche
Sale
Yenangyaung
Magwe
Taungdwingyi
LAOS
BAY OF
BENGAL
Prome
Rangoon
THAILAND
Moulmein
Night Rhubarb
20 February 1945
Strafed M/T North of Prome
Time out: 5hrs 10mins
Myitche - Prome - Taungdwingyi
- Magwe - Sale - Yenangyaung
MALAYA
Kumbhirgram - Prome
450 miles
pch

a river crossing at Nyaungu where the Irrawaddy is two thousand yards wide. The 17th Division was on its way to Meiktila, an important road junction and large town with two airstrips, seventy miles south of Mandalay. The capture of Meiktila on 4 March cut off the defenders of Mandalay from their main avenue of retreat. 221 Group, using all the available aircraft to support the Allied Divisions encircling Mandalay, mounted continuous attacks on the defences with bombs and rockets. By day and night all movement seen on Japanese lines of communication to Mandalay was under sustained attack from the air.

Our 20 February night patrol turned out to be our last operation in a Beaufighter before moving back to Mosquitos. We flew a sortie of five hours and ten minutes in KW32T covering over five hundred miles from base. As we crossed the bomb line, we scoured the roads adjacent to the Irrawaddy between Magwe, Taungdwingyi and Prome. We were well south of the 17th Division's advance to Meiktila as we searched for motor transport moving with reinforcements or supplies. It was a dark night, no moon, but no mountains in the vicinity either. We spotted, by their headlights, seven motor transport travelling south towards Prome, a railhead from Rangoon and an important crossing point on the Irrawaddy. They were promptly strafed with one truck exploding in flames. Returning north we dropped leaflets (code name Nickels) in the local language, in the Yenangyaung area. As an additional diversionary tactic we also dropped 'pintails', which were automatic firing Verey cartridges activated on impact. The 'pintails' dropped on the east bank of the Irrawaddy at Sale south of Chaulk were to confuse the Japanese on the location of our troops' crossing point over the river in the advance to Meiktila (Operation CLOAK). Return to base over the Chin Hills was uneventful.

Two days later 'A' Flight was assigned newly delivered and hopefully airworthy Mosquitos FBVIs. 'B' Flight was still with Beaufighters. Tommy and I had completed twenty two Beaufighter operational missions. We were never to fly operations in a Beaufighter again. Some crews in the Far East were always going to prefer the Beaufighter to the Mosquito, being rather fearful of the effect of heat, humidity and monsoon rain on the wooden airframe. For us, it was now the turn of the Mosquito, hopefully with its structural problems behind it. Later experience on several squadrons was to prove in the months ahead that this was not quite the case.

Another little non-operational diversion at this time was ferrying a nursing sister, Sister J Snodgrass, from Kumbhirgram to Comilla in the squadron Harvard, returning from Comilla with the SEAC Newsletter. 'SEAC News' was a popular publication, very professionally edited by Frank Owen, ex editor of the Daily Mail and distributed throughout the ACSEA operational area. Comilla, situated on the east side of the Ganges Delta, was in 1943 the 3rd Tactical Air Force Headquarters alongside Slim's 14th Army Headquarters. By late 1944 and into 1945 this base was an integrated joint US/British Air Transport Command HQ with substantial resources in support of the army and airforce in the front line. Overall control was by Eastern Air Command who between January 1944 and April 1945 (inclusive), using Dakotas and Commando (C-46) aircraft of the RAF and USAAF, carried 594,164 tons of supplies to forward airfields and the 14th Army. They also transported 315,125 personnel into Burma and evacuated 110,761 wounded, sick and urgent postings.

As the 14th Army advanced it was essential to bring captured airstrips into use as rapidly as possible. Without air supply in great quantity forward progress would soon grind to a halt. There was a race on against the onslaught of the monsoon due to arrive in May bringing with it torrential rain and massive cumulus clouds. Rangoon had to be reached by May if the greater part of Burma was to be cleared of the enemy. Failure could well see our forces in central Burma bogged down, unable to advance. Aircrews on 47 Squadron, as on other squadrons, had much to be thankful for from the Indian Army engineers who brought the forward airfields and emergency strips into use exceptionally quickly as they were captured from the Japanese. Not to be forgotten was the RAF Regiment, assigned to guard these airfields, the men often living and travelling in very difficult

G Thewlis

82 Squadron at 14,000ft, February 1945. Going home to Kumbhirgram, Assam over Kennedy Peak, 10,000ft, the Chin Hills.

G Thewlis

G Thewlis

An 82 Squadron crew at Kumbhirgan, Flight Lieutenant Vic Hewes (right) and Flying Officer Gordon Thewlis (above).

conditions, always to be on the alert from attack by small groups of the enemy bypassed as the 14th Army advanced. We will never know the privations and hardships endured by so many supporting personnel who made it possible for sophisticated aircraft to operate in conditions very different from a European conventional airfield.

We air tested our new Mosquito Mk Vl fighter bombers in late February 1945. Tommy and I were allocated Mosquito HR518, 'D' for Dog, which was to prove to be an exceptionally reliable aircraft. 'B' Flight continued with Beaufighters for several more weeks. Pilots and navigators were aware that there had been structural problems with Mosquitos after our conversion to the type at Yelahanka in October 1944. We were not to know at the time, which was probably just as well, that the climatic conditions would continue to cause structural and serviceability problems in the months ahead. The aircraft with their new reflective silver paint, instead of European type camouflage, and with inspection panels installed gave us total confidence that we had a first class aircraft to fly. The only note of caution expressed in handling the returned Mosquitos was not to dive in excess of the maximum speed when high dive-bombing. The pilot was instructed to allow at least one thousand feet for the pull out from a dive-bombing manoeuvre with the navigator calling out the air speed and height during the descent and the pilot concentrating on hitting the target with the 500lb HE bombs carried for that type of operation. As a further precaution, and as a reminder to the pilot, the maximum speed of 400mph considered safe in a dive was indicated on a note attached to the instrument panel. The bomb bay held four 500lb bombs or if carrying an extra fuel tank in the bomb bay the load was reduced to two 500lb bombs. Depending on the type of operation, fuses could be instantaneous or have up to an eleven second delay. For a bomb sight the pilot used an adaptation of his gun sight, which was not really very satisfactory, requiring much practice on the range to obtain a fair degree of accuracy. An alternative to the bomb bay fuel tank was a 50 gallon or 100 gallon drop tank on each wing, but these were in chronic short supply.

Burma, as far as flying conditions were concerned, was a far cry from our experiences in the Eastern Mediterranean. It is an enclosed country cut off from its neighbours by extensive mountain ranges of seven thousand feet and over to the west, north and east, with the only easy access to the central plain by sea from Rangoon Bay. The mountains, which have kept Burma relatively isolated, are covered with a great variety of trees, bamboo and thick vegetation difficult to penetrate. The foliage could be quite breathtaking with the red and orange tints of flowering trees among which are the flame of the forest. Central Burma is a wide alluvial plain which in many areas turns to bog and swamp in the monsoon season from April to September. The four main rivers, the Chindwin, Irrawaddy, Sittang and Salween, draining the central plain, flow from north to south terminating in the Andaman Sea. The roads and railways, which we were trying to deny to the Japanese, also generally ran north to south ultimately leading directly to Rangoon. The climate out of the monsoon season, though quite hot, can be pleasant enough, but with malaria endemic and high humidity when the rains come, conditions in the field can deteriorate very quickly for both the 14th Army and its supporting airforces.

By the end of February 1945 the Allied Air Forces were harrying the Japanese military bases, airfields and communications over the whole area of Burma up to and beyond Rangoon and down to the Burma/ Siam Railway. For our first operation in Mosquito HR518 on 23 February 1945 a long range sixty three gallon fuel tank was installed in the bomb bay. A signal on 24 February to 221 Group from the CO of 908 Wing, Group Captain L E Whiteley, stated that there was a severe shortage of both 50 gallon and 100 gallon drop tanks for the Mosquito, thus restricting our range. This operation was a daylight ‘Rhubarb’ with another Mosquito, crewed by Flight Lieutenant D A (Bill) Bailey as pilot and Warrant Officer F W Poree as navigator. We flew from Kumbhirgram over the Chin Hills at ten thousand feet, skirting the mountains to the east of Mandalay at Maymyo, then south west to Kyaukse on the main railway line thirty miles south of Mandalay.

Continuing south we had reasonable success on this four hours and twenty minute sortie, catching and strafing a locomotive in sheds on the railway at Pyanangazu, thirty miles east of Meiktila. Three days later on 26 February in the same Mosquito, we had another successful two aircraft daylight 'Rhubarb', flying in loose formation at around one thousand feet after clearing the Chin Hills, again with Bill Bailey leading. The two aircraft made a successful strafing run on a staff car on the road from Meiktila to the Heho airfields. We were four hundred miles from base and had to watch our fuel. Moving west across country we caught a group of closed wagons on the main north/south railway line at Nyaungyan. Four strafing runs were made with cannon and then it was to Thazi, a forward landing ground, to refuel completing a four hours and fifteen minute sortie. It was another forty five minute flight to Kumbhirgram for de-briefing. As an intruder aircraft we were very versatile, although the four .303 machine guns housed in the nose were not nearly as effective as the four 20mm cannon against ground targets, especially if they were stone buildings. Our most satisfactory weapon against stone built targets proved to be rocket projectiles. When required we carried eight of the 60lb version on racks, four under each wing, generally used against pre-determined targets.

On 28 February 1945, still flying 'D' for Dog, Tommy and I were back as night intruders. We were briefed to land and refuel on the return leg again at Thazi, a forward strip just to the east of the Chin Hills, north west of Mandalay, near Kalemyo. This emergency strip of two thousand three hundred yards was not all-weather but had been levelled and given a light tarmacadam covering by army engineers. The runway lighting was the very minimum comprising a 'Chance' floodlight mounted on a lorry together with a few goose neck paraffin flares to indicate the line of the runway. Landing at Thazi at night was far from easy with the strip sloping away as you touched down. We approached the runway in a long and steady descent not daring to overshoot, touching down as close as possible to the 'Chance' light situated to the right at the near end of the strip. The landing lights in the wings were full on. As soon as the pilot could see the ground from the illumination of his landing lights then was the time to level off and effect a landing. This refuelling exercise at Thazi was done on several occasions during the next few weeks, sometimes in the dark, but always with a sigh of relief when successfully completed. If staying overnight, it was in tented accommodation, hoping to find a spare camp bed on which to snatch a few hours sleep, still in full flying kit. Breakfast would be lots of tea, bread and probably fried Spam before taking off for base and de-briefing.

On this particular night 'Rhubarb' on the last day of February 1945 we took off from Kumbhirgram with another Mosquito piloted by Flight Lieutenant A C (Al) Scott, a very popular Canadian and the new CO of 'A' Flight. We left together in daylight but as darkness fell on clearing the Chin Hills, we went our separate ways. My route was down to Tatkon and Pyinmana covering the main railway line and roads running south from Meiktila to Rangoon, over four hundred miles from base. It was a clear moonlit night as we spotted a locomotive which was duly strafed at Kume Road Railway Station south of Tatkon. Light ack-ack came up from the railway station but we escaped any hits on our aircraft. Despite a diligent search for nearly two hours no more targets were spotted. Then back to Thazi and a successful landing using our landing lights to supplement the meagre illumination on this forward strip. After refuelling, back to base the next day.

We were now into March when 47 Squadron was to fly its greatest number of sorties of the Burma campaign as part of the 908 Mosquito Wing of 221 Group. March was later described as the crucial month for the 14th Army when the very maximum air support was required. Air Vice-Marshal S F Vincent was to state that:

'Almost every aeroplane exceeded the maximum degree of operational intensity laid down by the Air Ministry for six consecutive months - a wonderful effort from the pilots and groundcrews and also of the aircraft depots back in India which kept us supplied with remarkably little waiting'.

Letters to Joan during March more than once mentioned how we lost track of which day it was. Our activity was generally described as tiring, strenuous and quite demanding, particularly the 4.15am calls for early take-offs before the cumulus clouds over the mountains had time to make the sorties even more hazardous. Heavy thunderstorms were particularly prevalent in the evenings and at night. The temperature ranged from 57§F to 93§F with humidity at 27% rising to 100% at dawn.

In early 1945 Lieutenant General Sir William Slim had six divisions from IV Corps and XXXIII Corps at his disposal with which to destroy the six opposing divisions of the Japanese army in Central Burma. XXXIII Corps, with 19 Division supported by the 2nd and 20th Divisions, advancing from the north, west and south reached the outskirts of Mandalay at Mandalay Hill on 9 March 1945. Several days of bitter fighting followed to clear the enemy from this hill. Fort Dufferin, a formidable fortified enclosure within the city surrounded by a moat, was repeatedly bombed by B25 Mitchells and Thunderbolts. On 20 March it was all over as Slim entered the city, with all resistance at an end. This is the background to the squadron operations during March 1945, as it supported the drive to Mandalay as well as the assault by 7th, 17th and 5th Divisions of IV Corps on the airfield and supply base at Meiktila to the south. The whole area around this very important strategic airfield was finally cleared of the enemy by the end of the month after several days of bitter fighting. In support of this crucial drive to capture Mandalay and Meiktila, thus opening the way to the south, 221 Group flew eight thousand seven hundred and forty five sorties during March, with every squadron at full stretch. The fall of Mandalay and Meiktila was a defeat that the Japanese 15 and 33 Army Groups never recovered from.

Air Vice-Marshal Vincent made sure that the Thunderbolt squadrons gave close support to the advancing troops with the Mosquitos of 908 Wing making repeated attacks upon communication lines, supply dumps and oil pipelines. 47 Squadron was more than satisfied that it was playing its full part from its base on the other side of the Manipur and Chin Hills. A good example was a very successful 'Rhubarb' by Tommy and I on the night of 6/7 March when we caught a convoy of fifty eight enemy Motor Transports retreating south from Madaya, ten miles north of Mandalay. We strafed at least thirty five trucks receiving a little small arms fire in return. One truck, possibly carrying ammunition, blew up. This operation from Kumbhirgram was of only two hours and thirty five minutes duration over enemy territory. We used a temporary forward strip at Sadaung twenty miles north west of Mandalay, to refuel going out and coming back. It was our second night 'Rhubarb' in two days, both of which involved instrument flying in cloud as we approached the target areas. The previous night, unable to find any targets and with thick cloud over the Chin Hills, we were diverted to Kalemyo which was a rather short strip of 1,700 yards with no better lighting than at Thazi. Good team work between pilot and navigator was essential on these night sorties if there was to be a successful conclusion.

On 9 March, this time in daylight, we were out again in a formation of two Mosquitos led by a Canadian colleague Flight Lieutenant Stewart flying down the Irrawaddy to Magwe and Prome. We severely damaged a forty foot sampan and strafed a lorry at Magwe. Squadron operations during March were a mixture of day and night 'Rhubarbs', all of which involved at least four hours flying. It was a most intensive time, flying virtually every day, with an operational mission every other day. The days between were taken up with flights back to base from forward strips such as Thazi and Kalemyo or on communication flights, air tests or practice bombing exercises.

Unless we were given precise targets during the pre-flight briefing, target finding was a process of search and a very quick response. A good example was a daylight 'Rhubarb' on 11 March as we participated in a formation of two Mosquitos with Wing Commander Filson-Young leading. We flew from base, over the Chin Hills and then south down the Irrawaddy following the road from Yenangyaung to Thayetmyo.

Flying over the jungle at about five hundred feet in loose formation and just after leaving Yenangyaung, we suddenly saw straight ahead a Japanese gun emplacement in a small clearing. The Japanese soldiers hurled themselves over the bank surrounding their field gun as I pressed the firing button of the four machine guns, and pulled the trigger of the four 20mm cannon with the gun sight firmly on target. Nothing happened, I had forgotten to activate the guns' master switch after crossing the bomb line. Too late, the target was behind us with Filson-Young's Mosquito way ahead. The jungle was very thick, relocating the target would be difficult. However, before I could call up Filson-Young to seek out this field gun there was a very loud explosion immediately above my head. Our cockpit roof was blown out; all voice communication within the aircraft and to our leader was impossible due to excessive wind noise. All I could do was to catch up and be thankful that the 'plane was still flying. Apparently three .20mm HE shells came through the aircraft floor exactly between myself and Tommy. We were only eighteen inches or so apart with the shells exploding upwards blowing out the cockpit roof. Japanese light ack-ack fire from 20mm guns, as previously mentioned, was known to be dangerously accurate against low flying aircraft. We were protected by our flying helmets although Tommy received minor burns on the back of his neck. We continued the 'Rhubarb' by strafing and hitting loaded rolling stock at Satthwa on the railway line south of Taungdwingyi. Until we landed after four hours and ten minutes in the air the CO was quite unaware that we had been hit when flying over a company of Japanese troops around a gun emplacement in the jungle. Losing our cockpit roof was not the first time we had suffered this experience. Only four days earlier, engaged on high dive-bombing practice over the range with Tony Norris, our Intelligence Officer in the navigator's seat, we were in for a surprise. After executing a stall turn and commencing a fairly shallow dive from 6,000 feet onto the range target, there was a loud bang and out went part of the cockpit canopy above our heads. Apparently we had an undetected cracked canopy. On landing at base we were to discover that the lost perspex panel had taken away a piece of the tail fin. Tony remembers the experience to this day.

Another example of the versatility of the Mosquito in support of our troops came on 14 March when we gave close army support, directed from the ground by a VCP (Visual Control Post) through R/T (Radio telephone). The targets were usually pinpointed by Force 136, operating behind enemy lines and communicating by radio telephone. Flying from Thazi the target on this strike mission was enemy gun positions twenty five miles north of Meiktila at Myittha on the main north to south railway. Apart from creating a very large fire with columns of black smoke rising to 500 feet it was impossible to see the result. As weather was poor over base we landed at Thazi, staying overnight. Twenty fours hours earlier, in formation with Bill Hughes, we strafed a large quantity of 40 gallon oil drums near the railway at Heho. We followed up with strafing runs on the neighbouring 'bashas' used for storing ammunition and supplies. A very large fire resulted with heavy black smoke to 3,000 feet. Further east on the supply route from Taunggyi to Chiang Mai in Siam we hit more supply dumps at Shwenyaung resulting in several small fires. We landed at Thazi ready for the following day's sortie on 14 March.

On 16 March, again as No.2 to the Wing Commander, we were out seeking targets around the Heho airfield and again on the road to Taunggyi and further south. Apart from strafing airfield buildings at Heho with some return fire this was not a very productive mission. With well over four hours in the air and fuel low we landed at Thazi. Each 'Rhubarb', even at night, usually achieved some positive result such as on the night of 24/25 March when a most spectacular explosion erupted from a truck we strafed, along with two others, on the outskirts of Minbu one hundred and seventy miles south west of Mandalay adjacent to the Irrawaddy. Flames rose at least three hundred feet into the air. It was either a petrol tanker or large ammunition truck.

In the middle of the month, much to our surprise, we were granted four days leave from 17 to 21 March staying at a tea planters bungalow in

GRT Willis archives

Left: 47 Squadron, 13 March 1945, supply dump strike at Keng Hean, from Kumbhrigram, Assam.

Below: 82 Squadron, March 1945. Jap Radar Station destroyed, Shan Hills, Burma.

G Thewlis

GRT Willis Archives

Above: 82 Squadron, Myindiak, 6 March 1945, hits by cannon on Jap rolling stock.

Below: 82 Squadron, 2 April 1945, strike on Thaukegat Road bridge.

G Thewlis

Above: 82 Squadron, Kumbhirgan, going for Jap trucks on a jungle track.

Below: 82 Squadron, cannon strike on three Jap trucks.

G Thewlis

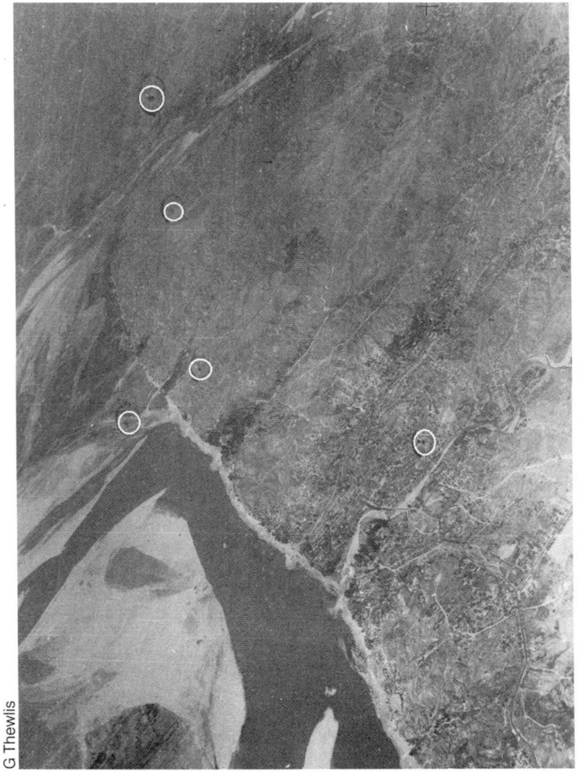

G Thewlis

Above: 82 Squadron, 2nd strafing attack on Japanese troops hiding in a Burmese village, 80 Japanese reported killed.

Right: Central Burma, Irrawaddy to the left with flak (ringed) coming up from Yenagyaung oil installation.

the hills close to Kumbhirgram. Filson-Young must have thought we required a brief rest, so off we went by RAF truck to the home of the McIvers on the Rukni Tea Estate in the Cachar Hills south of Kumbhirgram. Mr and Mrs McIver, whose family hailed from Scotland, couldn't do too much for us. We were truly feasted, enjoying a welcome change from RAF soya sausage, dehydrated potatoes and Spam. There was the inevitable tour of the tea plantation with tea plucking and grading taking place. The war against Japan was far away. The special treat the McIvers laid on was to take us into the jungle by a pick-up truck along with bearers carrying several guns. Arriving at a large clearing in the nearby jungle as darkness was falling, we quietly ascended a ladder onto a tree platform. Below us was a tethered goat as bait for a leopard which was prowling in the district. The goat bleated long and hard despite being protected from direct attack inside a wire cage. We silently waited on this tree platform with guns at the ready for two nights. The leopard never came. Much to our surprise on the journey back to the bungalow, just before dawn on the second night, the leopard, caught by our headlights, calmly crossed the road in front of our pick-up truck. At least we saw the animal and could only speculate upon its ultimate fate. On the fourth day it was back to the squadron and on with the tasks in hand. It was not unknown for a black panther or a leopard to cross the runway at night as aircraft prepared to take-off. At Cholaveram it had been cattle.

Towards the end of March were all sorry to see Tony Norris posted to a Thunderbolt squadron No.261 part of 910 Wing based at Wangjing near Imphal. Tony had been a great supporter of the squadron aircrew not only as the Intelligence Officer but also as a counsellor and friend. He had served the squadron well during its hectic and traumatic days in 1943/44, as the squadron moved along the North African coast in search of targets for its torpedo carrying Beauforts and Beaufighters, and then to India for operations in Burma. He and Doc Bill Bamford, had always supported the aircrew in times of crisis and stress. Tony as a convivial colleague would be sorely missed in the months ahead. I flew him along with his kit on 25 March in the squadron Harvard to join his new squadron at Wangjing. Many years later we were to meet again, both at our homes and on squadron reunions. Joan and I were to enjoy the most delightful holidays at his bungalow in Northumberland to which he and his wife Joyce moved on their retirement. Tony's successors, Flying Officer Barter, then to be succeeded by Flying Officer Johnny Banks, never had the time cultivate the close links with the aircrew Tony had enjoyed. Flying Officer R J Humphries was also close at hand as the Intelligence Officer for 908 Wing.

The day after I had flown Tony out of Kumbhirgram, March operations for Tommy and I took on an even greater intensity. From 23 March to 1 April we flew eight long 'Rhubarbs' in ten days, three of them at night, carrying two fifty gallon drop tanks to give well over four hours flying time on each sortie. The main targets were the oil fields at Yenangyuang, Japanese troop concentrations around Toungoo and the airfield areas of Toungoo and Heho. On at least four of these seven sorties anti-aircraft fire was encountered of varying intensity and type. Quite heavy ack-ack from the oil fields with lighter small arms or machine gun fire from other target areas was the normal experience on these intruder missions. Our aircraft Mosquito HR518 was patched up on more than one occasion by the servicing echelon at Kumbhirgram, but fortunately no vital parts were hit. The results of these operations in late March were quite good. We flew a typical daylight sortie on 27 March leading a formation of two Mosquitos on a strike against Japanese troop assembly areas around the Yenangyaung oilfields. This was our second strike against the oilfields on two successive days. On both occasions we came under heavy and light ack-ack fire. HR518 was hit again, this time by .303 bullets causing no serious damage. It was soon repaired and back in service.

During the four daylight sorties on 26, 27, 28 and 30 March results included damage to the oil pipeline and an oil dump and Japanese billeting areas, both burnt out. Rolling stock was damaged at Dalangyun, and the destruction of an oil storage dump at Shwenyaung resulted in large fires with dense black smoke rising over 3,000 feet. The sorties against billeting areas and supply facilities around Toungoo town and railway station on 28 March was particularly successful, leaving many buildings burnt out. Daylight sorties were in formations of four or two aircraft with ourselves as formation leaders on two of these occasions. On the three night 'Rhubarbs' on 23, 24 and 30 March, road transport was hit on all three operations with at least one 'flamer' every night, along with a substantial tally of damaged transport. We were operating at maximum range from Kumbhirgram, alongside 45 and 82 Mosquito squadrons of 908 Wing. Each round trip from base covered approximately nine hundred miles. We were hitting the enemy hard as they retreated in confusion from the Mandalay and Meiktila areas.

March closed with the squadron completing two hundred and twenty six sorties in the month and contributing to 221 Group's considerable tally of 4 locomotives destroyed and 25 damaged, 25 rolling stock destroyed and 458 damaged, 46 motor transport burnt out and 273 motor vehicles including 4 tankers damaged plus many river craft either destroyed or severely damaged. Casualties inflicted upon the Japanese forces, whilst considerable, could not be exactly quantified. All the aircrew of 908 Wing, in support of the drive south towards Toungoo and Rangoon, had similar experiences to our own, particularly of the hazards involved, the most feared being the unpredictable weather and fire from light machine guns or 20mm guns against low flying aircraft. With the continuing shortage of serviceable Mosquitos, 47 Squadron was still equipped with Mosquitos only in 'A' Flight and with Beaufighters in 'B' Flight. My old friend Bill Powell flew Beaufighters in 'B' Flight whilst I enjoyed the faster Mosquito. Which was the better aircraft in the conditions prevailing in Burma will always be a matter of debate. In the conditions of weather and terrain the Mosquito did have the edge, being a much better performer on one engine than the Beaufighter. Bill takes up the story in his own words of one of his Beaufighter sorties in February and another in March 1945.

'Late January and February of 1945 saw Beaufighters of No.47

Squadron maintaining night patrols over Japanese artillery positions and over Japanese held airfields whilst the 14th Army advanced towards and then across the Irrawaddy. My log book records such operations on the nights of January 27th and 28th, then February 1st, 3rd and 6th, so it was something of a relief to be flying one of two Beaufighters on a daylight offensive patrol behind the Japanese lines on February 17th. We patrolled the Irrawaddy from Sinbyugyun to Prome, the road from Prome to Satthwa and the road and railway from Satthwa to Kyaukpadaung to Meiktila to Myingyan, carrying out cannon strikes on rivercraft and motor transport. We then found ourselves over Ywatung airfield, where this operation became of special significance to me.

There were no Japanese aircraft, vehicles or troops to be seen and the airfield appeared to be deserted but as we turned away my navigator called up on the intercom "You'd better start weaving as some tracer bullets have just passed by!" I immediately did so, then heard a loud bang followed by a cold draught of air behind, but the Beau's two engines purred merrily on and eventually we returned safely to our base at Kumbhirgram.

A few days later I was down at 'B' Flight when the CO, Wing Commander Filson-Young, drove up in his jeep. He got out, came over to me and said, "I think you'd like to have this as a souvenir" and handed me a 20mm armour piercing shell. This had caused the bang at Ywatung and apparently it had hit my aircraft on the port side, passed about two inches behind my neck and then buried itself in the starboard engine from where the groundcrew had dug it out!

I make no claims to fame, but I don't suppose there are many aircrew who have amongst their memorabilia the shell that bloody nearly cut them off in their prime!'

Bill goes on to recall: *'We were based at Kumbhirgram in Assam with a forward re-fuelling base established at Thazi in Burma, which enabled the range of our Beaufighters to be greatly increased, thus allowing much deeper penetration behind the Japanese lines. Intelligence information had been received that the retreating Japanese Army had set up a temporary HQ, including a telephone exchange, at Toungoo, some 200 miles behind their lines. On 13 March four Beaufighters of the squadron, each armed with 8 x 60lb rocket projectiles in addition to the normal armament of 4 x 20mm cannons, took off from Kumbhirgram to attack this target. Having cleared the formidable mountains on the Assam/Burma border, we landed at Thazi to refuel and then set off for Toungoo. The CO, Wing Commander Filson-Young, was leading the operation, I was his No.2 and the third aircraft was piloted by a Canadian, Flying Officer Hardy (known inevitably as 'Judge' because the Lew Ayres 'Judge Hardy' films were very popular at the time!) with Flying Officer George Lidgitt as his navigator/wireless operator. Neither my log book nor my failing memory can reveal the names of the crew who were in the fourth aircraft.*

The 8 rocket projectiles were mounted on metal rails fixed under the Beaufighter's wings - 4 port and 4 starboard - and they could be fired as a salvo or in pairs. At the time, a salvo of 8 R/Ps was likened to a broadside from a 6" gun cruiser of the Royal Navy. When we reached the target area there was no way of knowing what was inside the various buildings so the CO ordered us to fire our rockets in pairs, which would have involved four separate attacks. The Japs were taken by surprise and the first attack was highly successful; on the second we were greeted with some light 'flak' but all four attackers released their rockets into the target area and we turned for the third run-in. My log book records that I fired my eight rockets in three runs and, although memory fades with the passage of time, I think I can safely assume that the CO wisely decided that the flak would get worse, as the element of surprise had gone, and ordered us to fire our remaining four rockets on the third attack.

The 'flak' ***was*** *worse and all four aircraft sustained some hits, but worst off was 'Judge' Hardy, whose Beaufighter was badly hit in the starboard engine. As we were re-forming to "get the hell out of here" we saw that*

'Judge' had feathered the starboard prop and was faced with the unenviable task of flying his aircraft some 200 miles on one engine - a task not helped by the considerable extra weight of the rocket rails under the wings.

I heard the CO try to contact 'Judge' on the radio but clearly that had been hit too, so I was instructed to escort the damaged aircraft back to our own lines and my navigator/wireless operator, Maurice Jones, conveyed this information to 'Judge' and George by Aldis lamp. We flew at about a thousand feet, carefully avoiding any spot where anti-aircraft fire might be encountered, with 'Judge's' aircraft maintaining its height successfully. The nearest "airfield" in our hands was a grass strip at Ywadon. When we got within R/T range I made contact, told them what had happened and asked them to ensure the strip was kept clear. The Aldis lamp was used again to tell 'Judge' to land at Ywadon and soon the strip was in sight. Down came the undercarriage of 'Judge's' Beaufighter and down went the nose as he started his approach: then to my utter astonishment I saw his port engine propeller come slowly to a stop and the undercarriage start to disappear again! This must have been a "panic stations" job for, of course, with both engines out of action there was no hydraulic power and the hand pump would have to be used. All 'Judge' could do now was to point the nose straight at the grass strip and hope for the best, which he duly did. Watching from about a thousand feet I saw the Beau pull out of its dive at the start of the grass strip but it clearly had too much flying speed and refused to stall. It floated the full length of the strip before it flopped onto its belly. It then skidded into a copse of trees, cutting them down like a scythe with the wings. Both port and starboard engines came out of their mountings and rolled away, looking from my vantage point rather like a couple of footballs. The Beaufighter eventually came to rest and, to my relief, I saw both 'Judge' and George climb out of the wreckage and wave to us, so I waggled my wings and flew on to the much better equipped airfield at Monywa to make my report.

When 'Judge' and George eventually rejoined the squadron, I learned that their Beaufighter had flown all the way from Toungoo on one engine at full revs and full boost in order to maintain height. Luckily, they were in sight of safety before the port engine seized up altogether and, apart from a nasty cut on 'Judge's' forehead where he had hit the gun-sight when his aircraft finally "landed", both he and George were unhurt.

There was much discussion about the incident on the squadron and I seem to recall that the general impression was that 'Judge' and George were lucky they had been in an all metal Beaufighter and not a balsa wood Mosquito! To some extent this was true, but the Mossy would easily have maintained height on one engine. Maybe, replied the Beaufighter 'buffs', but would it have survived the 'flak' over Toungoo?

Suffice to say that this incident proved yet again the incredible strength of the Beaufighters, which gave so much confidence to the crews who flew in them - they were, indeed, Flying Cruisers.'

Still using Thazi as a refuelling or overnight stop on our way to and from Kumbhirgram, sorties continued in April but with not quite the same intensity as in March. Thazi, despite its meagre facilities, was always a welcome stop over, situated as it was just over the Chin Hills from Kumbhirgram, near the river Myittha, a major tributary of the Chindwin. The convergence of these two rivers provided a key navigational pinpoint when clear of the Chin Hills. This pinpoint was keenly sought out by our navigators, as the tallest mountain in the Chin Hills, Mount Kennedy of nearly 9,000 feet, was just off the direct path to Kumbhirgram from Thazi.

By 30 March Tommy and I had clocked up 39 sorties with a few interesting interludes in between. Drinking gin and orange as a thirst quencher with beer always in short supply, hardly encouraged much conviviality in the mess as we gossiped and discussed the day's events. Most of the crews were just living from day to day - not worrying too much but certainly not enjoying the experience of jungle flying. Apart from operations, there were other hazards too, such as on 10 April when

I was detailed to conduct an air test on Beaufighter 'O'. On checking with Flight Sergeant Beanland 'A' Flight 'Chiefy', I was informed that the aircraft would not be ready until after midday. In the mess, over the usual rather monotonous midday meal, I sought out a volunteer to carry out this air test as I was playing football that afternoon in an inter-section match for the officers and sergeants team. Flight Lieutenant H D Mackay, who had been on the squadron since operations commenced over Burma, volunteered to take my place. Halfway through our football match we were startled by a loud explosion, followed by a column of thick black smoke from the direction of the airfield. All play ceased. We piled into our assorted transport, jeeps and pick-up trucks and sped to the airfield. There we were to learn that Mackay and his navigator Flying Officer H Smith had crashed on take-off in the Beaufighter to be air tested. The aircraft had climbed about fifty feet and then dived straight into the ground at the edge of the airfield. Both crew members were killed instantly, much to the sorrow of the whole squadron. Why was an experienced crew lost in this way? There was some speculation that it could have been a maintenance fault relating to the elevator trim. As Mike Mackay our engineering officer admitted some time later, it was so easy to make mistakes in the servicing echelon under the pressures and conditions prevailing at the time. There was also the additional strain imposed on the groundcrews in having to service two aircraft types on the squadron, the Beaufighter and the Mosquito. I could only feel that 'there but for the grace of God........'

We returned to the mess, much saddened by this event, but for me the day was not quite over. I was a sole passenger in a jeep driven too fast along a causeway leading from the airfield to the domestic areas. Nobody thought of being strapped in - anyway safety straps were not provided. The corner came up too fast, down the embankment went the jeep, the driver and me. How we escaped serious injury I will never know. I was thrown clear suffering only a few bruises, likewise the driver, who was an officer from one of the other units on the station who had offered me a lift. I don't believe we spoke as we trudged to the mess.

CHAPTER 10
THE RACE TO RANGOON

With the 14th Army now in control of Mandalay and all the area towards and around Meiktila, there was still three hundred miles to go to reach Rangoon with the monsoon weather only a few weeks away in early May. The 5th Division was given the task to reach Toungoo by 25 April and capture its two airfields only one hundred and sixty miles from Rangoon. Short range fighters, particularly Spitfires, could then operate from Toungoo releasing airfields further back but still in Burma for the longer range Thunderbolts and Mosquitos of 910 and 908 Wing.

April 1945 was our last month at Kumbhirgram, with night 'Rhubarbs' generally ruled out. The distance involved to reach the 'bomb line' and the weather risks over the mountains at night were too great. As the monsoon weather approached huge banks of cumulus cloud, rising up to thirty thousand feet, built up during the day over the Chin Hills. The order of the day was close support to the army as it drove forward towards Rangoon. During the month the seven sorties Tommy and I undertook again achieved quite good results, usually with other Mosquitos making up formations of two, three or four aircraft. Each aircraft carried two 50 gallon drop tanks, one on each wing to give us a little extra range. Unless in severe difficulties drop tanks were never jettisoned. On 1 April, flying 'D' HR518 in a formation of three Mosquitos led by Al Scott, we strafed with 20mm cannon enemy dumps and assembly areas identified around Heho. On 4 April, again with Mosquito 'D', we led a similar operation against similar targets at Kalaw twenty miles west of Heho, leaving behind after both sorties several fires. We were hitting a major escape route into Siam.

On 7 April quite spectacular results were achieved when, as part of a formation of four Mosquitos led by Bill Bailey, set at least eight trucks on fire with many others damaged after attacking a large concentration of motor vehicles at Mawchi fifty miles east of Toungoo. Operating at maximum range we returned to Thazi to refuel. On 11 April in another formation of four Mosquitos, again led by Bill Bailey, we inflicted much damage by cannon fire on supply dumps camouflaged as 'bashas' in the Minbu, Migyaungy area. Further targets were the oil pipeline near Yenangyaung and a substantial wooden bridge at Pynbye. Two days later on 13 April with three other Mosquitos led by Bill Bailey we strafed motor transport shelters and ferry crossing facilities at Bawlake on the Sittang River near Toungoo. We left behind many damaged buildings and two fires, landing to refuel at Sinthe south west of Mandalay. Sinthe had only been in our hands since the end of February, but was very quickly brought into use. I don't believe any of the squadron crews enjoyed this attrition by cannon fire on supply dumps and assembly areas behind the front line. What casualties were the civilian population suffering with whom we had no real quarrel? At the beginning of April, 17 Division and 5 Division broke the back of the last major Japanese defended positions at Pyawbwe 22 miles south of Meiktila, on the direct route to Toungoo and Rangoon. By 14 April the 14th Army had just 300 miles to go to Rangoon. The Japanese 33rd Army had been decimated and was now down to a mere 8,000 men. The enemy was scattered in pockets, striving to regroup in southern Burma or Siam.

With a desperate enemy, small arms fire from these retreating troops was always going to be a hazard. This risk was vividly brought home when we lost our 'A' Flight Commander, Flight Lieutenant Al Scott on 14 April. 'Scottie' was probably the most skilful pilot on the squadron, quite happy to perform aerobatics in his Mosquito. As an outgoing Canadian he was very popular with both groundcrew and aircrew. His Mosquito was hit by small arms fire as he, along with Flight Lieutenant Sid Parker flying as his No.2, strafed Japanese positions on Toungoo

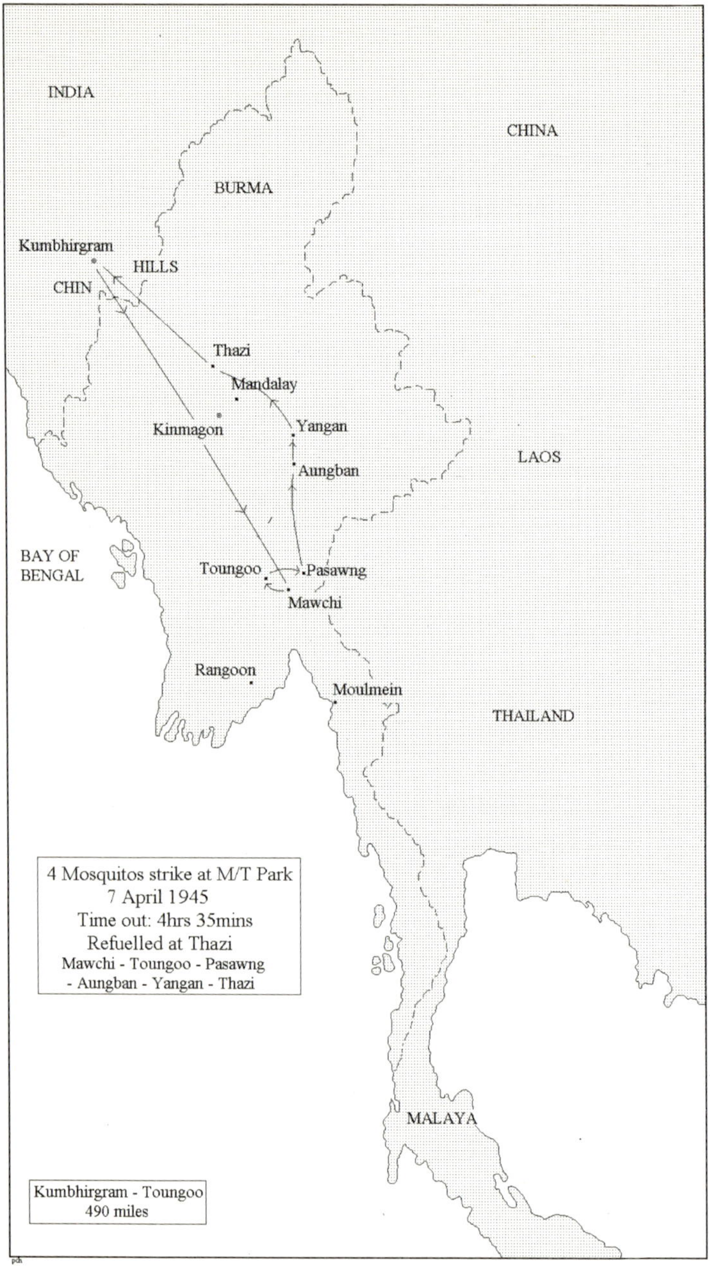
INDIA
CHINA
BURMA
Kumbhirgram
HILLS
CHIN
Thazi
Mandalay
Kinmagon
Yangan
Aungban
LAOS
BAY OF
BENGAL
Toungoo
Pasawng
Mawchi
Rangoon
Moulmein
THAILAND
4 Mosquitos strike at M/T Park
7 April 1945
Time out: 4hrs 35mins
Refuelled at Thazi
Mawchi - Toungoo - Pasawng
- Aungban - Yangan - Thazi
MALAYA
Kumbhirgram - Toungoo
490 miles

airfield. He was severely wounded. He managed to gain a little height and ordered his navigator, Flying Officer Eric Fisher, to bale out. Scottie too managed to bale out, both men reaching the ground safely. Unfortunately Scottie was to die almost immediately through loss of blood. Their aircraft crashed in the jungle over one hundred miles behind the front line in enemy territory. Eric Fisher, as he later recalled, was very surprised when approached by a young Burmese man who made friendly signs. Apparently Eric had come down in an area controlled by Force 136. Force 136 promoted, trained and supported resistance groups behind the Japanese lines. Secrecy was so obsessive that it wasn't until you were down in the jungle, as Eric was, that aircrew knew of their existence. By 1945 Force 136 agents were giving invaluable help in identifying targets and sending back reports on the results achieved by the attacking aircraft. Many aircrew who baled out over the jungle were guided by members of Force 136 back to the Allied lines. It was all so secret that most of us who flew on operations knew very little of this guerrilla activity in Japanese held territory. It was perhaps as well. If captured and tortured, which very sadly did happen, we had little to give away. Eric was shuttled from friendly village to friendly village and eventually, quite casually, walked back into our mess at Kumbhirgram only three weeks later, a cheerful but rather subdued individual.

Perhaps it was just a coincidence but on 16 April, just two days after losing 'Scottie', all available aircrew attended a lecture on the escape organisation behind enemy lines, from Flight Lieutenant R H Huxtable and Flight Lieutenant K McVicar, who came especially to Kumbhirgram from HQ RAF Burma to update us on escape tactics. The message was still the same. If you crashed in enemy territory and suffered severe injury the .38 Smith and Wesson was there as a last resort.

On 15 April, as an interesting diversion, Tommy and I, missing the 'escape organisation' lectures, were flown by Dakota (DC3) to Dum Dum outside Calcutta, and then on to Poona, still by Dakota, to collect and fly back a brand new Mosquito RF672 as one of the replacement aircraft for the Beaufighters of 'B' Flight. Long range drop tanks were fitted, with another supplementary tank in the bomb bay. The flight across India took five hours and thirty five minutes, covering one thousand three hundred miles nearly equal to a flight from London to Sicily. We were glad to be back but very sorry to hear that we had lost yet another experienced crew killed in a Mosquito crashing on a night take-off on 17 April carrying two 500lb bombs which exploded and burnt out the aircraft. Flight Lieutenant Butler and Flight Sergeant Robson, who had just joined the squadron, were killed. Within the space of ten weeks we had lost five crews on operations and one crew through a flying accident. Two of the pilots killed were 'A' Flight Commanders. Over twenty five percent of our operational crew strength lost in just a few weeks was quite a sobering thought. Many other crews flying over Burma, in a great variety of aircraft and in all manner of roles took risks too, which were compounded by the terrain and the climate.

On flights out of Kumbhirgram we kept our VHF receiver switched on to receive any message, particularly weather reports, diversions to other airfields or courses to fly back to base. On the flight from Poona to Kumbhirgram in RF672 we heard a 'Mayday' from an American Army Airforce B17 (Flying Fortress) flying over the 'hump' to Kunming with supplies for Chiang Kai Shek's forces in China. Flying the 'hump', was a distance of over eight hundred miles, with nearly half over the mountains of Yunnan Province and its peaks of over twelve thousand feet. We understood B17 crews were only allowed thirty minutes spare fuel in order to maximise the load. An inevitable tragedy followed if you strayed off course. Flying from bases in Bengal to China was a hazardous business and done by very courageous USAAF crews. Not all survived to relate their experiences. Many years later I was able to visit the USAAF Museum at Travis Airfield, north of San Francisco, where the story of the tremendous logistical support given by the USAAF to all the armies fighting for the Allies in the Far East is recorded and remembered. Nothing was possible in Burma without the total commitment of the crews both in the air and on the ground who flew and serviced the vast number of transport aircraft, both RAF and USAAF, supplying the 14th Army and the front line squadrons.

On 22 April with Warrant Officer Jimmy Gibson and his navigator Warrant Officer Pete Rostance flying as our No.2, Tommy and I led a very successful strike against Bamwegu railway station south of Meiktila, starting large fires with many explosions in the target area, probably from fuel or ammunition stores. These intensive harrying operations in April against lines of communication continued right through May and June from our future base at Kinmagon in central Burma. The next day on 23 April, leading a formation of two Mosquitos each carrying two five hundred pound bombs, we bombed and strafed two Japanese encampments at Taunggyi and Shwenyaung identified as holding areas for Japanese troops and motor transport retreating east from Meiktila, the vital road and rail junction and airfield complex 80 miles south of Mandalay, which the Japanese 33rd Army had desperately tried to defend. We left several large fires adding further harassment to the retreating Japanese. The airfield at Meiktila, with its two parallel strips, was finally cleared of Japanese troops by the end of March. This was our last sortie out of Kumbhirgram flying Mosquito 'D' HR518. We flew a total of eighteen sorties in this aircraft before it was crash landed by Flight Lieutenant Bill Hughes on 17 May, following flak damage to the landing wheels. Both Bill and his navigator John Kent escaped unhurt.

On 9 April 1945 Air Vice-Marshal S F Vincent sent a signal to all squadrons of 221 Group congratulating 'all wings and squadrons on the remarkably satisfying month's operations in March. January and February figures were good, but the figures for March in every respect have beaten all Group records'. He goes on to say, 'The numbers of sorties and hours flown by pilots, and hours worked by groundcrews, are in direct proportion to the successes gained against the enemy'. [G R T W1] The signal also indicated that a small reduction in activity during April would be essential to give a little time to regroup and to be ready for the final push to clear the Japanese out of central Burma. The

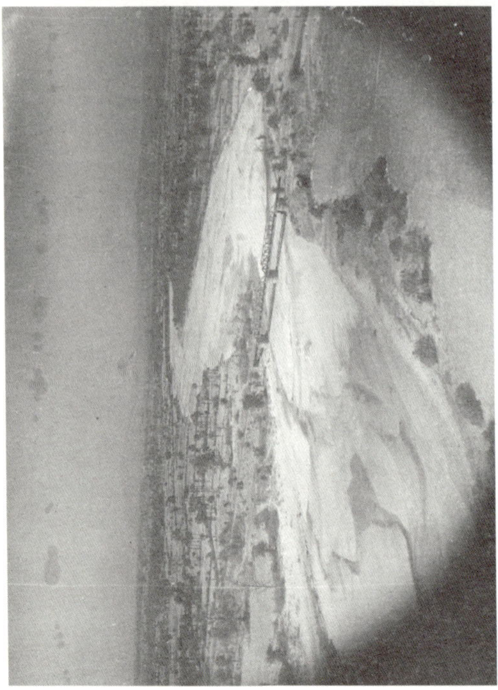

G Thewlis

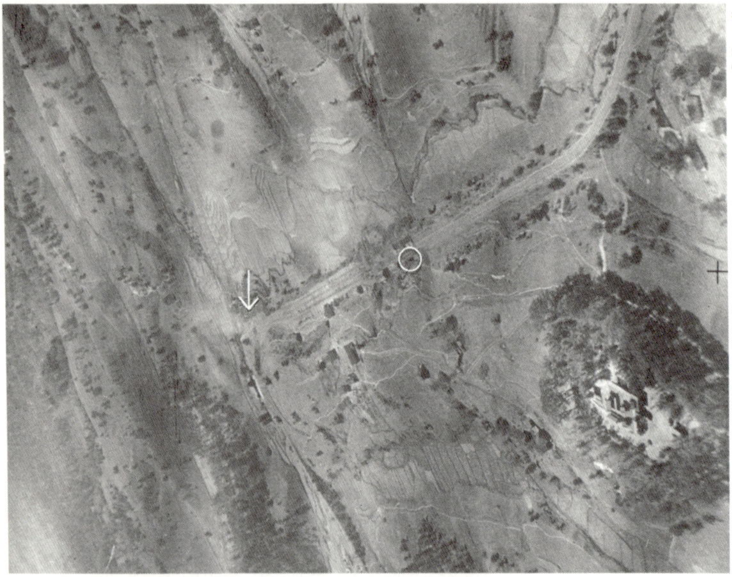

G Thewlis

Above: 82 Squadron, target ahead, bridge over the Chindwin.

Right: 82 Squadron, onto a train (arrowed) and an engine (circled), Central Burma.

47 Squadron, June 1945, Officers' lines at Kinmagon.

GRT Willis Archives

J Gibson Archives

J Gibson Archives

July 1945, monsoon weather at Kinmagon.

GRT Willis Archives

Above: 47 Squadron, May 1945, Mosquito FBVI at Kinmagon, Central Burma with the cockpit door open.

Below: May 1945, Kinmagon, Tommy Thompson and the artist Frank Harding.

GRT Willis Archives

future strategy to be pursued by 47 Squadron, as part of 221 Group, was to continue attacks by day and night on troop concentrations, gun emplacements, enemy transport and encampments on road, rail or river.

April closed with the loss of three aircraft together with their experienced crews. However, by the end of the month the squadron had received twelve new Mosquitos which were checked out and passed as fit for operations. These new aircraft enabled 'B' Flight to convert back to Mosquitos, giving us at long last an all Mosquito squadron. The remaining Beaufighters were ferried away to a Maintenance Unit by various non-operational aircrew. The pressure on aircrew and groundcrew, in the difficult climatic conditions, clearly played a part in the losses which befell the squadron as it responded to the needs of the day. The servicing of aircraft was now easier for 47 Squadron Servicing Echelon there being no need to carry two sets of spares.

As April operations continued from Kumbhirgram, preparations were put in place to move the Mosquito squadrons further forward. It was operationally vital to maintain air support for the advancing ground forces if they were to reach Rangoon by early May. Spitfires and Hurricanes moved into Sinthe, with its twin runways of two thousand yards each, situated 110 miles south west of Mandalay and some twenty miles to the north west of the Irrawaddy. Kinmagon, sixty miles south west of Mandalay, designated to be 47 Squadron's new base, was just over fifty miles from Sinthe. We would now have fighter protection from any intruder Japanese aircraft. Before leaving Kumbhirgram Daily Routine Orders displayed messages of congratulations to all personnel, which had been received from His Majesty the King, the Prime Minister and the Supreme Commander, following the capture of Mandalay. It was particularly pleasing to receive at the squadron a copy of the Order of the Day from Lieutenant General Sir Montagu Stopford, Commanding XXXIII Corps, sincerely thanking all units of the Royal Air Force and USAAF who had supported XXXIII Corps as they crossed the Irrawaddy and went on to capture Mandalay.

During April, when activities were not nearly so intensive as in March, the squadron flew one hundred and forty four sorties from Kumbhirgram for a total of six hundred and forty two hours, dropped eighty seven 500lb bombs and fired one hundred 60lb and four 25lb rockets together with over one hundred thousand rounds of all types of ammunition.

On 18 April, with operations continuing from Kumbhirgram, a large party left by seven Dakotas to prepare Kinmagon for our future arrival. On 19 April a further party left in a convoy of nineteen 3 ton trucks, with some of the squadron's heavy lighting units and the outdoor cinema equipment, on the long and tedious road journey over the Chin Hills to Kinmagon. Filson-Young made sure that the Group, to be based at Kinmagon, would not be deprived of its cinema, despite a signal that only essential equipment went into Burma. On 26 April we parted company with 45 and 82 Squadrons who left to join 901 Wing at Joari, to be deployed in direct support of the planned assault by amphibious forces landing on the banks of the Rangoon River, downstream from Rangoon, Operation DRACULA. Following the capture of Rangoon on 2 May, 82 Squadron moved to 47 Squadron's old base at Cholaveram to prepare for the planned invasion of Malaya, operation ZIPPER. From 24 April to 30 April inclusive, the rest of 908 Wing and 47 Squadron, including 7047 Servicing Echelon, were moved by a flight of five Dakotas to Kinmagon to join the first party sent out on 18 April. Much to the credit of all personnel, many of whom had experienced several moves with the squadron over thousands of miles, operational flights were recommenced immediately on arrival of the aircraft at their new base. By the end of the month all three hundred or more squadron personnel, together with their aircraft, tentage and equipment, were well established on this new airfield.

Kinmagon was a typical Japanese forward airfield with a 2,000 yard strip and complete with anti-blast shelters for the aircraft at dispersal. When the monsoon arrived the whole area was subject to severe flooding. Nevertheless, Kinmagon was to be home to 47 Squadron until the end of hostilities in Burma. This base, a tented encampment, located fifteen miles east of Myingyan, a town of around fifty thousand people on the Irrawaddy, had at least moved us much nearer the enemy. Forty miles to the south west was Mount Popa rising five thousand feet from the central plain. Containing a monastery and a shrine this mountain was reputed to be the home of King Cobras. It was to prove to be a very useful landmark from the air. Unless on official duties, all towns and civilian areas were out of bounds. There was too much of the legacy of war around for any personal ventures away from the airfield. Conditions were very basic, again with groundcrew of up to six men housed in small ridge tents sleeping on ground sheets and makeshift beds. We too felt a little cramped, Tommy and I sharing a similar sized tent with our camping kit and a few luxuries such as books and records we had flown in with us. We all had to do our bit, including erecting the tent and digging trenches around it, hoping we would not be flooded out. The mess was a large marquee with its inevitable 'bar'. Temperatures during the afternoon could reach 110°F. Most work on aircraft maintenance and arming for sorties during the daylight hours was done stripped to the waist. Fuel came in by Dakota in 44 gallon drums, along with new postings, mail, rations and spares. Refuelling was a tedious task using hand pumps, carried out as far as possible in the comparative cool of the evening. Covering up came at dusk, essential to avoid the onset of mosquitoes. If no duty called, we escaped under the mosquito net, sitting on the camp bed, writing letters back 'home' by the light of a pressure lamp or just sleeping. Drinking and washing water came from a local chaung, which despite being heavily chlorinated, initially resulted in diarrhoea amongst most of the personnel. Fortunately after two to three days most of us had recovered. The Doc made sure we were all up to date with our inoculations against cholera and smallpox and that the deeply cut latrines, dug by locally recruited Burmese, were kept under control. Small marquees served as the Operations Room, squadron headquarters, parachute store, equipment store, flight offices, medical centre, and for the officers', sergeants' and airmen's mess. Operational needs were also changing as all our Mosquitos were now modified to carry 500lb bombs. We were expected to shoot straight, fire rocket projectiles and drop 500lb bombs, as and when needed, all with a high level of accuracy. Quite a mixed bag of skills.

Letters written to Joan from Kinmagon said very little about flying operations apart from how tiring they were. Operational secrecy did prevail. The climate was described as being very hot and humid, with the minimum of clothing worn during the day. Squadron reports to 221 Group sometimes complained of mail delays and poor food but as everybody knew we were winning, morale was very good. If the airfield was temporarily flooded mail was dropped by parachute. Sport figured largely in all letters with rugby, football and handball still the main active leisure pursuits. When in India, either near Madras or in Assam, there were always bearers (registered followers) to hand to attend to all our domestic needs, particularly tea making (char) and clothes washing, pressing and mending. Once in Burma it was a rather different story as it was forbidden to take Indian servants into that theatre. However, friendly Burmese soon infiltrated from the local villages anxious to earn a little by washing our clothes, with much pounding in the nearby 'chaung'. Further letters to Joan spoke of the great satisfaction I had in having continuous correspondence with a girlfriend far away in Scotland. The lack of female company, as reflected in letters home, was certainly felt quite keenly by most squadron members. The sending and receiving of letters was an essential element in maintaining everybody's spirits as we flew on operations against a stubborn and cruel enemy, which in one letter written at this time I described as being 'an uncivilised and sordid business'.

On 14 April the squadron received another signal from Air Vice-Marshal Vincent congratulating all personnel on the achievements of the past three months. Reverting to the wider picture, we hardly realised that the defeat of the Japanese forces in Burma by the 14th Army had depended very largely upon the skill and commitment of the hundreds of pilots and aircrews of the joint US/British Air Transport Command. As previously noted, they kept the forward forces supplied by air with all the essential elements of war as the advance towards Rangoon was pushed ahead. The XIV Army did not waste any time. From 12 April the advance from Chauk on the Irrawaddy and Pyawbwe south of Meiktila made steady progress south against varying levels of resistance. 5th Division reached Pyinmana on 19 April occupying the airfield at Lewe the next day. Two days later came an attack on that airfield by eight Oscars, a defiant and rare appearance by the Japanese Air Force. On 22 April 5th Division were in Toungoo with its two important airfields which were quickly brought into use, bringing in supplies by the 24th of the month. On the 29th twelve Oscars made their last attempt in Burma to disrupt the supply of men and materials moving into Toungoo and southwards towards the ultimate prize, the capture of Rangoon before the monsoon brought its own problems. Spitfires and Hurricanes based at Toungoo quickly established unchallenged air superiority essential in maintaining protection of the air supply routes to the forward troops pushing on towards their goal. There was no time to waste. For 47 Squadron the escape routes out of central Burma were now the prime targets.

On 2 May, with Operation DRACULA in full swing, troops began to go ashore on the banks of the Rangoon river, 20 miles downstream from Rangoon. Following a heavy aerial bombardment of the landing area, there was no opposition. Troops were in Rangoon later that day. The Japanese had moved out to regroup around Moulmein or escape into Thailand.

Tommy and I flew our first operation out of Kinmagon also on 2 May, flying 'D' HR518 in a formation of six Mosquitos. The monsoon weather was already upon us. Huge thunderstorms, with storm clouds rising well over twenty five thousand feet, built up in the afternoon when the heavens opened. This monsoon weather forced our return to base with both the primary and secondary targets impossible to reach. Immediately on landing we enlarged the ditches around the tent which we had previously moved to a gently sloping site to give us better drainage. The rain came down in torrents, tent floors were awash, and the open latrines overflowed. Everybody learnt to cope, helping one another and generally managing to keep reasonably dry. It was quite remarkable at how quickly the sun dried out the ground the moment the thunderstorm passed. After the rains spirits were restored once again, stripped to the waist, the groundcrew did all they could to keep us flying. The open air cinema was established but cigarettes, fruit drinks and canteen amenities were in very short supply. The food or 'rations', as it was normally termed, were generally felt to be poor both in quality and quantity. The comradeship fostered in those days has stayed with many old squadron members, of all ranks, still meeting in reunions at least once a year.

As for operations against the enemy we became very expert in assessing the weather hazards and seeking out secondary targets when monsoon clouds blocked our way as we flew south. Extensive briefing was given by the Meteorological Officers from the 717 Weather Forecast Centre on the dangers of flying into monsoon clouds. For many it was quite important to know whether the likely weather would affect the evening film show at the open air cinema. For aircrew it was essential to avoid, if at all possible, monsoon cloud, particularly cumulo-nimbus which were always treated with grave suspicion and given a wide berth. Aircraft flying on some operations had been known to become totally uncontrollable due to the severe turbulence encountered when venturing into heavy monsoon cloud. Squadron Leader G L Gotch, 'A' Flight Commander of 82 Squadron had circulated a memo on his experience of loss of control in cumulo-nimbus cloud when he was lucky to escape in one piece. Fortunately, for our airfield in central Burma, the south-west monsoon was less severe than in the hill regions and in the Irrawaddy delta. We could expect heavy thunderstorms with extensive turbulence over base every five to seven days with widespread low cloud and haze prevalent on many other days.

Back to operations, we had better luck with the weather the next day 3 May. In a formation of four Mosquitos, still flying 'D' HR518 and led by Bill Bailey, the targets were Japanese supply bases and assembly areas on the railway at Pegu and on the Peg river at Kawa twenty miles north east of Rangoon. Many buildings were hit, each aircraft carrying two 500lb bombs. A medium sized sampan spotted on the river was strafed and damaged. The Pegu valley was a major line of retreat and supply for Japanese forces moving away from Rangoon. This route was very important to them in evacuating a reasonable fighting force into Thailand or Malaya. Adverse weather conditions the next day, 4 May, caused another sortie we were engaged in to be abandoned despite all our efforts to reach alternative targets. Rising at 4.30am for an early start to beat the build up of storm clouds and then to be thwarted by adverse conditions was a frustration we had to put up with. The very next day on 5 May in 'J' HR516 we tried again, leading a formation of two aircraft, successfully damaging or sinking several camouflaged river boats at Henzada on the Irrawaddy eighty miles north west of Rangoon. Small groups of Japanese were moving down the Irrawaddy and then striking east towards Pegu. Japanese forces commanded by Major-General Matsui were retreating from Pegu, a major town forty miles north-east of Rangoon, that had been captured by the 17th Division on 30 April. There was now only one way out for the enemy and that was eastwards to the Sittang River and then south to Moulmein. We were to pay particular attention to all lines of communication, river crossings and bridges on this line of retreat as the Japanese tried to slip away.

On 8 May Germany surrendered unconditionally and the war in Europe was over. When the news of the German surrender reached the squadron the reaction was a little muted. We had no reason to believe that the end of the war in the Far East was near. In many ways VE Day was a non-event with everybody carrying on as if nothing of significance had happened. The southern strip of Burma, all of Malaya, Siam and Singapore were still in Japanese hands - not to mention all of the then Dutch East Indies, and the many thousands of POWs and civilian detainees. We continued with our mail censoring, as a rather embarrassing chore, with most letters home reflecting the general wish to get back to the UK as soon as possible. Many squadron servicemen felt forgotten and unappreciated, particularly if they had been away from their family for three or four years - which many had. These thoughts were well summed up by Wing Commander G Mayland the CO of 908 Wing reporting at the end of May on the victory in Europe and the fall of Rangoon that *'everyone is anxious to clear up the mess out here and get home'*. Despite all these anxieties there was certainly no lack of keenness and commitment towards defeating the Japanese as quickly as possible. Everybody, groundcrew and aircrew, much to their credit, continued to get on with making their individual contribution to the squadron's objectives.

After the capture of Rangoon it was estimated that there were still at least fifty thousand enemy troops in Burma. The RAF Commander-in-Chief, Air Chief Marshal Sir Keith Park, signalled that every effort should be made to prevent their escape into Siam (Thailand) or Malaya where they could re group and fight another day. On 11 May the squadron received yet another 'Order of the Day' from Air Vice-Marshal Vincent, congratulating all concerned on the achievements of the Group in its major contribution to victory in Burma. He went on to say, *'it has been a race to beat the Jap and the monsoon and double victory has been achieved in time. I congratulate every Officer and Airman and am extremely proud to have commanded such a group. All units have been cheerful in their most uncomfortable conditions. All group records for monthly flying and bombing, strafing, and reconnaissance have been beaten two or three times.'* Peace had broken out in Europe, but our war had to go on.

Continuing close co-operation with the army's advancing forces, coupled with intelligence information from Force 136 infiltrated behind the Japanese lines, was essential for the identification of targets in the very fluid situation following the capture of Rangoon. Targets which had been pre-determined were monitored by a Visual Control Post using R/T to communicate with the aircraft formation leader. Given the go ahead signal by the VCP, with the target clearly identified, we then bombed through a high dive technique. This tactic involved forming a 'cab-rank' formation to one side of the target at four to six thousand feet, with each aircraft in turn executing a stall turn followed by a shallow dive adjusted to obtain an accurate path onto the target. HE bombs with an 11 second delay were released at 1,500 feet to give at least one thousand feet of air space in which to pull out. Height and speed were called out by the navigator. Much depended upon the skill of the pilot in the use of his gun sight to obtain accurate hits in the target area.

On 6 May in 'R' HR444 we made our fourth successive sortie in as many days. In a formation of four aircraft, each carrying two 500lb bombs, led by Bill Hughes we were under VCP control over Hlegu north east of Rangoon. Bombs fell in the target area followed by several strafing runs. Two large fires resulted with the target buildings virtually destroyed. A 'well done' message was received from an army colonel on the ground.

With ourselves leading a formation of two aircraft early on 11 and 16 May, down lines of communication in the Salween river valley ranging from Mawchi in the north and down past Papun to the south, we attacked store areas, transport shelters and enemy assembly areas, all pre-determined targets. We were crossing and re-crossing the escape routes to the north east of Rangoon leading across the mountains into Siam (Thailand). The most visible results on these two sorties were four motor transport strafed with one six tonner set on fire together with small fires in the target areas. On the 19 May in 'G' HR486, again leading a formation of two aircraft and guided by an army VCP, we bombed and strafed a Japanese encampment at Wutgyi in the Sittang valley. The same routine was followed on 23 May in 'G' HR486 leading two aircraft on a bombing strike, each aircraft with two 500lb bombs against Augban, an enemy assembly area in the mountains just ninety five miles south east of Kinmagon. Several strafing runs were made with cannon and machine gun on the surrounding trenches. Troops on the ground later reported many Japanese casualties from the attacks on the enemy by 221 Group in the Sittang River area which had to be crossed if the comparative safety south to Moulmein was to be reached.

On 27 May in a carefully planned strike led by Bill Bailey, now the 'A' Flight Commander, we were briefed as a formation of four Mosquitos to bomb and sink a reported two thousand ton coaster recently arrived in Moulmein harbour, a major port and supply point, across the Andaman Sea to the south east of Rangoon. The briefing for this operation was a reminder of our activities eighteen months before in the Eastern Mediterranean. As we expected substantial anti-aircraft fire in defence of this vessel, surprise was essential. For Tommy and I this was our fifty fifth operational sortie and perhaps one of the most dangerous. As we drove out in an open truck to our aircraft 'R' HR444 stress, which I did not normally show, brought about an urgent desire to go to the toilet. Fortunately there were plenty of scrubby bushes and bamboo readily available for this kind of emergency. Perhaps, as this was our fortieth successive operation over Burma, the inherent tension was beginning to show.

Fully kitted with 'Mae Wests', .38 revolver, emergency packs and maps we approached from the west low over the sea, climbing to fifteen hundred feet ready to attack as the harbour came into view. To our surprise and disappointment there was no large coaster, it had departed, probably during the previous night. The lead aircraft immediately targeted another smaller ship in the harbour estimated to be about three hundred and fifty tons. Each aircraft carrying two five hundred pound HE bombs with eleven second delay fuses bombed this secondary target with many near misses. We had come a long way with little to show for it. Bill Bailey signalled that, coming in again, we would make a strafing run on two schooners in the harbour plus the small coaster we had just bombed but was still afloat. This we did, up came the flak, quite intense, both light and heavy. By good fortune no aircraft was hit. This was just as well, as knowing how accurate the Japanese could be in firing at low flying aircraft, it had been resolved at the pre-flight briefing that a second strafing run would not be attempted against this well defended harbour, once the element of surprise had been lost. Nevertheless, disappointed that our main target had departed, Bill decided on a second run. All the formation followed without a second thought. Coming in low, climbing to one thousand feet and then diving onto the targets all four aircraft hit the two schooners and the coaster with cannon and machine gun. We broke away low over the sea and set course for home.

Not all such operations were completed without loss. Twelve days before on 15 May eight Mosquitos led by Wing Commander Filson-Young with navigator Flight Lieutenant R C U Waters were briefed to hit a supply point and a river crossing encampment at Lagunbyo, a small hill town on the road between Bilin and Dapu on the east bank of the Bilin River. Through Lagunbyo ran an escape route from the Sittang River valley south towards Thaton, Moulmein and ultimately into Malaya. All eight aircraft in two formations of four arrived over the target as planned. Warrant Officer Bill Powell in close formation as No.2 to Filson-Young takes up the story.

"The weather was reasonable and we found the target without much difficulty. Lagunbyo was situated in a valley and each of us was to drop our two 500 pounders in a dive bombing attack. The CO waved to me in the No.2 position and then peeled off to the left diving on to the target area at an angle of about 45ø. I followed suit and as I looked down, half way through my diving turn, saw to my horror the CO's aircraft crash and explode in a colossal fireball. My navigator's view must have been partly obscured by the angle and partly perhaps by me. In the Mosquito the navigator's seat is on the right of the pilot and about two feet behind. Maurice was completely unaware of what had happened."

Bill goes on to say, *"I must have been in something of a daze as I made my attack, dropping both my bombs into the target area and then carrying out a strafing attack with the cannon on buildings which came into the gun sight as I pulled out of the dive. Only then was I able to switch on the intercom and let the other two crews in the first flight and the leader of the second flight, which was now close to the target, know what had happened. All seven aircraft carried out their attacks and returned safely to base. The whole squadron was devastated when they heard the bad news of the tragic deaths of our gallant Commanding Officer and of Flying Officer Waters, who fate had deemed should be the navigator on that fatal operation."*

Filson-Young's regular navigator Flight Lieutenant D T P O'D McGlory had only days before been declared tour expired and had left the squadron on leave. Wing Commander Filson-Young was also tour expired with two hundred and thirty two operational sorties to his credit, but he could not resist having one last go before leaving the squadron. It truly was, as Bill later described it, "One 'Op' too many."

Again Bill takes up the story. *"Much later the news filtered through to us that the headman of the village of Lagunbyo had been questioned by some of our guerrilla friends shortly after our attack. He said that at the time many Japanese troops were in the village and they had been defending themselves with 40mm anti-aircraft guns and machine guns. The obvious conclusion was that the CO's aircraft had been shot up as he dived towards the target area giving him and his navigator no chance to bail out. Neither body was ever discovered and little trace of the Mosquito was ever found; possibly much of the wreckage would have been carried rapidly downstream by the Bilin River which is deep and swift during the monsoon season. Apparently the surviving Japanese troops pulled out into the narrow southern strip of Burma crossing the River Salween shortly after the attack destroying all their documents beforehand so no details of what had happened from their point of view ever became available."*

Later intelligence confirmed that there were around two thousand five hundred Japanese troops in Lagunbyo when the attack took place in two waves over five minutes.

Bill, who, as already noted, joined 47 Squadron with his navigator Maurice Jones at the same time as myself at Gambut in Libya, goes on to speak for all the squadron's personnel. *"So ended the life of Wing Commander W D L Filson-Young, DFC and Bar. A very gallant gentleman, a courageous and fearless pilot and a superb Commanding Officer of No. 47 Squadron during both the Aegean Sea and the Burma Campaigns of the Second World War. We who were privileged to know him and to serve under him will never forget his qualities as a leader."* Bill went on to stay with 47 Squadron to the very end of hostilities in Burma, completing over sixty operational sorties. He received a well earned DFC.

Filson-Young as a successful commander had always led the squadron by example. It was a great tragedy that this quality proved to be his undoing. He will always be remembered with great affection by all who knew him and served with him on the ground and in the air. He had courage, competence and compassion in abundance.

When these tragic events took place the squadron was still awaiting a new Commanding Officer. Flight Lieutenant J H E Etherton, DFC, Commanding Officer of 'B' Flight took temporary command until Wing Commander Victor Duclos DFC, our new Commanding Officer, arrived following a posting from 45 Squadron. Even though the new Commanding Officer's time with the squadron was comparatively short he proved a popular and most effective leader, unofficially referred to as 'The Duke'.

To both aircrew and groundcrew the loss of the Filson-Young and his navigator Roger Waters was a severe blow. Within the space of just over three months we had lost two flight commanders and now the Commanding Officer, all shot down over Japanese held territory. When news came into flying control at Kinmagon on 15 May from Filson-Young's formation that he was lost, I was standing on top of one of the aircraft anti-blast shelters in dispersal watching the returning aircraft. Thousands of miles away from home and with the war in Europe over, there was much speculation in the mess as to how our war would end. Knowing that there was still a hard slog ahead, the squadron's morale stood the test arising from the loss of Filson-Young remarkably well. There was no pause in our operational tasks with Tommy and I despatched the very next day, 16 May, in 'D' HR518 to lead a formation of two Mosquitos down the lines of communication in the Sittang river valley area as previously described. This continuing activity in May and June, through bombing sorties under VCP control and against lines of communication, led to further reports to 221 Group from IV Corps, 5th and 17th Divisions that we had inflicted many casualties on the Japanese 28th Army Group which was trying to break out across the Sittang. I felt no elation at our apparent success. We all wanted the war in the Far East to be brought to a successful conclusion as quickly as possible. On 31 May flying RF701 carrying two 500lb bombs and long range tanks, as part of a formation of four Mosquitos led by Flight Lieutenant Etherington, we bombed Japanese positions west of Kaywe on the escape route running south to Paung and Moulmein. We followed with strafing runs on the target area. It was our fifty sixth operational sortie.

The squadron had been operating on its own out of Kinmagon during early May. On 20 May 110(Hyderabad) Squadron, under Wing Commander A E Saunders, joined us with their Mosquitos. On 2 May the wing commander had landed his Mosquito on Mingaladon airfield on the outskirts of Rangoon, noting that the Japanese had stolen away. He had arrived before the 14th Army coming up the Rangoon River under Operation DRACULA. 110 Squadron were a welcome addition to our strength. Kinmagon was a far from ideal airfield in heavy monsoon weather, the runway becoming unserviceable after heavy thunderstorms. To partially overcome this problem a detachment was based at Meiktila with its all-weather strip, flying from 16 May to 19 June many sorties against enemy lines of communication. Tommy and I stayed in Kinmagon. The weather, together with the loss of the CO and his navigator, were not the end of our troubles. On 21 May Mike Mackay, in charge of the squadron's servicing echelon, grounded all the squadron Mosquitos for inspection, following the discovery of a fault in the woodwork of one of the main planes. Out of our strength of only sixteen Mosquitos nine were rendered unserviceable pending further investigation and repair. As with the monsoon weather we took these setbacks in our stride as Mike sent urgent signals to Group requesting replacement aircraft. On 23, 24 and 25 May the rain came down in torrents. Even our jeeps could not get about, although it was remarkable to see how quickly the ground dried out in the hot climate during the dry spells.

Wing Commander Victor Duclos joined the squadron on 15 June, together with several replacement crews direct from the UK. With the war in Europe over, long-serving Canadian and Australian crews were being withdrawn for posting back home. There was a large pool of newly trained aircrew available in the UK anxious to take their place. June came in with preparations at the highest level to attack and defeat the Japanese left in Burma south of the Bilin river, and then on to Malaya and Singapore. 221 Group HQ was now based at Mingaladon on the northern edge of Rangoon with a new AOC, Air Vice-Marshal C A Bouchier, taking over from Air Vice-Marshal S F Vincent. Despite very difficult weather conditions there was no pause in operations against the enemy by the squadrons of 221 Group. June, following the pattern in May, turned out to be very wet, with temperatures up to 110øF in the afternoons and humidity often at 100%. Flying often involved going through heavy rain with the reduced visibility making it far from easy in trying to judge the way forward through towering masses of cloud. The windscreen wiper worked overtime. Further backup came to Kinmagon with the arrival on 1 and 4 June of 34 and 113 Squadron Thunderbolts, who immediately commenced their own operations, bombing and strafing the enemy in retreat. We saw little of these squadrons dispersed as they were at the other side of the Kinmagon strip.

With the monsoon weather in full swing, we put in much effort scouring the escape roads south down the Salween river valley towards Moulmein, often guided to targets by Force 136 operating in the area. On 2 June, in RF757 carrying two 500lb HE bombs with 11 second delay fuses, as part of a strike force of six Mosquitos including two from 110 Squadron, led by Flight Lieutenant Gus Gieselman, a Canadian from 47 Squadron, we bombed and strafed Japanese gun positions at Pauggyi. On this same sortie we also strafed camp areas at Duyinzeik and Pa-an to the north of Moulmein. A further typical operation in RF713 was on 5 June, as part of a formation of four Mosquitos, on this occasion carrying four 500lb bombs, and led by Flight Lieutenant Milroy, another of our Canadian pilots. We bombed a concentration of approximately five hundred Japanese infantry together with a large Wireless Transmission station at Nyaungbo, ten miles north of Thaton. Thaton, a town with a population of over fifty thousand, is situated on the main escape road and rail route south to Moulmein. The weather was 5/10 cumulo nimbus cloud up to fifteen thousand feet. With long range tanks fitted we left just after dawn hoping to escape the storm clouds which would build up later in the day. The mission was highly successful with all the bombs exploding in the target area. The W/T station was set on fire after a sustained attack by cannon and machine gun. A total of thirty one strafing runs were made causing extensive damage to the Japanese camp. Our aircraft fired four hundred and fifty 20mm shells and one thousand rounds of .303 machine gun bullets. As on other occasions, a later report indicated that we had very effectively dispersed the Japanese troop concentration, inflicting many casualties.

Returning from this operation in loose formation at around ten thousand feet, between the most picturesque cloud formations towering over the mountains to the east and with the river Salween glistening below, it was difficult to believe that behind us was a Burmese village which, having sheltered the enemy, was now quite devastated after being heavily bombed and then blasted by our cannon fire. The country below, a jungle covered green and hilly landscape between the Sittang and Salween rivers with the mountains of western Siam in the distance, looked so peaceful and attractive. On the lower slopes of the hills and in the valleys were the terraced paddy fields green and lush with large stretches of water shimmering in the morning sun. Down there the Burmese were striving to grow their staple food, rice, in a country recently conquered and over-run by a cruel and ruthless army, now in desperate retreat after suffering heavy losses. Flying back that day I was all too aware of the havoc and destruction this war had brought to the towns and villages of central Burma. The towns which straddled the main roads and railways down the central plain had suffered appalling damage with numerous stone buildings totally wrecked and many of the bamboo 'bashas' in the villages burnt out. Liaison meetings with the army and journeys to supply points by pick-up truck, as the advance into Burma continued, brought us face to face with this destruction in town and village. It was sad to see, as we drove past, the bewildered homeless children and the ubiquitous Buddhist monks, in their saffron robes, wending their way on foot in silent contemplation along the unmade rutted roads, as the machinery of war passed them by.

It was not long, taking advantage of a short break in the monsoon weather, before we were back again down the coast to Moulmein. On 18 June in RF757 with two 500lb bombs, in a formation with two other Mosquitos, led by Bill Hughes, we bombed an identified Japanese camp east of Moulmein, with further attacks on stores areas south of Thaton. Accurate light ack-ack was encountered damaging aircraft 'O' flown by Bill Hughes who made an emergency crash landing at Hmawbi, a recently captured airfield thirty miles to the north of Rangoon, later to be home to 47 Squadron.

Amid all this activity South East Asia Command was anxious to remind the world that Burma, or at least most of it, had been liberated and a crushing defeat imposed upon the Japanese forces. The Supreme Allied Commander, Lord Mountbatten, decreed that there should be a Victory Parade, including a flypast by the RAF, over Rangoon on 15 June. This parade was to be held on the western side of the world famous Shwedagon Pagoda. Lord Mountbatten would address the parade from a raised dais at the western entrance to the Pagoda. The Shwedagon Pagoda is a two thousand five hundred year old, world famous and much revered, shrine of the Buddhist faith. Standing three hundred and twenty six feet high, with its gold covered dome gleaming in the sun, it would be a truly impressive backdrop to the victory celebrations.

The victory flypast was planned to include formations of Spitfires, Thunderbolts and Mosquitos of the RAF together with B25 Mitchells, P38 Lightenings and Liberators of the USAAF. Over the parade ground the aircraft were to descend to five hundred feet in salute then regain height to fifteen hundred feet after the flypast. The Mosquito formation was to be made up of twelve aircraft drawn from 47 and 110 Squadrons. On the day, 15 June, the monsoon weather was awful with towering cloud banks between Kinmagon and Rangoon. Tommy and I felt it was quite an honour to be a part of our formation led by Squadron Leader J H E Etherington, the temporary CO. We took off mid-morning along with the Mosquitos of 110 Squadron flying in four sections of three and all carrying long range tanks with our IFF (Identification, Friend or Foe) switched on. Flying through heavy rain and skirting the towering cloud banks we arrived at the assembly area just north of Rangoon to discover that only the Spitfires, based at Mingaladon airfield close by our rendezvous, had managed to arrive. Nothing daunted, with the Spitfires in the lead, the flypast proceeded. The perseverance of the Mosquito formation, covering well over seven hundred miles through and around the monsoon storm clouds, was duly acknowledged by a personal signal to 47 and 110 Squadrons from 221 Group's new Air Officer Commanding, Air Vice-Marshal C A Bouchier, simply saying: *'Well done. Your splendid effort and good formation maintained in appalling weather for the Rangoon Parade greatly appreciated. Please convey my congratulations to all aircrews.'*

CHAPTER 11
AFTER RANGOON: VJ DAY AND BEYOND

Following the capture of Rangoon, the liberation of Malaya and Singapore were the next strategic objectives for South East Asia Command. For Japan the war was still very much a fight to the bitter end, with many of the Japanese forces prepared to make supreme sacrifices to impede or push back the Allied advance.

Instructions from the Supreme Allied Commander, Lord Mountbatten, to the squadrons of 221 Group were quite unequivocal; seek out and destroy the retreating Japanese and as far as possible prevent them from re-grouping. During June, despite the monsoon weather, with the strip unserviceable for five days from 8 - 12 June due to severe thunderstorms, Tommy and I successfully completed five long distance sorties. They were generally strikes against pre-determined targets in formations of four aircraft or with another Mosquito as our No.2. The area of operations on which the squadron concentrated was to the east of the Sittang River and down the coast roads towards Moulmein. About thirty thousand Japanese troops, mainly from the 28th Army, were reported to be trying to re-group, prior to moving east over the mountains into Siam or south past Thaton and down the Burma-Siam Railway. It was interesting to learn that our old forward landing ground at Thazi had been abandoned and along with many other rear area strips was to be 'returned to cultivation'.

After our sixtieth operational sortie on 23 June whcn we led two Mosquitos on a bombing strike against road bridges east of Bilin, Tommy, who had flown with me on every sortie to date, learnt that he was on an immediate posting to the UK. This was an urgent assignment to familiarise navigators, coming out to the Far East, on the very different conditions to expect in Burma. This posting, certainly most pleasing to Tommy, was quite a shock to me. I was now on my own in our small ridge tent. An experienced crew who had flown together since July 1943 in Beaufighters and Mosquitos was broken up without warning. I was still required to carry on. My new navigator Flight Sergeant Churchill, just out from the UK, was a very pleasant and keen individual but quite new to operations in Burma. Without Tommy, but quite confident in my new navigator's skills, operations continued.

Our first sortie together was on 28 June. We were briefed to fly as No.2 to Squadron Leader J H E Etherington on a search and destroy mission over the Burma-Siam Railway south of Moulmein. The weather was awful with towering banks of thunderstorm clouds in the Moulmein area. We had to be satisfied with secondary targets on the road between Thaton and Pa-an, strafing pre-identified Japanese holding areas. On 3 July, with my new navigator, and leading a formation of three Mosquitos with two five hundred pound HE bombs on each aircraft, we bombed and strafed Japanese quarters and stores twelve miles south of Mokpalin on the coast road running south over the Bilin river towards Thaton and Moulmein. Large fires were left in the target area.

What was to be my last operational flight with 47 Squadron was on 5 July 1945 when I led a formation of two Mosquitos on a bombing mission to Kyaikto, quite close to the target hit two days before. Both aircraft, each carrying four 500lb HE bombs, took off from base as dawn was breaking to get the best of the very difficult weather conditions. Kyaikto was an important Japanese assembly area on the main highway and railway running from Rangoon to Moulmein, just to the north of the river Bilin. All the bombs fell in the target area. Other targets we were briefed to strafe were covered in thick cloud and abandoned. That same day, on returning from this mission, I flew the squadron Harvard down to Toungoo airfield which had featured so much in our operational activities over the previous months. I picked up and returned to

Watercolour painting of Mosquito D HR518 at Kinmagon by Frank Harding.

GRT Willis Archives

J Gibson Archives

84 Squadron Mosquitos on flooded standing, operating over Java 1945/46.

G Thewlis

Above: 82 Squadron, Madras, July 1945, Mosquito RF792 fitted with RP rails.

Below: 47 Squadron, Kinmagon, Officers and Sergeants team - Intersection Cup Winners. Back l to r: Doc Bamford, Bert Reich, Maurice Jones, Jack Wallace. Middle l to r: Jimmy Gibson, Ron Watson, Ernie Bevan. Front l to r: Johnny Rogers, H Fishwick, Fred Poree, Bill Powell, Les Francis.

GRT Willis Archives

R Davis

47 Squadron, Meiktila, September 1945. Back l to r: F/L Pete Cardno, F/L Van Weede, F/O Mike Saunders, W/O Fred Poree, F/Sgt Flower, F/L Watson, W/O Maurice Jones, Sgt Wright.
Middle l to r: F/Sgt Greenhill, W/O Pete Rostance, F/L Powell, F/O Reg Davis, S/L Bill Bailey, S/L Dunlop, W/O Tommy Thompson, F/Sgt Horton, Sgt Doyle.
Front l to r: Sgt Barker, F/Sgt Reich, F/L Wise, W/O Sturt, W/O Smith, W/O Pardoe.

Kinmagon a fellow squadron pilot, Warrant Officer Jimmy Gibson. Jimmy was returning to base after attending an army liaison briefing at Toungoo. A couple of days later he was on a flight by Dakota from Kinmagon to Mingaladon with Bill Powell, both to attend a commissioning board in Rangoon. He and Bill were lucky to make it as the Dakota, in landing, hit a pot hole on the not fully repaired airfield, tipping the aircraft over onto its back. Luckily nobody was seriously injured although Bill turned up with a heavily bandaged head after being struck by some of the cargo which flew past as the plane came to an abrupt stop.

The very next day, 6 July 1945, I was summoned to the CO's tent where Wing Commander V Duclos asked me to make ready for immediate departure to England by air. I was to be posted to an Operational Training Unit for Mosquito crews in England, joining up with Tommy, who was still in Calcutta. We were to be flown to the UK, without delay, to pass on our experience of flying Mosquitos in the very different conditions to those prevailing in the European theatre. Forty eight operational sorties over Burma, many by night, covering just over five months and often in very poor weather conditions, were enough for any Mosquito crew as my second tour came to a close. Over two tours I had clocked up 274 hours in 64 sorties.

My last letter to Joan before leaving the squadron, written on 1 July, was full of good cheer with the usual comment about the sultry weather, the flies and my sporting activities, especially football. There was no hint of any possible return to the UK. Having been with 47 Squadron since 20 November 1943 for a period of over nineteen months, I was certainly feeling like a survivor. Then, when least expecting it, came the good news that I was on my way home. What a joy to be getting away from the heat, humidity and rather rough living conditions.

Sunday 8 July 1945 began with an early breakfast in the officers' mess marquee with the 'Doc', Bill Bamford, there to see me off. The Doc had already served on the squadron for over two years, joining at

Misurata, east of Tripoli in April 1943. No officer was held in greater affection by both groundcrew and aircrew. We shook hands as he wished me 'good luck' with tears in his eyes. It was a moment I shall never forget, quite emotional, as I walked out to the waiting Harvard for the first leg of the journey home, with my kit already loaded aboard. Years later the Doc and I were to meet again at squadron reunions and have many happy meals together with his wife, family and old colleagues. For all the years to his retirement and after, his home in Wandsworth, where he had a general practice, always offered an open door to ex-47 Squadron members. For the Doc, 1943-1946 squadron members were his boys, who he supported and counselled in good times and bad until the day he died.

Leaving 47 Squadron meant not only leaving aircrew colleagues, but also many groundcrew friends who under all conditions serviced our aircraft and were proud of our achievements. It was with mixed feelings that messages of good luck were exchanged. I wished my navigator of recent days all good fortune, with a good pilot in the future. Addresses were hastily scribbled down, with promises to keep in touch and then it was 'chocks away' as we took off with the usual wave from the attending groundcrew. Particularly memorable were friends such as Nick Colley, an LAC engine fitter in 'A' Flight, and Bob Barrett, also an LAC engine fitter in 'B' Flight. Bob had been with the squadron since 1942 moving along the north African coast from Shandur to Protville, back to Gambut, and then onto India and into Burma. Nick had been with the squadron even longer, joining the unit in the Sudan when it was flying Vincents and then Wellesleys, taking part in all the moves from the Sudan to Eritrea, across North Africa and finally to India, from where after four years overseas he caught the boat home. Bob Barrett left for home from Rangoon. Another friend was Frank Harding, an LAC airframe fitter, who had worked as a commercial artist for J Walter Thompson, before volunteering for the RAF. Using home made paints he created two watercolours of Mosquito 'D' HR518 at Kinmagon, giving Tommy and myself a copy each. This was the aircraft in which we completed nineteen sorties. The original water colour is still in perfect condition and much treasured. Grant Flook from the armaments section was another long serving airman who came out from England in 1941 on the 'Empress of Australia', joining the squadron the same year on a four year posting. Perhaps we have never paid sufficient tribute to the airmen who toiled on the ground in the monsoon conditions of Burma, largely unsung and back home quite unappreciated. These were some of the men who kept the 'planes in the air despite the rain, heat, humidity and rough living conditions, knowing that aircrew lives depended on their care. Morale was always high as they coped with the chances of heat-stroke, dysentery, 'dhobi itch', malaria and the inevitable boredom in being so far from home. Too much tribute cannot be given to these men who re-fuelled, re-armed, checked radios and signal equipment, checked engines and airframes, all to ensure that every aircraft as it came back from each mission was ready, if at all possible, before the day was out, for the following day's sorties.

With the war in Europe over, the Dutch government was anxious to re-establish their presence in the Dutch East Indies - later to become Indonesia, an independent nation, much sooner than was at that time foreseen. There were many Dutch pilots and navigators who required training on Mosquitos prior to going out to Java and Sumatra. We were just a small cog in the plans which had been formulating since early May at SEAC headquarters in Kandy to capture Malaya - code name, operation ZIPPER. With the capture of Malaya, through a seaborne invasion, the way would be open to recapture Britain's primary far eastern establishment, Singapore - code name, operation MAILFIST. Preparations were under way for several new Mosquito squadrons to move from Europe and to be available in August/September to support the landing in Malaya. Substantial Japanese forces still remained across much of South East Asia. They were expected to offer fierce resistance rather than surrender. Aircrew from the Far East, who had experienced the conditions in Burma, were an essential element in the training of these planned reinforcements. Not even the most senior commanders were to know how all these plans would be brought to an abrupt halt and re-assessed by the cataclysmic effect of the atom bomb dropped on Hiroshima on 6 August 1945 just four weeks after I was posted back to the UK.

Through June and July the planners at SEAC pushed ahead with implementing operation ZIPPER. D Day was scheduled for 9 September 1945 with amphibious landings on the beach between Port Swettenham and Port Dickson on the coastline facing Kuala Lumpur. A supporting strike force of five Mosquito squadrons, together with Thunderbolt and Spitfire squadrons, was to be deployed along with carrier-borne aircraft. Air supply would be provided by Dakotas from RAF Transport squadrons. Little wonder that we were dispatched in a hurry to the UK in early July, to give some familiarisation training to aircrew going out to a hostile and unfamiliar environment for the first time.

Write-ups of operational experience were requested from squadrons in the field. Commanding Officers submitted to SEAC an official report each month, for transmission to the UK, in order to give aircrews some understanding of the conditions to be faced on arrival at an operational squadron in Burma or elsewhere in SEAC. Reports were selected and written up of sorties regarded as being more worthy of mention than the many others carried out. Wing Commander Duclos submitted a report of an operation by 47 Squadron in July 1945.

No one had any idea, as squadron operations continued in July that plans were in motion, through the authority of the President of the USA, Harry Truman, for an atomic bomb to be used against a city in mainland Japan. Several new crews, now available from the UK following the end of the European war, had joined the squadron only too anxious to make a contribution to the final defeat of Japan. With the capture of Rangoon and the release of prisoners held there, every effort was needed to effect the release of the tens of thousands of prisoners of war still held in the camps and jails of Malaya, Siam (Thailand), Singapore and many other Japanese held territories. Flying in all weathers over Burma the squadron did not forget the suffering and hardship being endured by these prisoners.

TACTICAL DETAIL OF OPERATION BY 47 SQUADRON JULY 1945

The highlight of this months operation was an attack on the town of MOULMEIN. A higher concentration of flak was expected and experienced.

In actual fact, this was a secondary target, the primary target being inaccessible due to an intervening line of thunder storms. It is customary during this season for crews to be briefed on a primary, secondary and a last alternative target.

Three aircraft carrying 4 x 500lb G.P. bombs, fused 11 seconds were briefed to bomb a hospital area in MOULMEIN which the Japs were using as a barracks - as a secondary target.

Only one attack was made, from South to North, which course lay at right-angles to a range of hills beyond the target, and allowed a clear breakaway to the West. The aircraft flew at roof-top height in echelon starboard and at a speed of 280mph. bombed simultaneously in sticks of four. 20mm and L.M.G. flak were experienced and the leader saw what appeared to be cannon strikes just in front of him. It was discovered at de-briefing however that No.2 & 3 had not fired their guns up to this point - the fire must have therefore come from the range of hills behind the target.

No.2 also carried out cannon and machine-gun attacks on two dhows being unloaded in the harbour and on one basha believed to be a flak position.

A Force 136 report dated 2nd August 1945 stated that nine direct hits, two near misses were scored on the buildings, and one direct hit on a flak position. Over 400 bodies were recovered from the debris.

V.S.H.Duclos Wing Commander
Commanding Officer 47 Squadron SEAF

Crews participating:-

Pilot	Navigator
W/Officer K. Byatt	W/Officer D. Horn
F/Lt. S. Powell	F/Officer B. Busby
F.Officer R. Davis	F.Sgt. B. Reich

6th August 1945

Years later, at reunions, we would reflect on just how difficult it had been to keep up the operational activity through the prevailing climatic conditions. Arriving at Kinmagon on 1 May 1945 the squadron never found it easy to keep the aircraft in the air. Kinmagon was not an all-weather strip. On more than one occasion, with the airstrip unserviceable after heavy rain, aircraft were diverted to Meiktila. Following the finding of further defects in the woodwork of the Mosquito main plane on 21 May, as previously mentioned, the squadron was down to only eight serviceable aircraft for several weeks. Urgent replacements were requested. Despite this setback, the squadron under its new Commanding Officer, Wing Commander Duclos DFC, maintained a full programme of operations from May to early August. Many bridges, river craft and motor transport were destroyed, to be followed up with sustained attacks on the retreating enemy and its supply points, all conducted in the middle of the monsoon season. It was an impressive record.

There was no fiercer advocate of the skills and care exercised by all the ground staff than Mike Mackay, our extrovert and very supportive Engineering Officer in charge of 7047 Servicing Echelon. Mike was under constant pressure from the CO and Wing to have the maximum number of serviceable aircraft available day or night. Fortunately, Mike was well backed up by a core of well trained ex apprentice Halton boy entrants, now senior NCOs or commissioned officers. Names from this impressive team that readily come to mind are Flying Officer Harold Fishwick, in charge of the Signals Section, Warrant Officer Smith the senior NCO responsible for general order and discipline, Sergeant Kershaw in charge of the Instrument Section with Sergeants Beanland and Frankie Salt of 'A' Flight responsible for general servicing. Others to remember with gratitude were Flight Sergeant Simmons and Sergeant 'Doughy' Baker. These were the men who kept us alive and in the air. They were all part of a very cohesive team which made 47 Squadron what it was - a very efficient fighting unit.

On 7 August the squadron received orders to move from Kinmagon to Hmawbi, a forward airstrip thirty miles north of Rangoon, arriving there on 15 August, VJ Day. On this day Emperor Hirohito broadcast his country's unconditional surrender, following the destruction of Hiroshima and Nagasaki by the atomic bomb. With this sudden and dramatic surrender of Japan all operations by the squadron ceased, with the last sortie flown on 12 August. The news that the war was over and decisively won was received with much relief by all ranks, with many still believing that they were part of a 'forgotten' army and airforce.

On the night of 16 August, having just settled in their new base at Hmawbi, and as victory celebrations were taking place in the officers' mess and amongst the rest of the squadron personnel, approximately eighty Japanese soldiers from the 5th Commandos made a quick dash at the officers' lines, throwing hand grenades and Molotov cocktails. Six officers of 47 Squadron and two officers of 110 Squadron were slightly injured and taken to hospital suffering from the effects of blast. One Mosquito was written off and some personal kit destroyed, but with most of the officers in the mess, a short distance from the area attacked, the casualties were of a comparatively minor nature. Both squadron personnel and airfield guards from the RAF Regiment were kept on full alert for the next few days as surrender for many Japanese, despite the capitulation ordered by the Emperor, was an experience some did not want to know.

On 21 August a signal was received from Headquarters RAF Burma confirming that DFCs had been awarded to Flight Lieutenant D A Bailey, 'A' Flight Commander, Flight Lieutenant D T P O'D McGlory, the squadron's long serving navigation officer, and to myself, for our individual contribution to the squadron's operations in Libya and Burma. I was sorry to miss the celebrations in the mess, when no doubt the squadron 'song' was rendered with much enthusiasm. It went something like this, to the tune of 'My Darling Clementine'.

47, 47, 47 is the name,
We fly Mosquitos,
Bits of plywood, fastened down with glue and twine,
Though on take-off, wings may break off,
It's a wonderful design.

47,47,47 is the name
All the aircrew and the groundcrew slowly going down the drain.

47, 47, 47 is the name,
When its mentioned down in ACSEA
Lord Mountbatten pulls the chain.
Came the monsoon, can't get airborne,
Runways deep in mud and slime,

Are we carping, no we're charping
Doc's got us all on number nine.

47,47,47 is the name,
All the aircrew and the groundcrew slowly going down the drain.

The fight, the fight, the fight, the fight, the fight,
The fight of Hmawbi field,
When 47 stood the ground and not an inch did yield.
When the fight was over,
Our casualties were nil,
But that was soon remedied by Doctor Bamford's skill.

47, 47, 47 is the name,
All the aircrew and the groundcrew slowly going down the drain.

With the occupation of Bangkok on 3 September, Dakota squadrons were soon flying from Hmawbi to base camps in India with POWs from Siam, who had also been rescued by Dakota. Many squadron members helped to welcome back these men who had suffered so much. For many the sight of these emaciated figures was something they would find very difficult to forgive or forget. The congestion at Hmawbi was so great that a detachment of six Mosquitos was sent up to Meiktila. This detachment provided a welcome respite for both groundcrew and aircrew, little flying being done. The weather was much improved as the monsoon season tailed off. The detachment returned to Hmawbi in the middle of November although conditions, particularly for the airmen, were far from ideal. It took some time for proper messing arrangements to be made and for an adequate cookhouse to be built. As ever, everybody made the best of the available facilities.

Wing Commander V Duclos DFC was repatriated to the UK at the end of October, his place being taken by Wing Commander Melville-Jackson DFC. Melville-Jackson had served with great distinction on 248 and 618 Squadrons in the UK flying both Beaufighters and Mosquitos. He was well equipped to cope with the repatriation problems now arising, as well as dealing with the messy situation developing in Java. During September ten new crews arrived on the squadron and with aircraft now up to strength the unit was available for any eventuality. Action soon came with a signal early in November requiring the immediate dispatch of four Rocket Firing Mosquitos to Batavia, Java, for policing operations to control insurgent activity threatening the restoration of the newly established government.

Warrant Officer Jimmy Gibson, with the squadron since Cholaveram, later recalled that on 17 November, flying one of these four aircraft from Hmawbi and now fitted with rocket rails, he arrived two days later at Kamiron airfield, Batavia (Jakarta), having refuelled at Butterworth in Malaya. There had been a number of recent atrocities following the Japanese surrender which prompted the arrival of HMS Sussex and the landing of a small force of Royal Marines.

On Sunday 25 November, following a reconnaissance the previous day, four Mosquitos from 84 and 47 Squadrons, each armed with eight 60lb rockets, flew two separate missions destroying W/T stations at Jogjakata and Surakata in central Java, held by dissident Indonesian nationalists broadcasting their opposition to the British and Dutch occupying forces. Four more aircraft from the squadron joined the detachment on 30 November. Leaflets were dropped from supporting Beaufighters giving warning of imminent rocket attacks thus hoping to encourage immediate evacuation to minimise the loss of life. Eight successful rocket operations were deployed. Additionally the squadrons flew about thirty reconnaissance and escort sorties to protect the convoys of internees moving from the interior of Java and including about thirty thousand Dutch citizens, who were being repatriated to Holland. For two of my old colleagues, Flight Lieutenant A Jacomb-Hood DFC and Warrant Officer Jimmy Gibson taking part in these activities, the war was hardly over. From Batavia Jimmy made his last escort flight on 15 December 1945, but did not return to the squadron until 26 February 1946. However, from the end of January the Batavia detachment was virtually grounded due to main spar defects in the squadron Mosquitos coming to light once again. By early March 1946 operational sorties in Java came to an end.

In November 1945 the squadron was pleased to learn that their sustained efforts in the early months of 1945 had been properly recognised. Ten more DFCs were awarded to squadron pilots, including my friend and colleague Bill Powell, and six DFCs to squadron navigators including Tommy Thompson. The squadron's operations from November 1943, mostly led by Filson-Young, over nearly two years from Gambut in Libya to Kinmagon in central Burma were acknowledged by the award of one DSO, nineteen DFCs, one bar to the DFC and three DFMs. These awards were a well-deserved recognition of the contribution made by all the squadron's personnel as they coped with the constant moves, over thousands of miles, in pursuit of the enemy in the more remote corners of the wider conflict. It truly was a mobile squadron.

On 12 January 1946 the squadron moved from Hmawbi to Butterworth, an old RAF base in Malaya. At Butterworth, until 21 March 1946 when the squadron was disbanded, very little flying was done apart from the operations by the detachment based at Batavia. Servicing routines were completed and aircraft left behind at Hmawbi were collected. This period must have been a very frustrating time for newly arrived aircrew, some of whom had come from disbanded Mosquito detachments in Australia. From a historical point of view the squadron had a long and honourable history to come, being re-formed in the UK at Fairford in Gloucestershire on 1 September 1946.

1946, Butterworth, Sergeant's Mess and tented quarters.

J Gibson Archives

GRT Willis Archives

UK 1945, Mosquito FBVI taxiing out for take off.

GRT Willis Archives

Middleton-St-George 13 OTU Mosquito Instructors, November 1945. Back row, far left Bob Willis, 2nd from right Tommy Thompson, centre front row Wing Commander Irving Smith.

CHAPTER 12
INSTRUCTING AND PLANNING A NEW LIFE

With Tommy already waiting in Calcutta, I wasted no time in packing my things, thankful to be leaving tent life, hopefully for the last time. In any case we had been on the move for so long that my personal possessions quickly went into my tin trunk and large leather suitcase, all ready to move out from Kinmagon early on the morning of 8 July 1945. Flown by Harvard to Meiktila airfield, just twenty minutes flying time away, I was soon aboard a Dakota bound for Calcutta. My kit was lashed down for the Dakota flight to Dum Dum. I, as the sole passenger, just hung onto a cargo ring in the aircraft floor. There were no seats for passengers as the aircraft had just unloaded 44 gallon fuel drums. Fortunately it was a smooth landing. I was soon on my way by pick-up truck to stay at the Grand Hotel in the city centre, used as a transit hotel for junior officers. Following a bath with a change of clothes, and joining up with Tommy, we were soon out to find a decent restaurant, normally Chinese. This was luxury indeed compared to the rather dreary rations we endured at Kinmagon.

Calcutta was a city of many contrasts, as it will be today. Cheek by jowl with the residences of the rich, surrounded by exotic gardens and high walls, were the poor, the beggars, the street vendors, the rickshaw wallahs which, together with all walks of life made up the crowded streets. Service personnel were necessarily restricted to the area of the city which contained a modern infrastructure such as piped water fit to drink and modern sewage disposal. As we savoured the sights and sounds of this rather restricted area around the Chowringhee thoroughfare, the Grand Hotel and Firpos Restaurant one of my most abiding memories was the exorbitant price of a haircut, European style.

No doubt it would have been far cheaper and a good experience to squat on the pavement, Indian fashion, and enjoy a shave by a skilled barber with a cut-throat razor. Taking full advantage of our short stay we enjoyed the bustle and clamour of this vast and diverse city. Never to be forgotten were the large numbers of homeless families sleeping in the confines and shelter of the central railway station. Coming down from the country seeking a better life, where else could they go?

After just three days in Calcutta we were up before dawn, to be taken by truck from the Grand Hotel to Dum Dum ready to fly to Delhi and then on to Karachi to pick up a BOAC flight to England. The RAF Dakota on which we were booked had imposed a luggage weight limitation. To get over this problem Tommy sent two trunks home by sea. My tin trunk also followed suit. The large leather case just came within the weight limitation. Unfortunately, I was obliged to abandon most of the books I had acquired over the past two years, leaving them behind in the Grand Hotel. No doubt they helped to raise a few rupees for the Indian room attendant.

It was still dark as we waited in the dimly lit hotel lounge for transport to the airport to arrive. We were a party of six RAF personnel, all bound for the UK. It was hot, humid, too early for breakfast and we were thirsty as we waited. There were no staff on duty, so we sought a drink of water in the hotel kitchen. As we opened the kitchen doors, much to our surprise, dozens of rats scampered off the kitchen tables. We beat a hasty retreat. A few weeks later we read in the press, that the hotel was closed down shortly after our stay due to a severe outbreak of cholera. The closure of the hotel was publicised as a visiting American band leader staying at the hotel, along with several other hotel guests, died in the outbreak. I suppose one could say this was just another escape from serious 'misfortune'.

As Tommy and I flew from Calcutta to Delhi on 11 July 1945, on a hot sunny day, passing over the limitless landscape of small villages, palm trees, rivers and green paddy fields, we had to acknowledge that India had proved a fascinating experience. Would we ever be back? Burma was different, we had no wish to return. Two days were spent in Delhi, waiting around at the RAF HQ India, a sprawling establishment of many temporary buildings, as our documents were processed. One of the HQ buildings had collapsed a few days before with some injuries to the occupants. Nobody seemed to express much surprise. The journey continued as we flew by RAF Dakota to Karachi, landing at Jodhpur en route. Still together with our kit we boarded a BOAC Dakota at Karachi early on 14 July, scheduled to arrive in the UK in two days' time. The whole flight was uneventful down the Persian Gulf, refuelling at Sharja and Baghdad, arriving in Cairo sixteen hours later. The next day on to Malta, with refuelling at El Adem bringing back memories of joining the squadron in November 1943. Leaving Malta after an overnight stay, and with the usual purchase of Maltese lace for the folks back home, we landed at Hurn Airport outside Bournemouth mid afternoon on Monday 16 July. It was a bright sunny day as we came over the coast with the countryside looking unbelievably green and so welcoming. What a relief to be back home in one piece. With most of my kit packed into the tin trunk left behind in Calcutta for shipment by sea, we were still in our crumpled tropical uniform as we caught a train to London. On arrival at Waterloo we were eyed with some suspicion by two RAF police (Red Caps), noting how disreputable we looked in our bush jackets and brown shoes. Fearing arrest, we beat a hasty retreat by taxi to Kingsway to report to the Air Ministry. Our arrival didn't raise an eyebrow - perhaps it was forgotten that there was still a war on far to the east - many thousands of miles away.

There was no great sense of urgency, three weeks leave was the first consideration; news of our posting would follow. I had two priorities of equal urgency, to let the folks at home know I was back and to get in touch with Joan at the Royal Infirmary, Edinburgh. I was also anxious to see Stan Perrett who was living at Buckhurst Hill, north east London, who I had not seen since our training time together in Southern Rhodesia and South Africa. By this time Stan had been invalided out of the Royal

Air Force. I would be assured of a warm welcome from his family if I gave them a call. A 'phone call home caused much surprise, and then the train to Sheffield with the final leg by bus for a family reunion. Nothing much had changed since I was last home nearly two years before. Father was still running a small car on business use with a very limited petrol ration. My sister Maisie was holding the business together and, despite having a heart complaint, was even helping in the garden and running the local Girl Guide troop. Mother, as ever, was coping with rationing and my rather unpredictable father. Three days at home and I was off by train to stay with Stan in Buckhurst Hill. There was a warm welcome from his parents and his sister Muriel. Tommy, who had promised to get in touch with Joan's parents, had rung to say that Joan was on holiday in Whitby - I did not know her address. How was I to arrange to meet Joan when her holiday ended, also knowing that she had very little free time away from ward duties? Stan's parents came to the rescue. His mother's sister Marion Archer with husband Bob, lived at Comely Bank in Edinburgh and would be only too pleased to put me up. Plans were immediately made for the journey to Edinburgh with letters and a telegram to Joan so that all could be fitted in before my leave ran out.

In the meantime, Joan had telephoned my home from Whitby after hearing from her father that we were back in England. An apology was due to Joan as our correspondence over the past two years was unknown to my folks at home. Following a 'phone call and assurances by me from Buckhurst Hill, the family soon came to terms with the news that I had a priority 'date' in Edinburgh! I arrived in Edinburgh on Saturday 28 July 1945. Joan was free for a few hours the next day, Sunday, in the morning. It was an overcast but fine day as we met outside the Royal Infirmary at the top of Middle Meadow Walk and walked down the hill towards Princes Street just happy to get to know each other after nearly two years correspondence. Five days later I had to return home. Joan managed as many hours out of the Infirmary as possible during these few days. The weather was sunny and warm as we walked the byways of Edinburgh catching up with all our news. We still remember travelling by tram out to Colinton and walking in the Pentland Hills. Marion and Bob Archer were very kind, welcoming both of us into their home. From the very first day of being together in Edinburgh Joan and I knew we were creating bonds for life.

Back home father and mother were also pressing to take as much advantage of my leave as possible. Travelling by train from Edinburgh to Doncaster on 3 August my sister Maisie met me in a small van at Doncaster station. The next day, 4 August, I was on my way to Somerset by car with father and mother who were anxious that I should see my grandparents, retired in Nether Stowey, Somerset and both in their late eighties. We were back in Barnsley on Sunday 6 August. A telegram arrived Monday morning. I was to report to the Air Ministry in Kingsway, London, on 8 August to receive posting instructions. Stan's parents at Buckhurst Hill again agreed to provide a bed for the night. I duly arrived at Buckhurst Hill that evening to hear on the radio that Hiroshima, a Japanese city in the south west of the main island of Honshu, had been virtually destroyed by an atom bomb the day before. Tens of thousands were killed instantly. The knowledge that a major city had been destroyed, with most of its citizens reduced to cinders, was quite an emotional shock. I felt at the time, and still do, that it was one of the worst moments of my life. I volunteered to be trained as an RAF pilot, never dreaming that the war would end with such terrible consequences. To this day, I know that I could never bring myself to consign tens of thousands of civilians to such devastation and suffering by the pressing of just one button. In a letter to Joan that same evening, 7 August, I wrote, 'we must all pray that the guidance of God is given to all those in power who now control this new and terrible weapon'. As the years went by and the Cold War became more threatening I was often to pray that world leaders would have the moral courage to turn away from the atom bomb and other methods of mass destruction. To turn human life on such a scale into little more than a crisp was too awful to contemplate. On 9 August the second atomic bomb was dropped

GRT Willis Archives

Above: 47 Squadron Association 40th Reunion. 18th May 1986. L to r: Bill Powell, Tony Norris, Bill Hughes, Bob Willis, Mike Mackay, Doc Bamford.

GRT Willis Archives

Left: Bob and Joan Willis on their wedding day, 24 November 1945.

on another Japanese city, Nagasaki on the west cost of Kyushu, with equally horrific results.

Following the surrender of Japan on 14 August 1945 how would our future turn out with Britain thankfully at peace once again? With all the country's cash reserves spent and millions of servicemen still in uniform the transition from war to peace was sure to be a mixture of hope and disappointment. On 24 August Attlee, the newly installed Prime Minister, told Parliament that the country was 'broke'. Rationing of food and fuel could be more demanding than in the war years. No longer was there a ruthless enemy in the far east to overcome. My expected role in the UK had turned out to be quite an anti climax.

Reporting to the Air Ministry at Kingsway on the morning of Wednesday 8 August my posting to No.13 Operational Training Unit for Mosquito aircrew, at Middleton-St-George, Tees-side was confirmed. Catching a train at Kings Cross I arrived at Middleton late the same afternoon. After settling in to my accommodation and reporting to station headquarters, I quickly learnt that I was off duty until Monday 13 August when I was to report to the Chief Flying Instructor, Squadron Leader Wright. The very next day I was on an early train to Edinburgh from Darlington. Joan was able to get away from the Infirmary for a few hours, which we spent enjoying the hospitality of the Archers. The following morning, Friday 10 August, we went for a long walk from the Infirmary, down the Royal Mile, past Holyrood House and on to Arthur's Seat, an ancient volcano over three hundred million years old, from which we had fine views of the city and the Firth of Forth. It was a fine sunny day, good to be out and about in the open country and such a welcome change from the heat and humidity of Burma. Arthur's Seat was a place we were to visit many times together over the years ahead. I plucked up the courage and asked the crucial question. We came back from Arthur's Seat engaged to be married as soon as arrangements with our families could be made.

On Saturday 11 August the ring was bought after a frantic search in the jewellers of Edinburgh. Attractive and good value engagement rings were in very short supply. The Archers had again, at short notice, made me most welcome over these few days, with Joan joining us as often as duty would allow. Back to Middleton St. George was by the last train on Sunday, 10.00pm from Waverley station to Darlington and then a cycle ride back to the officers' quarters at Middleton. This journey was repeated several times in the weeks ahead, always returning by the latest possible train, usually crammed full with servicemen returning from leave. I had yet to meet Joan's father and step-mother. Joan's father wrote wishing us all happiness, inviting me to their home in Dewsbury as soon as I could make it. It was most fortunate to be based at Middleton, within easy reach of Edinburgh and Barnsley, my home town.

From October 1942 to May 1945 Middleton-St-George had been home to 419, 420 and 428 Royal Canadian Air Force Lancasters of No.6 Group. On 31 May 1945 they were given a special send off by Air Chief Marshall Sir A T 'Bomber' Harris as the Canadian aircrew and groundcrew prepared to leave for Canada. Two months later the Station under Group Captain Paul presented a very different picture, away from the pressures of Bomber Command, with the arrival of No13 OTU and its Mosquitos. It was not going to be easy to keep up the level of wartime commitment from both aircrew and groundcrew in the months ahead. The majority of officers and airmen had their thoughts firmly fixed on their future prospects, following a return to civilian life, and in speculating on what jobs would be available. I missed the comradeship we had forged with all ranks in the Middle East, India and Burma. Mess life and inter-personal relations, particularly with senior officers, were more formal than on overseas squadrons. I was assigned to the air tactics section of No.2 Squadron. This section largely involved instructing in low flying, either singly or in formation and demonstrating target approach and evasive action to combat return fire from the target or enemy aircraft. I was the only pilot in the section of about twelve ex-operational pilots with experience of the Far East, the other instructors being veterans of the European theatre. Separated from our friends and colleagues we did not really have much in common to reminisce over. Sadly one or two of the instructors were determined to do as little flying as possible, pending their release. Not knowing of their experiences I could not be too critical but more than once volunteers were required to participate in certain exercises or air tests when for one reason or another qualified pilots for these duties were difficult to find. I did my share in these rather difficult circumstances, still finding flying Mosquitos an enjoyable experience. Perhaps this attitude prompted the Chief Flying Instructor, Wing Commander Irving Smith, to urge me some months later to accept a posting to Little Rissington, the Royal Air Force's Central Flying School, to qualify as a certificated instructor. With the training programme during August, following the Japanese surrender, being in some disarray much time was spent waiting around in the crew room at dispersal. We were ensconced in the usual Nissen hut with the only concession to comfort being a coke stove and a few battered armchairs. Around the walls, still pinned up, were the rather tatty and torn posters featuring Pilot Officer Prune exhorting 'care' in the air. Many a Canadian Lancaster crew had walked out of this crew room over the past three years for the last time. Thankfully, we still remember them.

With the sudden end to hostilities in the Far East, we junior instructors were to have a much reduced training role at Middleton during the ten months I was stationed there. In June 1945 I had been posted as a matter of urgency to assist in the training of Royal Air Force and Dutch aircrew to reach operational efficiency, prior to a posting to the Far East. These aircrews were destined to be re-inforcements to operation ZIPPER for the planned assault on Malaya and Singapore following the liberation of Burma. The surrender of Japan on 14 August changed this plan overnight.

By the time of my first flight at Middleton on 12 August, comprising two air tests, the training programme had lost all its urgency. There was no more flying until 20 August, when with Flying Officer McConochie as navigator and participating in a formation exercise of two hours and forty minutes duration, I had the dubious pleasure of landing Mosquito 835 without an airspeed indicator. My introduction to Middleton as an instructor was very casual reflecting the 'end of term' feeling now that all hostilities were over. I was just handed the Instructors Handbook of Advanced Flying Training. There was no check on my ability. This was taken for granted! I did read that the technique for single engine landing in a Mosquito had been modified since my training days. Through to early September there was no formal flying training; only various exercises by the instructors themselves along with our navigators, designed to prevent us from going stale. I managed just seven hours and forty five minutes flying in August which was hardly enough to maintain personal enthusiasm. From September, with a much reduced throughput, we demonstrated to and taught, as enthusiastically as possible, a wide range of RAF pilots and navigators, including some Dutch and Naval personnel, all destined to fly the Mosquito in squadrons policing the old theatres of war. Some trainees were ex prisoners of war who required refresher training and presumably were staying in the RAF. The objective was to pass on our experience flying the Mosquito, to both pilots and navigators, who would have to cope with any operational need which may arise in the future. Although the Mosquito was to serve the RAF for many more years we already knew it would be superseded as a front line aircraft by the new post-war jets just coming into service.

An additional duty, which befell us at Middleton, was to collect the odd Mosquito left behind as airfields were closed down. Such exercises took me to St. Athan in South Wales, Edzell north west of Montrose in Scotland and to Finmere, an airfield just to the west of Buckingham. Taken to Finmere as a passenger on 8 November 1945 in a Middleton Mosquito flown by Flight Lieutenant Rix, I was briefed to collect a Mosquito Mark ll DD301 and bring the aircraft back to Middleton. This aircraft had been standing outside in all weathers, alone on an airfield abandoned soon after VE Day. There was a sergeant with four or five supporting airmen of various trades in attendance. I was handed the Form 700 all completed for my signature and which certified that the aircraft was fully serviceable and airworthy. I made the usual visual checks that the undercarriage locks were out, the pitot head cover off and the wheel chocks in place. I climbed up the ladder to the cockpit. Then followed the visual check of all the flying controls before starting the engines and again making the usual engine and instrument checks before taxiing out to the end of the runway for take-off. I was on my own, no control tower, no navigator, no crash wagon - it was to be hoped all would be OK.

Accelerating down the runway it was quickly apparent that it was becoming nearly impossible to keep going straight ahead. As the aircraft gathered speed the swing torque became nearly impossible to hold. It was too late to abort the take-off. I became airborne with the starboard engine virtually throttled right back and full rudder applied to contain the torque and prevent loss of control. Immediate action was 'wheels up', 'flaps up' followed by a wide circuit of the airfield as the aircraft was just about impossible to fly. With only the port engine able to give full power, plus my locked leg on the rudder bar a near single engine landing was successfully accomplished. I taxied up to the dispersal area, switched off and climbed out rather shaken. Taking the Form 700 again I endorsed it saying - 'this aircraft is unserviceable due to severe airframe distortion'. I can only assume that, due to prolonged exposure to rain and lacking any form of cover over many weeks, the aircraft frame had warped. There were no airframe jigs on the station to diagnose any structural fault. Nobody there at the time appeared to know how long this particular aircraft had been abandoned. One thing was certain, this aircraft would only be made airworthy again if moved on the back of a lorry to a fully equipped Maintenance Unit. The sad thing about this incident is that the verdict of any crash enquiry, if I had failed to control the aircraft, would probably have been 'pilot error'. We lost aircrew, particularly in the Far East, due to Mosquito structural problems which were not always recognised, on what was in many respects a very fine aircraft. That ten minute flight made me ask myself - would my luck run out one day? Many of the pilots were alert to the possibility of maintenance standards falling at this time.

The experience at Finmere reminded me to be extra vigilant, especially when undertaking the pre-flight checks prior to signing the Form 700. On one occasion, I enquired from the duty airframe fitter, a young lady in the WAAF, whether the undercarriage wheel locks had been extracted. This was a last minute task for the groundcrew immediately prior to the pilot's pre-flight check. I was assured that the locks had been removed. Experience and the standard pre flight drill made me look for myself. The wheel locks were still in place. In the event of an engine failure on take-off, being unable to retract the undercarriage with the wheel locks still in place could result in total disaster. Small flags were attached to these locks to allow a visual check to be made by the pilot from a reasonable distance.

Men who had experienced unemployment through lack of jobs in the 1930s were understandably anxious to get back to civilian life as soon as possible. Employers were obliged to take back their old employees who had been called up, but even with this safeguard civilian life for many would pose difficulties. I was to find out from personal experience lack of available and affordable housing was a major problem. Despite having a new government, for many service personnel these were quite anxious times.

Back at Middleton it was important to plan what Joan and I intended to do with our lives. Where were we to live and should I stay in the Royal Air Force? In the meantime wedding preparations went ahead. We were married on 24 November 1945 at St. Mary's Church, Worsbrough near Barnsley, with the reception at my parents home, Hyland House, situated half a mile from the church. Tommy, my long-suffering navigator, was 'Best Man'. Granted just seven days leave for our honeymoon, we chose the Yorkshire Dales, staying at the Wheatsheaf Inn, Carperby, near Aysgarth in Wensleydale. Despite the time of year the weather was fine and clear. We explored Wensleydale and Swaledale by bus and in the car of a retired lady, also staying at the Wheatsheaf, who had a little petrol available for her Austin 7. Through this lady's kindness we were able to see much of what is now the Yorkshire Dales National Park. Driving from Hawes towards Ingleton and Ingleborough was particularly memorable. On another day we walked from Hawes to Hardraw Force and then half way along the Buttertubs Pass. It was a glorious day and the views were stunning. There were no tourists, just a very infrequent car or bus, with the sheep as ever grazing quietly on the hillsides. No aircraft flew overhead, the country was at peace. No medieval castles, stately homes or tourist centres were open; we just enjoyed the open fields, the stone walls, the isolated stone barns and the splendour of Aysgarth Falls. An abiding memory was the austerity of the accommodation at the Wheatsheaf, with war time rationing still in place, and only one coal fire to heat the inn. It was greatcoats on the bed - perhaps that is how honeymoons should be!

Joan was able to resign from nursing pending her marriage. We rented two rooms at 245 Yarm Road, Darlington. The house, occupied and owned by a Miss Florrie Suttill living on her own, provided comfortable accommodation outside the station. No.2 Squadron was not involved in any night flying so it was usually back to Yarm Road each evening. As often as possible we entertained colleagues from the Officer's Mess. Flight Lieutenant George Baker, a fellow pilot and instructor trained in Canada, was a welcome visitor. Whilst in Canada he had become very attached to Margaret who lived with her parents, the Scrimgeours, in Calgary. Concerned about responsibility for his parents in Suffolk, George was always very grateful in later years that we encouraged him to return to Canada where he married Margaret. We received an invitation to their wedding which, much to our regret, having neither finances nor time and with two small children, we had to decline. Years later we stayed on several occasions with George and Margaret in Ottawa, getting to know quite well their three children, now with families of their own. George worked until retirement for the Federal Government promoting farm exports. They both came to stay with us in Yorkshire meeting all our family. He was a great friend we were very sorry to lose when he died of cancer, after a long illness, in 1992.

George had flown on daylight bombing missions in Lockheed Hudson twin engined aircraft, with 487 (RNZAF) Squadron. On one such daylight mission, on 3 May 1943, of twelve aircraft over Amsterdam, only his and one other aircraft made base back to England. He was a devout practising Christian who sorely missed his friends lost in the RAF. Speaking of his own experiences he was convinced that some of the missions undertaken were not worth the loss in lives so sacrificed. On one mission his navigator was wounded dying later in hospital. Subsequently he was to fly Mosquitos with 605 Squadron. In pursuing the objectives of Bomber and Coastal Command we now know how great were the sacrifices made over Europe. George Baker, from his earliest days in Canada, never lost his enthusiasm in support of his local church and the community at large. He was certainly driven to try in his own way to compensate for the ravages of war.

Life settled down into a steady routine over the months ahead, reporting to the squadron crewroom each morning. Exercises were usually low level demonstrations, often in formation or low level navigational exercises. Weekends were usually free. Joan and I found our rooms quite convenient, just a short cycle ride from the airfield. Miss Suttill asked me if I would demolish the Anderson air raid shelter in the garden. This I was happy to do. Her father had made such a good job of the concrete floor that, despite using a borrowed sledge hammer, the floor withstood all attacks upon it. As the shelter had been constructed with the concrete floor at least two feet below ground level, it is probably still under the garden of number 245 Yarm Road. We were particularly pleased to hear that Tommy too had become engaged to his girl friend, Ethel, who had written regularly to him while we served together overseas. The wedding was on 10 November 1945 at Thornhill Parish Church, Dewsbury, where it was my turn to be 'Best Man'.

Our regular flying programme was restricted to the designated low flying area over the Yorkshire Wolds to the south of Loftus, Guisborough and Stokesley, bounded to the west by the main London to Edinburgh railway line. Making sure that we knew exactly the position of the pylons and lines of high voltage electricity cables, we simulated as closely as we could, low flying below 200 feet, designed to avoid detection by radar and with the maximum element of surprise. Perhaps from time to time passengers travelling on the main London to Edinburgh line would be surprised to see how low a Mosquito could fly. One morning on 17 April 1946 we were engaged on just such a low level formation exercise with four aircraft, flying on a southerly course to cross the River Humber, when unfortunately our lead aircraft overlooked the fact that three hundred feet above the river high voltage cables were directly in our path. There was a sudden cry from the formation leader 'Break, cables ahead'. We were flying just below heavy cloud. I instantly broke away into cloud climbing steeply and praying that all would be well. The four aircraft in the original formation came back to base individually to receive a most contrite apology from the formation leader. We can all make mistakes but this hazard should have been foreseen. High tension cables were clearly marked on our maps.

I could also make mistakes. On 18 January 1946 whilst carrying out an air test in Mosquito 973 I decided to do a practice Standard Beam Approach to the airfield, listening to the signals in my headset. On landing I was called to report immediately to the Control Tower to be confronted by the Station Commander, Group Captain Paul, who informed me that I had crossed his flight path as he was coming in to land. Despite carrying out a practice Beam Approach I should have been much more vigilant. He was not best pleased and stated that I was grounded immediately, pending disciplinary action by the Chief Flying Instructor. Called in front of Wing Commander Smith a few days later he just said, "Back to duty - keep a better look out in future". I had spent a miserable few days since the incident, it being my first 'black' as a pilot. From Wing Commander Smith I received the benefit of doubt.

I soon acquired a good knowledge of the landmarks adjacent to the airfield at Middleton, particularly the contours of the River Tees which flowed in a zig zag pattern close by. More than once the river was a good guide onto the runway when, a sudden shift of wind blowing from the east brought with it the smog and near nil visibility from the ICI works at Wilton; or when a sudden snowstorm shut the base down and you were still out there with little fuel to spare.

Despite the personal adjustments most people were making, we did enjoy, from time to time, a few high jinks in the mess. A party one Saturday evening in February was always remembered as the occasion when 'Bluey' Webster, on Australian Flight Lieutenant instructor, enquired of a very high ranking military officer, attending as a guest and attired in dress uniform, if by any chance he was in the 'Mounties', as the uniform did bear some resemblance to the Canadian Mounted Police. 'Bluey' was in front of the Station Commander the next day and grounded indefinitely. A few years later he and his wife and two children stayed with us. 'Bluey' was still in the RAF and enjoying the life. On another occasion we were entertained by the Wing Commander demonstrating, in the mess, his skill in handling a motorbike.

Overall my ten months at Middleton were a welcome change from Burma, taking a variety of RAF and Royal Navy aircrew on low level and formation training flights. The instructors were kept in a reasonable state of competence through various ground programmes and simulated exercises on the Link Trainer. With an over-riding wish to return to civilian life as soon as possible it was still difficult for some of my colleagues to keep up any real enthusiasm for our training programme. Many aircrew, who were wartime volunteers, realised that now hostilities were over the population at large appeared to have very little interest in their current or even their past activities. Peace time priorities were taking over. However, there was the opportunity to stay in the RAF for at least the next three years, although generally the prospect of civilian life was too strong for many of the wartime volunteers. I have always admired those aircrew of my old squadron who stayed in, such as my last 'A' Flight Commander, Squadron Leader Bill Bailey DFC. Our training programme as an Operational Training Unit in early 1946 was a very uncertain affair as the service tried to come to terms with its future operational requirements. Much of the problem was finding a proper role for the large number of recently qualified aircrew, most of whom wanted release when their turn came. It was difficult to create a proper course structure with the wide variety of aircrew passing through our hands from Wing Commanders to Sergeant Pilots. In the summer of 1946 Middleton held an open day for the general public to show off our Mosquitos during which Tommy and I gave a hand. Probably due to lack of transport and publicity the turnout was very modest. It would be many more years before the Mosquito was recognised as a truly historic aircraft.

Letters arrived from time to time from old 47 Squadron colleagues still overseas. Maurice Jones, Bill Powell's navigator, writing in April from Hong Kong after the squadron was disbanded at Butterworth, informed us that the aircrew we knew had been scattered far and wide. Maurice, a cheerful unflappable fellow, ideal qualities in a navigator, who I was to meet again many years later at squadron reunions, remarked in one of his letters that "47 was pretty clued up and all in all did a good job". Sentiments with which I fully agreed. He and Bill were now part of a communication flight with Beaufighters, one of whose main tasks appeared to be keeping the re-opened British Consulates in China well supplied with beer.

By May 1946 it became clear that Middleton's role as an Operational Training Unit was going to be diminished. The airfield did in due course become Tees-side Airport. The Chief Flying Instructor, Wing Commander Smith, a cheerful and popular New Zealander who had served in Europe with great distinction, sent for me and said he had posted me to the Central Flying School at Little Rissington to train as a fully qualified flying instructor. I had the option of staying in the Royal Air Force, initially for three years. I would be able to apply for a permanent commission and look forward to a long term career. It was good news to be given such a posting, which I promised to consider, although I also had the choice to leave the service as a wartime volunteer. It was rather flattering to be given a vote of confidence in my flying ability and to be offered further training and promotion in the post-war Royal Air Force.

Joan was expecting our first baby in August. Father had offered me a full partnership, along with my brother Derek and sister Maisie in the family business. I found the decision whether to accept the RAF posting a difficult one to make as I knew father was far from easy to work with. After much discussion with Joan, I saw father and agreed to join him after obtaining assurances on the future plans for the business. I also knew that my sister, who had largely kept the business going during the war, was far from being a fit person. She was to die of heart disease just a few years later in 1949. In many ways she was a casualty of the war, keeping the family business going as the men of military age were called up. She had worked long hours, driven in the blackout and undertaken all manner of roles, all of which eventually took their toll. I will always remember the Girl Guides of her troop weeping as she was buried in the family grave at Worsbrough. She had been their leader during the war years and is still remembered as she touched so many lives. To Joan, myself and her immediate family she was a very sad loss.

It had been a hard choice in deciding on the family business. There were risks involved either in continuing my RAF career or working with a rather unpredictable father. I hoped I had made the right decision. I was sorry when the day came to say good-bye to the Royal Air Force on 3 June 1946. The return to civilian life was quite an anti-climax, involving a journey to Wembley to be kitted out with a 'demob suit' and trilby. Then came a brief medical check, followed by a handout of demobilisation papers, ration book, clothing coupons, civilian identity card and a railway warrant to Barnsley.

I was proud of the modest contribution I had been able to make in the struggle against Germany and Japan. Joan and I knew that many challenges lay ahead which were difficult to foresee, in a country which still had substantial food shortages and had lost the immediate economic support of the USA through the cancellation of Lend-Lease. Thankfully Marshall Aid was to arrive from America in late 1947. My RAF story was over, but the friendships and achievements of those years were to touch our lives in so many ways as the future unfolded. We had to keep alive the vision of trying to make the world a better place for all nations, particularly in memory of those who did not return.

CHAPTER 13
REFLECTIONS AND ASPIRATIONS

I had been flying continuously for over four years clocking up one thousand and ninety five hours as a pilot on eight different aircraft types, and of which four hundred and ninety five hours were flown on 47 Squadron. At least I had achieved what I set out to do after volunteering in late 1940 for pilot training. For many years from 1946 these experiences were put behind us as Joan and I concentrated on finding a home, providing for the family and pulling a business together which the war had much diminished. Without Joan's unfailing support over those immediate post war years of long hours and very few holidays, later success would have never materialised. We still kept in touch with not only Tommy, but also my old friends from training days in Southern Rhodesia, Stan Perrett and Charlie Tomalin. We never lost sight of George Baker in Canada nor with my friends on 47 Squadron, Bill Powell, Maurice Jones, Bob Milne, Jimmy Gibson, Reg Davis, Bill Hughes in Australia, 'Doc' Bamford, Tony Norris and that inimitable Irishman Mike Mackay, all of whom feature in this story.

Leaving Middleton on 3 June 1946 I was given fourteen weeks leave following my overseas service and so was not due for discharge from the Royal Air Force until September 1946. Such was the pressure on father's business that I was in his warehouse in Eckington, south of Sheffield, just a week after leaving Middleton with all thought of leave put on one side. The business of food distribution, in which this warehouse was involved, was practically non-existent due to rationing and neglect by father and the management to obtain the necessary supply registrations. Prior to my arrival, father had not visited his Eckington warehouse for over six months. The staff comprised just a manager, a salesman, a lorry driver and two warehouse assistants. The manager was immediately discharged by me on the grounds of gross negligence over several years. I now had a business to develop when all our basic products were subject to rationing. With virtually no registrations at the warehouse for supplies it was to prove very difficult to find sufficient products to sell just to pay the wages. The pressure was so great that all thoughts of squadron reunions were out of my mind. In any case, Joan and I had to find a house in which to live. With scant house building for the past five years or so this was far from easy, but is another story.

In 1947 Bill Powell along with Doc Bamford, Tom Miles and Reg Davis, ex-47 Squadron colleagues, formed the 47 Squadron Association welcoming all ranks to an annual reunion in London. It was not until 1960 that I found time to even consider meeting up with my old RAF colleagues. Father had died five years previously, but the business had been transformed and substantially enlarged. From 1960 to the present day, I have attended every squadron reunion but one, always held in London on the third Saturday in May. One highlight was meeting again the Commanding Officer I had left in Burma, Group Captain V S H Duclos, CBE, DFC, AE, who assumed the Chairmanship of the Squadron Association. 'The Duke', as he was affectionately known, was remembered by all his friends and colleagues at a memorial service Joan and I attended on 7 December 1989, after his sudden death in November 1989. The 'Duke' was succeeded as the Association Chairman by Group Captain Harold Fishwick MBE MID who it was a delight to meet once again. He served on the squadron as Signals Officer during my time and went on to enjoy a most successful career in the service during the post-war years. Attendance at squadron anniversaries has always been most memorable, particularly as the distinguished history of 47 Squadron has continued to the present day. Now based at Lyneham in Wiltshire and flying C130 Hercules in a transport support role, involving global activities, it was an honour to be welcomed at the 60th 70th and 75th anniversary celebrations of the squadron at their Station.

Volunteering for aircrew training in 1940, besides being an escape from family constraints and expectations, was quite exhilarating in being able to feel that at last I had taken some control of my life. I well remember the feeling of rest and relaxation I had on the voyage to Southern Rhodesia on the 'Empress of Russia' in 1941. On this six weeks voyage, for the first time in my life, I was able to pause a little and reflect on what life was about and what meaning it had. I was to be much influenced by the dedication and desire for a better world demonstrated by many of the colleagues I flew with, who fought so hard, many giving their lives. Certainly I emerged from the Royal Air Force wartime experience with a wider vision of the world at large. Confidence had grown in my ability to play an active part in whatever level of society I was drawn into. This personal narrative of a career in the Royal Air Force, nearly sixty years ago, does I hope, reflect the spirit and sacrifice so freely given at that time by so many fine people and which still prevails in such units as 47 Squadron to this day.

GRT Willis Archives

Above: Beaufighter TF X with torpedo.

Below: A few 47 Squadron personnel, North Africa 1943.
l to r Sergeant Ken Thomas, LACs 'Dodger Green', 'Taff' Phillips, Nick Colley and Ray Pratt.

GRT Willis Archives

Top l to r: Sgt Fred Poree (N), W/O Ray Wapshot (P), Sgt Curly Wallace (Fitter).

Middle l to r: F/L Al Scott (P) lost over Burma 14 April 1944, F/O Arthur Unwin (P) lost over the Mediterranean February 1944, Sgt Frank Salt (Fitter), Malta, North Africa and India 1941-45.

Bottom: Sgt 'Doughy' Baker, North Africa 1943-44.

All photographs courtesy of GRT Willis Archives

BIBLIOGRAPHY

Published Books

Allen, Louis: *Burma The Longest War 1941-1945*, J M Dent & Sons Ltd 1984
Bingham, Victor: *Bristol Beaufighter*, Airlife 1994
Bishop, Edward: *Mosquito - The Wooden Wonder*, Airlife 1980
Bowman, Martin: *Mosquito Bomber/Fighter Bomber Units 1942-45*, Esprey Publishing 1997
Bowyer, Chaz: *Beaufighter at War*, Ian Allen Ltd 1976
Bowyer, Chaz: *Beaufighter*, William Kimber & Co Ltd 1987
Bowyer, Chaz: *The Royal Air Force 1939-1945*, Pen & Sword 1996
Calvert, Mike: *Slim*, Pan/Ballantine 1973
Collier, Basil: *Japan at War*, Sidgwick & Jackson Ltd 1975
Curtis, Des: *A Most Secret Squadron*, Skitten Books 1995
Golley, John: *Aircrew Unlimited*, Patrick Stephens Ltd 1993
HMSO: *The Campaign in Burma*, HMSO 1946
HMSO: *Wings of the Phoenix*, HMSO 1949
Howe, Stuart: *The de Havilland Mosquito*, Aston Publications 1992
Innes, David J: *Beaufighters over Burma (27 Sqdn)*, Blandford Press 1985
Murray, Dr Williamson: *The Luftwaffe 1933-45*, Brasseys 1996
Nesbit, Roy Conyers: *The Armed Rovers*, Airlife 1995
Nesbit, Roy Conyers: *RAF An Illustrated History from 1918*, Sutton Publishing 1998
Nesbit, Roy Conyers: *The RAF in Camera 1939-1945*, Alan Sutton Publishing Ltd
Overy, R J: *The Air War 1939-1945*, Macmillan Publishers Ltd 1980
Philpott, Brian: *German Fighters over the Med*, Patrick Stephens Ltd
Probert, Air Commodore H: *The Forgotten Air Force*, Brasseys 1995
Rooney, David: *Burma Victory*, Arms and Armour Press 1992
Sharp, Martin C & Bowyer, Michael J F: *Mosquito*, Faber & Faber 1967
Thomas, Antony: *Rhodes*, BBC Books 1996

Public Record Office

Air 2/9659	47 Squadron Decorations 1945/46
Air 15/42	Operational Training Units policy January 1939-April 1942
Air 15/571	Training Aircrew for Torpedo Bombers
Air 15/575	Operational Training Units policy April 1943-August 1944
Air 15/575	Training in Coastal Command Operational Training Units
Air 15/576	Flying in Monsoon
Air 20/2859	Length of Operational Tours
Air 22/499	Kumbhirgram January 1945
Air 23/1114	Castel Benito No 17 Staging Post, El Adem No 12 Staging Post
Air 23/1120	Bahrein No 43 Staging Post
Air 23/1938	221 group Operations Record Book August 1944-March 1945
Air 23/2058	Marking of Targets by Agents and use of VCPs April 1945
Air 23/2065	Headquarters RAF Burma June 1945
Air 23/2266	To SACSEA from Air Ministry
Air 23/2283	Operation Dracula, signal from Prime minister
Air 23/4350	Mosquito Long Range Tanks April 1945
Air 23/4350	Grounding of Mosquitos
Air 23/4682	221 Group 1945
Air 23/6743	Notes on Operations Aegean Sea September/October 1943
Air 24/178	German Air Force Eastern Mediterranean Deployment
Air 24/478	Air Headquarters Eastern Mediterranean
Air 24/970	Casualties 8 November 1942-29 February 1944
Air 25/796	Gambut Operations Record Book December 1943
Air 25/962	Headquarters 225 Group
Air 25 1068	Rhodesia Air Training Group
Air 25/1069	47 Squadron Movement Order No3/42
Air 26/301	235 Wing Operations Record Book El Adem/Gambut 1943
Air 26/499	908 Wing Operations Record Book September 1944 -September 1945
Air 27/164	201 Group Operations Record Book
Air 27/463	47 squadron Operations Record Book 1939-1941
Air 27/464	47 Squadron Operations Record Book 1942-1943
Air 27/465	47 Squadron Operations Record Book 1944-1946

Air 27/466	47 Squadron Appendices 1927-1945
Air 27/467	47 Squadron Appendices June 1940-February 1941
Air 27/2418	47 Squadron Appendices January-March 1946
Air 27/2866	47 Squadron Miscellaneous
Air 27/2928	47 Squadron Miscellaneous
Air 27/3082	47 Squadron Miscellaneous
Air 28/57	Belvedere, 125 Castle Kennedy, 143 Cholaveram
Air 28/176	Croft Operational Training Unit 1945/46
Air 28/177	Croft Operational Training Unit 1945/46
Air 28/295	Gambut, Summary of Events 5 7 March 1944
Air 28/648	Port Ellen 1943
Air 28/658	Ranchi 1944
Air 28/701	Shallufa December 1940-August 1945
Air 28/702	Exercises with HM Ships January 1944
Air 28/966	Yelahanka 1944
Air 28/1618	Middleton St George, Little Rissington
Air 29/330	Habbanya
Air 29/331	Habbanya
Air 29/634	Scarborough ITW 1941
Air 29/684	Crosby on Eden OTU June-August 1943
Air 29/705	47 Squadron Operations Record Book June-August 1943
Air 29/796	Gambut Operations Record Book 3 December 1943-23 December 1943
Air 29/1174	908 Wing Operations Record Book April 1945
Air 30/158	Promotion of NCOs to Officers
Air 41/4	Flying Training, Aircrew Training 1934-1942
Air 41/37	Air Supply Operations Burma
Air 41/53	The Dodecanese, Eastern Mediterranean
Air 41/61	The Dodecanese, Eastern Mediterranean
Air 41/71	Operational Training
Air 41/76	History of East Mediterranean Activities

HO/196	Bomb Census
HO/199	Air Raids United Kingdom
HO/203	Blitz on Sheffield December 1940

DEFE/2/890	Special Boat Squadron Aegean
DEFE/2/1019	VHF Equipment 1943

APPENDIX

47 Squadron Honours and Awards September 1943 - August 1945

Pilot Officer G R T Willis

The following recommendation was made on 10 May for the award of the Distinguished Flying Cross to Pilot Officer G R T Willis by the Commanding Officer of 47 Squadron, Wing Commander W D L Filson-Young.

"This officer has carried out 45 operational sorties totalling over 200 hours. He has been conspicuous at all times for his keenness and determination.

By straight shooting and pressing home his attacks he has inflicted considerable damage on enemy equipment. This includes three enemy aircraft destroyed in the air, one destroyed on the ground, 66 M/T destroyed and badly damaged and considerable amount of small shipping and supply dumps.

On several occasions P/O Willis' aircraft has been hit by flak but he has always shown great coolness under fire and has pressed home his attacks and completed his mission. By his cheerfulness and enthusiasm he has set a high example of courage and devotion to duty."

Further awards in the period were:

Distinguished Service Order

Squadron Leader G F Powell

Distinguished Flying Cross

Flying Officer C Adams
Flight Lieutenant D A Bailey
Flight Lieutenant C E Gieselman
Flight Lieutanant R P S Harridence
Flight Lieutenant A J Jacomb Hood
Warrant Officer A Howard
Flight Lieutenant W L Hughes
Wing Commander J A Lee-Evans
Flying Officer R L Lowman
Flight Lieutenant D T P O'D McGlory
Warrant Officer R Meredith
Warrant Officer W C Outhwaite
Squadron leader K R P Painter
Flight Lieutenant S R Parker
Flight Lieutenant P A S Payne
Warrant Officer F W Poree
Flying Officer G W Powell
Flying Officer G L Reneau
Flying Officer Sharwood Smith
Flying Officer D P Thompson
Flying Officer R Wapshott

Bar to the Distinguished Flying Cross

Wing Commander W D L Filson-Young

Distinguished Flying Medal

Flight Sergeant G T Craven (seconded from 603 Squadron)
Sergeant H A Milne

Mentioned in Dispatches

Flying Officer H Fishwick
Flying Officer H A Milne

Index

Military Units
RAF and Allied Squadrons, Wings and Groups

Naval Units

Japanese Burma Forces

A

B

C

D

E

F

G

H

I

J

K

L

M

R

S

T

V

W

Y